HOLD ON TO
hope

CHRISTIAN ART
PUBLISHERS

Published by Christian Art Publishers
PO Box 1599, Vereeniging, 1930, RSA

© 2018
First edition 2018

Cover designed by Christian Art Publishers

Artwork by Amylee Weeks

Edited by Amanda Cowles

Printed in China

ISBN 978-1-4321-2562-2

18   19   20   21   22   23   24   25   26   27   –   10   9   8   7   6   5   4   3   2   1

THIS BOOK BELONGS TO:

_____

FROM:

_____

DATE:

_____

Introduction

The beautiful psalms remain ever popular because of the typical human element – we can identify with the emotions and situations, and we ask the same questions today: Why did it happen? Where is God? What should I do?

Together with the psalmists we work through our own fears and obstacles, our doubts and insecurities, but in the end we rediscover our faith and trust in God again. Through the psalms we rejoice and sing praises once more.

The concise and powerful devotions in *Hold on to Hope* remind us that we will always have ups and downs, but the best life is lived in a relationship with God. Such a relationship is examined, explained and exercised in many practical ways. Let your relationship with God grow deeper this year – day by day.

The Psalms will be covered in chronological order – from Psalm 1 to Psalm 150 – without regard for special days like Easter or Christmas. If you, however, want to read special psalms for these Christian celebrations, look at the following:

Easter. The eight devotions from Psalm 22 are meant for Holy Week and have been marked for that purpose.

Christmas. The jubilant Psalms 96, 97, and 98 are traditionally used over Christmas.

As you're reading, the following tips will help and guide you to make the most of your daily quiet time:

Purposefully make time to become still. Get out of bed a little earlier, or close your office door over lunch time. Five minutes are enough, but ten or fifteen are even better!

ty to read through all the psalms in a year by following the reading plan each day. When you read, read audibly, slowly, and deeply, focusing on the rhythm and poetry of the beautiful songs. Realize that you're reading God's words!

Meditate on it. Scripture meditation means to intentionally reflect on what you've read, to ponder its meaning, to explore its depths and application. The short discussions will introduce you to all the main topics of the psalms and get you thinking.

React in prayer. Agree with the short prayer that follows each discussion, but also pray whatever is in your heart. The psalms are prayers in themselves, of course, and this year you'll definitely see your prayer life deepen!

> Yes, my soul, find rest in God; my hope comes from Him.
> Truly He is my rock and my salvation;
> He is my fortress, I will not be shaken.
> PSALM 62:5-6

This year, hold on to hope with a song in your heart!

~ Jimi le Roux

January

Blessed is the man who walks not in the counsel of the wicked, nor stands in the way of sinners, nor sits in the seat of scoffers;

but his delight is in the law of the LORD, and on His law he meditates day and night.

He is like a tree planted by streams of water that yields its fruit in its season, and its leaf does not wither. In all that he does, he prospers.

The wicked are not so, but are like chaff that the wind drives away.

Therefore the wicked will not stand in the judgment, nor sinners in the congregation of the righteous; for the LORD knows the way of the righteous, but the way of the wicked will perish.

PSALM 1

JANUARY 1
THE WAY TO BLESSING

*Blessed is the man who walks not in the counsel of the wicked,
nor stands in the way of sinners, nor sits in the seat of scoffers.*

PSALM 1:1

The purpose of the book of Psalms is indeed to show the way to a blessed life. Such a life is always a life *with* God, a life in relationship with Him. Blessings cannot be had apart from God, because it is *He* who blesses!

This psalm says we cannot allow anyone or anything to detract us from living a life with God. If we "walk" among those who do not know God – and our world is filled with unbelieving and even wicked people – we may later "stand," that is become comfortable, with those who do wrong. After all, "everyone does it." Before we know it we will "sit," in other words be at home with people who have turned their backs on God.

No, that must never happen! It is true that believers have unbelieving friends, and that is good and necessary. But our friends should see our faith, be drawn to God, and be changed. Then they, too, will be blessed!

*God who blesses, I want to live in Your blessing.
Let my walking, standing, and sitting glorify You! Amen.*

LEARN TO MEDITATE

His delight is in the law of the LORD, and
on His law he meditates day and night.
PSALM 1:2

In the Old Testament the *righteous* are distinguished from the *sinners*. Where sinners are drawn to people who don't care for God and prefer to spend time with them, the righteous are drawn to God. They enjoy learning more about Him and spending time with the Word. They "meditate" on the Word of God, says the psalmist.

The word *meditate* literally means "to mutter" the Scriptures – to recite subvocally from memory. It also has the general meaning of pondering or contemplating. Let's learn here something for our own spiritual journey. Regularly read the Word – about a chapter at a time – in a whisper or audibly, because we need to hear the Word. As you read, open your spiritual faculties and ask God, "What do You want to tell me, Lord?"

If the Holy Spirit highlights certain words or phrases, stop, or return to them, and repeat them several times, slowly. Roll them about in your mind and contemplate their meaning. Let their richness, depth, and application open up to you. This is Scripture meditation! Keep the Word in the back of your mind as you go through your day.

Holy Spirit, open the Word up to me.
I also open my spirit up to the Word! Amen.

A TREE BY THE STREAM

*He is like a tree planted by streams of water that yields
its fruit in its season, and its leaf does not wither.
In all that he does, he prospers.*

PSALM 1:3

If you abide in the Word and the Word abides in you, you will develop depth, maturity, wisdom. You will become stronger as your knowledge of God increases. Your fullness of the Spirit – of which the water here is a symbol – will become apparent in your fruit: love, joy, peace, patience, goodness, faithfulness, etc. (Gal. 5:22-23).

People will want to be near you because they will recognize your faith, your love for others, your words that instill hope. You will prosper in all that you do, the Bible says. Take note that prosperity or blessedness in the Bible is not just about material wealth – it is especially about having God with you.

Living with God means to draw from *His* strength and peace in both the ups and the downs of life. It means that you can handle anything! Now *that* is wealth and blessing, *that* is prosperity! Having God with you is shalom – the peace of the righteous, the result of a deep relationship with Him. What a privilege!

*Lord, let me abide in You, as You abide in me;
and let me bear fruit to Your glory. Amen.*

THE HOME OF MY HEART

Therefore the wicked will not stand in the judgment,
nor sinners in the congregation of the righteous.
PSALM 1:5

Everyone is looking for a place to feel at home, a place where they can relax and be themselves. The question is, where is your place, your home base, your comfort zone? We read here that sinners feel at home in places where God is kept away. In the "congregation of the righteous" they feel uncomfortable, ill at ease.

They shy away from God's presence, because His holiness is too much for them. It's a sad fact that some believers are so judgmental that very few people, believing or not, can feel at ease with them. Yes, some unbelievers make better Christians (as far as love and grace is concerned) than some believers! Let's forget about such believers for now. In general, the righteous do feel at home in the company of those who serve God. Of course they do!

Ultimately, however, we feel at home with the Father Himself. We are not afraid of Him. He does not judge us; He loves us and we love Him. He is the home of my heart!

Lord, You alone are my rest, my peace, my joy.
All my desires are in You! Amen.

TWO PATHS - CHOOSE ONE

For the LORD knows the way of the righteous,
but the way of the wicked will perish.
PSALM 1:6

Psalm 1 can be seen as a summary of the entire book of Psalms. It deals with the two paths that lie before every person: the path of the righteous and the path of the wicked.

The psalmist wants us to choose, and of course he wants us to choose God's path. He says God "knows" the path of the righteous, which means that God is intimately present in the life of His child. That path leads to God! On the other hand, on the path of the sinner, God is nowhere to be found. Also, that path leads you nowhere. It "perishes." It simply disappears – a striking image of being lost.

You might think that you're heading somewhere, but then suddenly there is just no road left. On what path are you? The simple truth is that we attempt to walk on both roads, a little of this and a little of that. We *want* to stay on God's way, but then we wander off. That is why we remain confronted by this choice. Choose again the right way, choose God's way, choose today!

Lord, I so want to walk the road that You want me to walk.
Take my hand and lead me closer to You. Amen.

MY SHIELD AND MY GLORY

But You, O Lord, are a shield about me,
my glory, and the lifter of my head.
PSALM 3:3

David wrote these words as he was fleeing from Absalom, who staged a coup against his throne. It was David's own doing, as his sin with Bathsheba was now catching up with him. Remember, he took another man's wife for himself and then had the husband die in the war – a terrible sin!

David was acutely aware of his shame, but had pleaded for mercy and forgiveness. And now, while being chased, he simply clung to God, because he had nowhere else to go. He radically believed that God would remain with him because of their covenant. So he just trusted and waited for God to save him and restore his honor.

Let's stay on the straight and the narrow – yes, by all means possible. Still, we stray, and sometimes we stray far. The lesson here, however, is that God does not stray away. God remains true, even when we are untrue. That's His character. Lift your head, therefore. God is still here; God is still involved!

Lord, save me from myself. Restore me when I fall. Amen.

JANUARY 7
MORNING PRAYER

I lay down and slept; I woke again, for the LORD sustained me.

PSALM 3:5

David woke up with the realization that he had slept well. Remember that he was a fugitive at this stage with his pursuers hot on his heels – not exactly cause for a good night's rest! Still, in the next verse he maintains that he will not be afraid of even ten thousand enemies around him. He has the peace of the Lord!

Nowadays, our stress is more psychological. Worry, failure, and relationship problems create tension in our bodies that prevent us from relaxing and rejuvenating rest. It does help to be physically active during the day (especially in natural sunlight) and to keep good sleep habits: avoiding coffee and electronic devices, and turning the lights low.

However, David's peace came from God. He felt secure, because his Covenant God was with him. Why wouldn't he sleep well – he had radical faith!

You, O Lord, are my shield and strength.
Teach me to trust You and to then relax. Amen.

MORE JOY THAN THIS

*You have put more joy in my heart than they have
when their grain and wine abound.*
PSALM 4:7

These words by David refer specifically to people who have just harvested, whose barns are filled with grain, grapes, and fruit. Harvest time is a joyful time in all agrarian communities, and harvest festivals are always filled with exuberance and abundance.

David felt, however, that he had even more joy than this. Of course we can rejoice over a plentiful harvest, a solid return, an unexpected bonus, or a time of financial security. Why shouldn't we? We should really be able to enjoy life and celebrate it with vigor – yes, let's do! Still, like David, we also know that there is more to life. There is a deeper joy.

What David felt with God surpassed all the festivals he ever attended! The fact is that we can long for more in the middle of the biggest celebration, or just be happy in God with relatively few earthly things, as long as *He* is in the picture – that's what's important!

Lord, You are my joy. To live with You is a celebration! Amen.

EVENING PRAYER

In peace I will both lie down and sleep;
for You alone, O LORD, make me dwell in safety.
PSALM 4:8

I used to stay in a city where we had to put a lot of security in place before we could retire for the night. We made sure the gate to the street was locked, the cars put away, the garage closed. We had security gates at the front and back of the house and burglar bars at the windows. We even had a gate in the passage to keep intruders from the bedrooms.

Then, many of us had dogs to be loosed, floodlights to be switched on, and an alarm to be set! Yes, that's the way we had to live. You cannot act irresponsibly but then claim you trust God. We must do what *we* can do. As the Arabs say, "Trust God, but tie your camel down."

This, however, is only half the picture. The other half is that prevention can only go so far. The rest is really in God's hands. After you have done what you can – and the above is about the most anyone can do – you can leave the matter with God and go to sleep in peace. Ultimately, it is He who takes responsibility for you! Yes, you are called to responsibility, but not to fear. Get into your warm bed, say thank You, and … have a good night!

Lord, keep Your hand over me tonight;
appoint Your angels to keep me safe. Amen.

DAYBREAK WITH GOD

O LORD, in the morning You hear my voice;
in the morning I prepare a sacrifice for You and watch.
PSALM 5:3

How wonderful the mornings are! Modern man has lost his natural day-and-night rhythm, because electricity now makes it possible for us to have the lights shining brightly until late. That keeps us awake, and we go to bed – and get up – much later than earlier.

When people were still synchronized to the sun's rhythm, they went to sleep when it became dark and got up at dawn or earlier. The people of old saw the sun come up every morning, while today we scarcely ever see that majestic natural miracle. Mornings, however, are the best part of the day: the air is fresh and cool, the colors are deep and bright, and the birds chirp about. Our first coffee should be had outside! Mornings are also ideal for spending time with God – reading, praying, and pondering. It's the most popular quiet time for a reason.

David spent time with God in the morning, and Jesus got up early to pray. So did almost all of the saints of the past and present. Let's rediscover mornings – and make God part of the picture!

Lord, I want to meet You in the morning! Amen.

A LIGHT IN THE DARK

The LORD has heard my plea; the LORD accepts my prayer.

PSALM 6:9

In this psalm, David was in a dark place emotionally: sick with worry, crying day and night, his body weakened and weary, his eyes blurry and teared.

Commentators believe that he was acutely experiencing God's turning away after his sin with Bathsheba. He was experiencing true remorse, absolute regret, embarrassment, and shame. However, right at the end of this lament – here, in verse 9 – David makes this strong statement. God heard him! Where did that come from? Well, it came straight from his spirit, because it's faith speaking! While David's body and soul were weary, his spirit still clung to God. In his heart of hearts he *knew* that God considered his anguish. What's more, he also believed that God accepted his pleas and forgave him.

He knew these things because he *knew* God! In his darkness, that knowledge was his ray of hope. Let us as well, wherever we are, confess and believe that God is good, that God hears, that God *knows*, that God will intervene. He will; He will!

Lord, in the darkness I see a light. It is You! Amen.

MY SHIELD IS GOD

My shield is with God, who saves the upright in heart.
PSALM 7:10

David complains about the unrighteousness around him – there is just too much godlessness, injustice, and violence! He pleads for God to intervene and set things right.

We have the same need, don't we? David finds consolation, though, in the fact that God is his "shield" – a common symbol in Scripture for protection or safety. For David, it is a given that God defends the "upright." What does *uprightness* mean, though? Uprightness alludes to *doing* right, but the essence is a heart that *is* right: authentic and sincere, without masks or facades.

It is what it is – you get what you see! Mistakes are not hidden away, but taken responsibility for. With such a person, as David indeed was, God can do much. However, with insincerity and artificiality one doesn't get far. Get under God's shield with the right attitude!

Lord, make me upright and be my shield! Amen.

JANUARY 13

LEARN AWE

*O Lord, our Lord, how majestic is Your name
in all the earth! You have set Your glory above the heavens.*
PSALM 8:1

"How majestic is Your name in all the earth." With this utterance of wonder this beautiful psalm starts and ends. It is all about God's marvelous creation and how anyone can see God's hand in it.

David is saying that he looks up at the sky, sees the work of God's hands, the stars and moon, and then sings, "How great Thou art!" Well, not in these exact words, but with the exact same feeling of wonder. He says even babies and infants see God in nature (Ps. 8:2). That's quite a statement, because it teaches us that experiencing God in nature is not so much a rational exercise. It's not about gathering evidence, for example. It's more of a feeling, a sensation, a knowing of the heart.

Only when we lose ourselves in nature, when we suspend the rational and analytical mind for a little while, can we experience the wonder, the awe, the flow. Children do it instinctively, but we can learn to be in awe before God. Marvel in the beauty around you – find Him there!

*Lord, teach me to look, teach me to see,
teach me to be in awe of You. Amen.*

JANUARY 14
HOW GREAT THOU ART!

When I look at Your heavens, the work of Your fingers, the moon
and the stars, which You have set in place, what is man that You are
mindful of him, and the son of man that You care for him?

PSALM 8:3-4

David looks up at the night sky and sees the moon, the stars, and the
Milky Way. He is overwhelmed by its immensity – and he of course
didn't know a fraction of the universe's true greatness!

All around him David sees the wonder of nature: the flight of the
birds, the marvel of a perfect birth, the circle of life. And then he wonders, What is the meaning of this fantastic creation? What is its purpose? Where do I fit in? His intuition and reaction is then to burst out
in praise to the Creator! It's true that the whole creation is one great
symphony to God's glory. All creatures add to the chorus of praise by
their mere existence and by faithfully living out their creation purpose

Listen! The fact that we cannot hear creation singing is because of
our own preoccupation and self-centeredness. In reality, God's praise is
thundering all around us. We must simply open our ears, hear this love
song, and then add our own little voice to the majestic chorus of which
we are a part. That will introduce us to the most wonderful harmony
we can ever know.

I will sing, Lord! I will sing about Your greatness and glory. Amen.

SADNESS AND GLORY

*Yet You have made him a little lower than the heavenly beings
and crowned him with glory and honor.*
PSALM 8:5

David is in absolute awe about the majesty of creation. He wonders where man fits into this grand scheme. "What is man that you are mindful of him?" (Ps. 8:4).

Our natural answer would be that man is completely insignificant, a mere speck in the greatness of the universe. But that is wrong! David correctly puts man right on top of creation – just below God and the angels. Yes, indeed! Man has been placed above the whole created world, including the sun, moon, and stars, because he is the image of God, the crown of creation. He was created to rule over it all! That is man's purpose. Therefore, whenever we see a destitute or broken person – degraded or defeated – it is a terrible contradiction, a far cry from the honor that God bestowed on man.

It is the tragic result of sin. It should make us exceedingly sad – and angry! God's will is that everyone should be restored to dignity and worth, that his or her crown should be returned.

*Lord, it is sad to see so many people dishonored
and fallen. Help me; help us! Amen.*

YOUR PURPOSE: TO RULE

You have given him dominion over the works of Your hands;
You have put all things under his feet, all sheep and oxen,
and also the beasts of the field, the birds of the heavens,
and the fish of the sea, whatever passes along the paths of the seas.

PSALM 8:6-8

In this psalm, David is asking about man's place in creation. He finds his answer in Genesis where God says, "Let us make man in our image … and let them have dominion" (Gen. 1:26). These are the first words that God uttered about human beings, that their purpose would be to rule over the animals and plants, the earth, the whole of creation. In principle, even the sun, moon, and stars!

We have been created to rule over creation but, of course, under God, on His behalf. Have we done a good job so far? No! On the contrary, instead of good and godly governance, we misused and plundered our home. Let's do better! There is also a personal spiritual truth in this. Our primal command to rule should bring order and purpose to our personal lives and relationships.

We were meant to control our personal chaos by discipline, planning, and working. Rule, then! Just remember that we rule in subordination to God, not independent of Him. Execute His will in your life.

Lord, teach me to rule in my life according to Your will. Amen.

GOD CHOOSES WHAT IS RIGHT

He has established His throne for justice, and He judges the world with righteousness; He judges the peoples with uprightness.

PSALM 9:7-8

One of the best known images of God is that of a judge. We often read in the Bible, as in this verse, that God is a "righteous" judge. We know that He also demands "righteousness" of us.

What is this righteousness? Well, it basically means "to be right," and it has two sides. First, we need to be right with God, meaning that we only do what He expects. Then, we need to be right with others, meaning that we act only with fairness and consideration. Be one of the "righteous" that the Old Testament speaks of! There is something to be added here, however: remember that God stands for what is right, and that He stands on the side of what is right – never on the side of what is wrong.

If your case is *right*, God will be on your side, or you on His. With such a case, you can proceed. Never find yourself on the side of wrong-doing – you won't find God there!

Lord, let me act in justness and fairness.
Also, let me add grace to justice, as You have done! Amen.

GOD WILL NOT FORGET YOU

For the needy shall not always be forgotten,
and the hope of the poor shall not perish forever.
PSALM 9:18

Sometimes people think God has forgotten them, but God cannot and will not forget. He is especially concerned for the needy and the afflicted, the humble and the lowly, as the word *poor* in this verse can also be translated. God is especially on the side of those who are in need and depend on Him.

That's His character! Why then, if we are needy, do we sometimes have to wait so long for His answer? Think of faith as sowing a seed. When you sow a field, it doesn't mean that there will be an instant harvest. Oh no, between sowing and reaping lie several seasons. The sowed field might look to you as if nothing is happening, but that's not true. The seed is there, under the ground, growing. Such a field has *all* the potential for a harvest, while an unsowed field has none! All the seasons that then come and go are necessary for the harvest to ultimately come.

God did not forget you! He is busy with you, but perhaps He intends more for you than you expected. Keep sowing in faith, for your harvest will come!

Lord, help me to faithfully keep on trusting.
I will wait for Your time to come. Amen.

NO PLACE IN HIS THOUGHTS

The wicked, through the pride of his countenance,
will not seek after God: God is not in all his thoughts.
PSALM 10:4 (KJV)

This psalm is about sinners. The poet is describing someone who exploits or deceives others. Others are pushed down in order for him to get ahead, because his own benefit and wealth is his only concern. He is self-assured and arrogant. Others are cursed left and right. Yes, he is "full of himself." Everything is about him!

What is worse is that there's no room in his thinking for God. He thinks he has discovered that he can do whatever he wants. There's no God to answer to. The poet's bitter accusation is that God is *nowhere* in the sinner's thoughts – nowhere! He has many plans, many thoughts, but God is not in the picture. That's sad! Let's put God in the picture, in our plans and our thoughts, and let Him take center stage!

Lord, be part of my dreams and plans.
I cannot be happy without You. Amen.

NO MORE FEAR

You defend orphans and everyone else in need,
so that no one on earth can terrify others again.
PSALM 10:18 (CEV)

God is a reality, says the poet, and where God is on the scene, terror and fear are dispelled. It is a well-known biblical fact that God wants to take our fears away. Still, we struggle to let go of fear, because it has a useful function in our behavior.

We must remember that fear is the body's primary mechanism for keeping us safe. When we are afraid, we are extremely conscious of danger and can avoid it. There are circumstances, though, in which fear becomes generalized, a habit. Fear can also become misplaced or expressed in inappropriate or damaging ways. How do we live wisely with fear? Of course, we need to take reasonable precautions against danger. After that, though, fear has no useful function. Then it becomes counter-productive and destructive.

Fear often then becomes the danger, and we become our own enemy! Confess the following: God is in control of what happens. God keeps me safe. God frees me from fear. Repeat it as necessary – it is the truth!

Lord, I will no longer fear; I will trust in You. Amen.

LOOK IN HIS EYES

The Lord is in His holy temple; the Lord's throne is in heaven;
His eyes see, His eyelids test the children of man.
PSALM 11:4

God's eyes are open, says David. He sees everything. Some people "confess" this truth out of bitterness and resentment: *God saw this! God is not sleeping!* It's rather sad, but it remains true. God sees everything, and one day there will be accountability for what He saw.

This truth has two implications for us. First, we don't need to take revenge, because God already saw what happened and will fairly judge it. We can leave it to Him. Second, God sees us as well! He discerns who are truly righteous, as David says here so eloquently. We praise God that our righteousness is not measured by our personal merit, but by Christ's righteousness that we have received by faith.

We can live freely and boldly because of *His* righteousness! Here is a final truth about God's eyes: God's eyes are full of love for you!

Thank You for looking at me in love,
Lord! Help me to see others like You do. Amen.

SILVER WORDS

*The words of the Lord are pure words, like silver refined
in a furnace on the ground, purified seven times.*
PSALM 12:6

In this psalm, David is speaking out about the corrupt and deceitful words of the godless. Opposed to that, he defines God's words as "silver, refined seven times." A beautiful image, isn't it?

God's words are pure, costly, the truth – worthy of seeking and finding! There is also a lesson for us in this. Our own words should likewise be "pure," even before we say them. The Word says that to speak without control is foolish. It also says that we should be quick to listen but slow to speak. Yes, let's post a guard before that mouth of ours! Let's think before we speak. A good start is just to say less.

Above all, let's be guided by the Holy Spirit, because self-control is His fruit. Allow the Spirit to filter out all falseness, self-centeredness, and harshness from our words. Then our speech will be gracious, pleasant, and powerful as well!

*Holy Spirit, purify my heart. Then my words
will be pure too. Amen.*

QUESTIONS, QUESTIONS ...

How long, O LORD? Will You forget me forever? How long will You hide Your face from me? How long must I take counsel in my soul and have sorrow in my heart all the day?
PSALM 13:1-2

So many questions! In our crises, questions like these just pour out of us as we search for meaning in what is happening. Pastors often hear questions like these: Why did it have to happen? Why did it happen to me? What have I done to deserve this?

We often ask these questions well knowing that no man can answer them. Often we just need a safe space to unload, empathy, and God's presence. The fact is that these are questions that only God can answer. Even so, for some of God's answers we have to wait long, and some will only be answered in eternity. That is where faith comes in. Somewhere in the process, we have to stop asking questions and start trusting God again.

Remember, God never promised to answer all our questions, but He promised to wipe our tears. He promised to be with us always. He promised that He has everything under control, that He can be trusted, that everything will work out well in the end. With His help, you *will* overcome! Take these as provisional answers to help you along.

Lord, I now leave my questions at the foot of the cross.
I trust in You! Amen.

THE FAITH OF FOOLS

The fool says in his heart, "There is no God."
PSALM 14:1

Even in David's time some wondered whether God actually existed. The reason for their doubt was that they could seemingly get away with violence and injustice. "See, we can do whatever we want – no consequences, no retribution, no God!"

David declares this a foolish notion, because it disregards the possibility of postponed retribution, of eventual judgment. Nowadays people are atheistic mostly because of "scientific" reasons. They feel God cannot be "proven." That's also foolish! God cannot be proven by scientific means, because He is not empirically provable *by definition*. The Creator is not subject to His creation's instruments to be proven or disproved by what *He* has made. If that were possible, God wouldn't be God at all. No, God must be accepted, believed.

He is approached in *faith*, which is to accept something in the absence of proof. However, when we do accept God in our lives, He becomes part of our reality, of our truth. A believer does not ask for proofs for God's existence – he experiences God every day!

Lord, I do not need proofs for You.
You are my greatest reality. Amen.

WRONG WAY, RIGHT WAY

They have all turned aside; together they have become corrupt; there is none who does good, not even one.

PSALM 14:3

In this psalm, David notices that all are sinners, all have "turned aside," meaning they have veered off. They have left the right way. He says the Lord looks down from heaven to see if there are any who seek after Him. The rhetorical answer is "no."

We, therefore, take as fact that all men are sinful. Remember that the core of our sinfulness lies in our ego, our self-centered and carnal nature. It means that our own personal needs, wants, and urges always come first in our lives. It also means that we want to be independent of God; we want to be our own master and do our own thing. That is human nature!

The answer to that is a radical submission to God. Jesus calls it "taking up the cross." The cross of discipleship means that we follow Him, the Crucified, away from ourselves. In the process, we forget and overcome ourselves more and more to live for Him and for others. Follow Him in the way of the cross – it's the right way!

Lord, help me with my cross. I want to be more like You! Amen.

ON MY SIDE!

But you will be frightened, because God is
on the side of every good person. You may spoil
the plans of the poor, but the LORD protects them.

PSALM 14:5-6 (CEV)

It's wonderful how simple David's worldview was – typical of those times. He says God is on the side of the righteous and that is it! Let's just accept this wonderful truth, without getting academic about the fact that God loves everyone.

Yes, simply take it as your personal truth. Write "God is on my side" in your journal, or put it on your notice board. David says this fact is true for anyone who is righteous, here translated as a "good person." Is a righteous person someone without sin or mistakes? Oh no, it is someone who knows his sin all too well and flees to God for *His* help. It is someone who is deeply dependent on God, who has made Him his refuge!

Such a one has been made righteous by God because of Christ. Go get your righteousness from Him and then remember, God is completely on YOUR SIDE. He is!

Thank You, Lord, for being so completely FOR ME. Amen.

COMPLIMENTARY TICKETS

O LORD, who shall sojourn in Your tent?
Who shall dwell on Your holy hill?
PSALM 15:1

David is thinking in a typical Old Testament way – some are worthy to approach God and others simply are not. He names ten things that will qualify the righteous: he lives blamelessly; he speaks truthfully; he does not slander or speak evil; he keeps his word, etc.

The New Testament perspective on this is different. No one is worthy to approach God, because no one does these things fully! For us, these are the facts. So, who can approach God? Jesus rejects any idea that we are at least better than some others – and therefore stand a better chance – and rather shows us another way. We can acknowledge our inability to God and find that, by His grace, His door is already open!

Yes, through grace we receive the right to be called children of God and receive entrance into His house and His feast. This makes us eternally grateful, eager to please God in all those ten ways – and more!

Thank You, Lord, for grace. Without merit
I find myself at Your table! Amen.

JANUARY 28
MY ALL IS YOU

I say to the Lord, "You are my Lord;
I have no good apart from You."
PSALM 16:2

David says to the "Lord" (his Covenant God, Yahweh) that He is his "Lord" (Adonai), in other words his master, his boss. God is the Master of his life. A beautiful confession!

Still, David takes it deeper. He not only submits to his Master, but absolutely rejoices in his submission. In fact, David declares that God is the only good he possesses. He means that nothing of the many good things that he had – being King of Israel – came close to experiencing God.

God is the only real source of David's joy and fulfillment. No wonder David was a man after God's heart! God can also be first in our lives – the first source of our joy, the meaning of our lives, and the best we can hope for. Where He is the Master, we have joy and peace and meaning and hope. He makes everything good. See it like David did!

God, You bring goodness to my life.
You bring me joy and purpose! Amen.

SEE? IT'S BEAUTIFUL!

The LORD is my chosen portion and my cup;
You hold my lot. The lines have fallen for me
in pleasant places; indeed, I have a beautiful inheritance.
PSALM 16:5-6

In this psalm David is full of joy and gratitude. He looks around him and feels absolutely blessed. He says, "What I have received, comes all from God." Everything that God has measured out to him is beautiful. Remember, this psalm is not about the fact that David was a king and had many treasures.

No, it's about David's heart and relationship with God. Other kings might reason that they still have too little or believe that they have obtained all their possessions by their own effort. David, on the other hand, gives the glory to God. We, too, can look around us and decide that our portion is too little or too inferior.

Remember, some people feel thankful and blessed with little while others are unsatisfied and angry amidst plenty. That's our choice – to feel blessed or not. Yes, indeed! Choose gratitude and contentment, choose blessing!

Lord, help me to look around and see Your blessings. Amen.

ALWAYS SOMETHING IN HIS HAND

You make known to me the path of life; in Your presence there is fullness of joy; at Your right hand are pleasures forevermore.

PSALM 16:11

What poetic words and phrases – the path of life, fullness of joy, pleasures forevermore. Yes, beautiful! These words form the climax of a lyrical psalm of praise in which David feels himself intimate and close to God. He describes God's blessings in three thoughts:

- God teaches him how to live – He shows him the path to a deep, authentic, and abundant life.
- God makes his joy "full," in other words complete – He satisfies fully. David asserts that he has almost no joy apart from what God brought him. Wow, what a focus on God!
- God gives him "pleasures" – God's "right hand" is God's hand of giving. One commentator says, "God's right hand is never empty."

Let's be like David, rejoicing in God! Our lives would be one great celebration.

Lord, I want to live with complete devotion.
I want to experience Your loveliness! Amen.

BE BLESSED

Keep me as the apple of Your eye;
hide me in the shadow of Your wings.

PSALM 17:8

David asks that God "keep" him, in other words protect or shield him, from his enemies and from dangers. The "apple of the eye" is the black pupil of the eye, which of course is a highly sensitive body part that needs to be protected at all costs. The origin of this term holds for us a special lesson.

The Hebrew literally calls it here the "little man of the eye." Several other ancient languages also call the pupil by this name, because you can see your miniature self reflected in it. In fact, the word pupil itself comes from the Latin pupilla, meaning "little doll."

Why do we stress this word's origin? Well, we see ourselves as God sees us! And the same goes for God, doesn't it? If He looks at us He sees Himself, because we are made to His image. Therefore, you are precious to God. He will always protect and guard you under His "wings" where you will always, always be safe!

*Thank You, Lord, that Your eyes are on me,
that You've seen in me something special. Amen.*

February

The LORD is my shepherd; I shall not want.

He makes me lie down in green pastures. He leads me beside still waters.

He restores my soul. He leads me in paths of righteousness for His name's sake.

Even though I walk through the valley of the shadow of death, I will fear no evil, for You are with me; Your rod and Your staff, they comfort me.

You prepare a table before me in the presence of my enemies; You anoint my head with oil; my cup overflows.

Surely goodness and mercy shall follow me all the days of my life, and I shall dwell in the house of the LORD forever.

PSALM 23

DRAW THE SWORD

Arise, O LORD! Confront him, subdue him!
Deliver my soul from the wicked by Your sword.
PSALM 17:1

It's an appropriate and biblical image to picture God with a sword in His hand. Yes, Scripture refers to the sword of God in several places. Also, in the New Testament Christ is depicted with a sword.

In Revelation, for example, He is seen with a sword protruding from His mouth – a sharp, two-edged sword that we associate with His Word (Rev. 19:15). Elsewhere, in Hebrews, we read that the Word of God is like a two-edged sword. Paul calls the Word of God the "Sword of the Spirit" (Eph. 6:17). We can learn from this that the Word can act like a sword: protecting us, but also piercing our hearts with the truth!

The Word challenges us and even stops us. We should learn to take up and use this sword ourselves in order for it to have this effect. Yes, draw God's sword and practice with it. The following two ways will be of help: meditating on the Word (meaning to ponder and reflect on it, letting it sink in) and memorizing the Word. Feel how empowering it is to know and use God's Word!

Heavenly Commander, teach me how to use Your weapons. Amen.

FEBRUARY 2
I LOVE YOU, O LORD

I love You, O Lord, my strength. The Lord is my rock and
my fortress and my deliverer, my God, my rock, in whom
I take refuge, my shield, and the horn of my salvation, my stronghold.
PSALM 18:1-2

What is the Great Commandment? The Great Commandment is that you shall love your God – with your whole heart, soul, and mind, and all your strength (Mark 12:30).

It might be a difficult thought, that God asks to be loved, but it's exactly what He asks for! So, do you love God? In this context do not try to feel love for God as a warm and fuzzy feeling. Rather, start by confessing that you do love God. Say it to Him as David did: "I love You, O Lord!" Declaring your love is your conversion and submission, your transformation, your sanctification! By confessing it, you will grow in it.

See how beautifully David then motivates his declaration of love. God is his fortress, his shield, his salvation, his stronghold. You can also tell God why you love Him. You know, that is what worship is!

Loving Father, I do love You! Teach me what it means. Amen.

YOU GET WHAT YOU GIVE

With the merciful You show Yourself merciful; with the blameless man You show Yourself blameless; with the purified You show Yourself pure; and with the crooked You make Yourself seem tortuous.

PSALM 18:25-26

There is a wonderful reciprocal principle in the Bible that we get what we give – that we reap what we sow. Those who give love will receive love, those who forgive will be forgiven, and the ones who bless become the blessed ones.

Here we read it again: the merciful ones will find mercy; the faithful will find faithfulness. And for the pure, everything is pure (Titus 1:15). With the measure you use it will be measured to you, Jesus declared (Matt. 7:2). Even if we give a disciple a cup of cold water because of Christ, we will receive the reward of a disciple. The opposite, however, is also true – as we judge we will be judged, and as we condemn we will be condemned. Here David says the crooked will also find God to be complex, "tortuous" – full of twists and turns.

Is that how God is? No, that's how the crooked person is! As you are, you perceive your world. I pray that your heart will be simple and pure, loving and kind! Then that will be the life you have.

Holy Lord, make me pure, kind, and true. Make me like You! Amen.

AGAINST THE WHOLE GANG

For by You I can run against a troop,
and by my God I can leap over a wall.
PSALM 18:29

Yes, sometimes we are up against a wall or feel ganged up on. The "troop" of this verse can refer to a company of soldiers or a band of robbers. Then we need the Lord!

Look again at this verse and answer these questions: Who runs against the enemy? Who leaps over the city wall? Well, it is "I," isn't it? "I" jump; "I" fight! In other words, when we face the enemy we must fight them, and if we face the wall, we must get over it. Most often there is no getting out of difficult situations – we need to get through them! Painful conversations need to be had, unpopular decisions must be taken, bad news must, unfortunately, be conveyed, and conflict must be tackled and resolved.

The Lord most often will not take away the difficulty or release you of responsibility. However, God will help you handle it. Do what you must do, and trust God to strengthen your heart, purify your motives, and give you the right words. Do so – it's spiritual leadership!

Lord, make me strong, keep my words true,
and help me to only act in love. Amen.

WHO ELSE IS A ROCK?

For who is God, but the Lord? And who is a rock, except our God?
PSALM 18:31

To describe God as a rock is a well-known metaphor in the Bible. We already see it, for example, in Moses' song at the end of Deuteronomy. What does the image mean?

Well, a rock always stands for solidity and security, because a rock is immovable, permanent. On a rock you can build your home; on a rock you can anchor your life. That is how God is! If the winds and storms come – for they will come – we will not perish, because He is stronger than any storm. It is interesting to often read in Scripture that the Rock is the only rock. There is just no other God onto whom you can anchor your life.

You could just as well anchor yourself to your own boat – it would mean nothing! No, there is only one Rock, and that is Elohim, our God. Whatever is not built on Him will surely perish.

Lord, You are the fixed point in this chaos around me,
my anchor in this storm. Amen.

STAND SECURE, LOOK DOWN

He maketh my feet like hinds' feet, and setteth me upon my high places.
PSALM 18:33 (KJV)

What does it mean that God sets us on "high places"? Other Bible translations render it, "You set me secure on the heights" (ESV), or "You help me stand on the mountains" (CEV).

Remember that David is referring here to the deer that inhabited the mountains, or Judea. From a height, they could look down. A "high place" in this context is a position of authority and dominance, of victory. In our faith-walk with God we need to get to a "high place" as well, meaning that we view the matter from above, that we see it as God sees it. When we move into God's perspective, when we take authority in His name, we are moving into victory. We weren't called to wallow about in the quagmires of hopelessness! Oh no, we're believers. We're children of the Most High!

Even though we know these things, we so often sink back into doubt and fear when we face hardships. Yes, we do! That's why it requires of us a new and definite decision every time. Decide again to take up a high position in Christ. Decide again to look away from your dark anticipations and fears. Decide again to focus on Him instead, to look up. Rise up, believer!

Most High God, show me how You see this situation. Amen.

THE DAY TESTIFIES, AS DO I

The heavens declare the glory of God, and the sky above proclaims His handiwork. Day to day pours out speech, and night to night reveals knowledge.

PSALM 19:1-2

David says that nature constantly declares God's goodness and glory. He poetically describes how one day pours its report of God's greatness into the next – from the first creation day right until this morning!

When the sun rises in its grandeur, it testifies about God's shining glory. When dusk sets in and the moon shines bright and clear, it affirms that God was trustworthy once again. Think of the rolling planets and the immeasurable stars, the powerful forces that hold atoms together and the ever-expanding universe. All of this testifies about God's fantastic power and might. Stand in awe thereof – see God in it! Then, pass the testimony on. Let people see your faith, hope, and love – it honors Him!

Then tell someone about God's goodness. Let them know about something God did. Encourage others to trust the good God you know!

Yes, wonderful God, I do want to be a witness of Your goodness and grace! Amen.

DESIRABLE, COSTLY, RICH

More to be desired are they than gold, even much fine gold;
sweeter also than honey and drippings of the honeycomb.
PSALM 19:10

This psalm starts off with nature as God's general revelation, but then it turns to His Word as His special revelation. David says, for example, that God's Word – referring to the Law – is perfect and trustworthy. It brings healing and shows the right path.

In this specific verse he says the Word is more costly than gold, even much gold, and tastier than honey. See God's Word from a modern perspective: What would computer equipment be without a program? Merely unusable metal and plastic. It needs a program, software. Similarly, God's Word supplies the program on which we live – the software that guides our behavior and life. Remove it, and we wouldn't know what to do. Program it in, and our life has meaning, direction, and purpose.

It supplies the facts of where you come from, what you're here for, and where you're supposed to go. Now you know what to do and how to do it! Program the Word daily into your soul, and experience its direction and purpose for yourself!

Lord, Your Word is indeed dear to me – like gold,
like honey! It gives meaning to my life. Amen.

IN THE UNKNOWN DEPTHS

*Let the words of my mouth and the meditation of my heart
be acceptable in Your sight, O LORD, my rock and my redeemer.*

PSALM 19:14

David asks here that his words and thoughts be "acceptable" to God, meaning "pleasing" or favorable, good. Remember, as we think, we talk – our words directly mirror what is in our hearts.

Let's unpack a bit this concept of the "heart" that David mentions. Of course he uses it in a very general way, but we can suggest that our heart contains our deepest motives: the reasons why we want what we want, feel what we feel, and think what we think. From out of our heart's motives – which should please God – our whole personality unfolds. There, in the unconscious depths of our psyche, God wants to do His work. There He wants to change us. That is the whole purpose of the Holy Spirit!

Work with the Spirit's work in your heart. Submit to it; give in to it – surrender to Him! Let Him do what He wants to do. Now that is pleasing to God!

*Lord, purify my heart. Then my words and
deeds will be pure as well. Amen.*

THE GOD OF YOUR FATHERS

May the LORD answer you in the day of trouble!
May the name of the God of Jacob protect you!
PSALM 20:1

In this psalm David announces seven blessings on the king. Amongst other things he asks that God will hear and protect the king – just as He did for Jacob, their forefather. Remember that Jacob experienced God intensely in his lifelong struggle to obtain the covenant promise. David, who is the king at this stage, wants to live his life in the same way.

Do you have a similar desire? Did you have a father or mother who truly served God – or a grandmother, or some other mentor or role model? Do you need to return to the "God of your fathers"? Yes, turn – turn back! You cannot relive their lives or their relationships with God, but you can have your own, in your own way. You can write your own story-with-God with the same passion, trust, and commitment that they had.

Yes, you can have God in your life, see Him working, hear His voice, and experience His guidance. Then your own children, one day, will want to follow the God of their father or mother too!

Yes, Lord, I do want to show my children how to
live with God. God of my fathers, help me! Amen.

GO DOWN INTO THE HOLY PLACE

May He send you help from the sanctuary and
give you support from Zion!
PSALM 20:2

This is one of the seven beautiful blessings of the Davidic covenant: "May He send you help from the sanctuary." What does "sanctuary" mean here? David is referring to Zion, which is the spiritual name for Jerusalem, the city of God. More specifically, he means the temple in Jerusalem.

The Israelites believed that God's presence resided on the Ark of the Covenant there in the Holy of Holies. That is the sanctuary from where God will help His people! That temple, however, as you know, does not exist anymore, which makes us wonder where God resides now. Yes, where is God's temple today? God's temple is in our hearts! Scripture is clear: our bodies are the temples of the Holy Ghost (1 Cor. 6:19). If you belong to God, His Spirit resides in you. What a wonderful truth!

From out of our heart, our deepest being, we experience His rule, His guidance, His encouragement, His confirmation, and His peace. Find Him there!

Holy Spirit, teach me to find You deep within my heart. Amen.

SUCH WORDS HAVE POWER

May He grant you your heart's desire and fulfill all your plans!
PSALM 20:4

What a beautiful blessing the Word pronounces here – over me and you! Remember, a blessing in Jesus' name, spoken in faith and accepted in faith, is a powerful confirmation of God's goodness and intention. It changes lives! Just think of the effect that it had on you when an adult or a teacher acknowledged your worth as a youngster, perhaps pointing out your strengths or assuring you of your future success.

It was very encouraging! We remember such affirmations forever. It's the same when we declare God's blessing over someone: "God loves you; God cares for you; God will fulfill your desires." Such pronouncements are empowering and faith building. Make sure to bless others with such words! Please, please avoid telling a child the opposite: that he will fail or that she is not good enough. It robs them of their very life; it binds them inwardly – and it's not true at all!

No, Jesus said to bless, never curse (Matt. 5:44).

Loving Father, make all my words a blessing! Amen.

HOIST HIS BANNER!

May we shout for joy over your salvation, and in the name of our God set up our banners! May the LORD fulfill all your petitions!
PSALM 20:5

The topic of this verse is battle, warfare. David is referring to the battles of Israel, but we also battle, don't we? Take note that David's battles are fought "in the name of our God" and that the victory is also God's. Therein we find our key.

Our struggles are most often only our private little struggles – often about a bruised ego. As we grow spiritually, however, we will learn that our ego is not the center of our lives. On the contrary, we learn to "crucify" our ego and to focus on God and His will for us. We also learn to just leave some battles for Him to fight. Let us ultimately learn, though, to fight His battles, to fight His enemies, to advance His interests, and to let His kingdom come.

When we fight this way, victory is assured – most definitely so! His banners will be hoisted over the battlefield!

Lord, fight for me as You have promised –
and let me also fight for Your sake! Amen.

TAKE UP HIS WEAPONS

Some trust in chariots and some in horses,
but we trust in the name of the LORD our God.
PSALM 20:7

David is reminding us of the fact that the battle is the Lord's, not ours. It is true that we need to fight from time to time – there is no escaping it! Let's learn from David, though, whose trust was in his God, not his weaponry. It doesn't mean that he entered the fray without anything, but that he realized that the victory was in God's hands – not in his!

As a young man David once discarded Saul's heavy body armor and approached – and won – Goliath with nothing more than a sling and five stones. In our personal battles, our own "weapons" are not worth much, anyway. Let's rather fight "in the name of the Lord," like David. What does it mean?

Well, it means that we fight as He directs us to fight, that we make it a spiritual fight, and that we leave the result in His hands. He is, after all, the Lord of Hosts, the Captain of the armies. That's how David fought – and won!

Lord, I will fight this fight in Your name.
What is my next move, Captain? Amen.

PRAISES AND THE PRESENCE

Yet You are holy, enthroned on the praises of Israel.
PSALM 22:3

This verse can be understood to mean that God "inhabits" or "indwells" the praises of His people – as some Bible translations have it. We really experience it as such: when we start praising God, in prayer or song, we sense His presence more and more.

Especially in our crises, when we so need God's presence, our praise-in-faith soon brings peace and victory. Like Paul and Silas who sang to God's glory in prison in the middle of the night, we can also experience God, even in our darkest hours. However, let's not think that mere words of praise can bring God near. It does not work mechanically! No, true praise is focusing our hearts on God, turning to Him who is already present anyway. Praise is becoming more and more aware of His presence!

Words that do not mirror the praise of our hearts will remain only words – they are not praise as such. However, if our hearts burn for Him even in our difficulty, we will experience His faith, His victory, His presence!

Lord, help me to win over the darkness
by focusing on the light. Amen.

SUDDENLY, THE DARK NIGHT

*My God, my God, why have You forsaken me? Why are You
so far from saving me, from the words of my groaning?*
PSALM 22:1

Without any warning, we suddenly find David at his lowest. In this psalm he experiences, as later authors would call it, the "dark night of the soul." It is the forlorn place we get to when we feel that God has withdrawn. We feel isolated. We cannot hear His voice anymore. Our prayers bounce off the ceiling. Our worship means nothing.

Some believers find themselves in such a valley for a long period. Looking back, they later realize that it made them grow spiritually. Even here, in David's desolate cry, he realizes that God is still there, because he still addresses God! He spells out how desperate he feels, but in spite of that he believes that God is there, that God is still in control. The problem is more within himself, with his own locked-up soul.

Let's confirm something most assuredly: behind God's silence lies God's love! It's still there, as it always has been. Just push through and find it again!

Lord, I struggle to experience You.
Unlock my heart through Your Holy Spirit! Amen.

LOW POINT, HIGH POINT

*But I am a worm and not a man, scorned by
mankind and despised by the people.*
PSALM 22:6

David's life was one of extremes. He was the youngest child, but destined to be a great king. He was a shepherd, a ruler, a general, a singer, a killer, and a lover. He was completely devoted to God, but because of his bloodshed God didn't allow him to build Him a temple.

Yes, David knew lows, and he knew highs! In this psalm he was probably fleeing again, as he often was: from Saul, from the Philistines, from Absalom, from his subjects. Once again he feels the humiliation of their rejection – even their loathing. Therefore, he's calling out to God.

Remember, in all of David's ups and downs one thing remained constant: his relationship with God. He had a covenant with God, and he simply kept on trusting God through everything that happened, even through his sin.

And God, true to His promise, restored David every time. Every time! Are you at a low point in your life? Make things right with God, and then see it through with God!

Yes, Lord, lead me out of here – to the heights. Amen.

FEBRUARY 18
HERE IS MY GOD

He trusts in the LORD; let Him deliver him;
let Him rescue him, for he delights in Him!
PSALM 22:8

David's thoughts are dark, because things are not going well at all. He is mocked and despised, rejected. He feels unworthy and humiliated. It is a bitter thought for him that God can intervene but doesn't.

This causes his enemies to ask, as always, "Where is your God now?" David is wondering the same! He pleads for God to prove Himself to the whole world, yet experiences the opposite. We can identify with David here. We also live as believers in an unbelieving world. We sometimes feel excluded or rejected, even ridiculed. It is especially bad when others make snide remarks about faith, believers, or God. Remember, that's part of our Christian life!

We so want God to prove Himself to the world, but it doesn't work that way. However, you can help people see God in your words and actions, in your life! Do that as well as you can – the Spirit will help you.

Lord, make me a living testimony
of Your goodness and power. Amen.

I AM POURED OUT

I am poured out like water, and all my bones are out of joint;
my heart is like wax; it is melted within my breast.

PSALM 22:14

David is at an absolute low. He is falling apart. How precisely he describes his breakdown! He says his heart is poured out like water. His defenses have crumbled; he is going to pieces. He is undone, finished, all is over!

David is breaking apart, his strength melting away like hot wax. He has no control left, none whatsoever. Helplessly, he sinks down to the ground. Most of us have, thankfully, never experienced such a complete meltdown. Many have an idea of what it means, though, while some know it all too well. Do you know what happens after you have broken down so completely? Well, you stay there at God's feet as long as you need. You just stay there. Then you get up, dust yourself off, and carry on.

Is it possible? Yes, it is! God gives you the strength! Are you weak, despondent, despairing? God will raise you up! Listen here: you are not weak anymore – you are strong, in Jesus' name!

Lord, when I'm weak You are strong.
Work Your strength in me! Amen.

AS GOOD AS DEAD

My strength is dried up like a potsherd, and my tongue sticks to my jaws; You lay me in the dust of death.

PSALM 22:15

We are busy with a dark topic, because David is at a dark place. He says here his enemies have encircled him like a pack of dogs and trapped him down. Now he finds himself in the hands of evil men. His hands and feet are tied up like an animal's, and he lies powerless between them. He is as good as dead!

It's bad to see how David ascribes all of this to God: "You lay me in the dust of death" (emphasis added). He means that God could have prevented this. Still, David is not pointing fingers with this comment. He is merely stating his total feeling of abandonment. Do you feel abandoned by God – sometimes?

Then listen to this: Wait, David! Yes, you're at your lowest point, but wait. It's not the end. You will go through this, you will be restored, and you will end your life with success and significance. Yes, that's how it was for David – and for you, most assuredly, if you trust in God. David's God!

Lord, I have little strength left – but You are with me! Amen.

HOPELESS, BUT GOD IS THERE

Save me from the mouth of the lion!
You have rescued me from the horns of the wild oxen!
PSALM 22:21

In this psalm we now come to a turning point. Even in David's darkest thoughts there remains an undercurrent of faith, because he is sharing his dark thoughts with God. He still believes! Perhaps it was this talking-it-through-with-God that built his faith, because now, right at the lowest point, his spirit lights up.

He now realizes that his deliverance is assured – he must only persevere; he must just see it through! Soon it will all be over. You and I can experience a crisis in two ways. If we are *without hope*, it can really feel as if God is gone and that everything is lost. We are fixed on the worst-case scenario. Then the realization can dawn, though, that God is still present, that He is still in control. That changes everything!

Suddenly we have *hope* – and biblical hope is a very powerful thing – and our strength returns. O, pray that your hope and strength reignites, because the fact is this: God is near!

Lord, switch on hope in my heart – renew my strength! Amen.

FROM DEATH TO LIFE

*I will tell of Your name to my brothers; in the midst of the congregation
I will praise You: you who fear the LORD, praise Him!*

PSALM 22:22-23

Everything has changed for David! This psalm moves from one extreme to the other, from deep despair to exuberance and joy! David's experience ends with his calling upon the whole world to praise God.

What this psalm teaches us is how easily circumstances can change when God gets involved. David had times where he really thought his life was ending, but then, at his worst, he realized that God was still near. Somewhere in his darkness he met with God, which changed his outlook completely. Even while circumstances remained the same (for a time), God's presence changed him *in* his circumstances. It gave him faith, renewed his hope, and turned his struggle into victory!

Ultimately, David went through his crises and lived a long and productive life. Don't accept that things cannot change – things *can* change! Take it as a fact. Believe it!

Lord, in spite of all my bad experiences, I trust in You! Amen.

EVERYTHING FOR TODAY

You, LORD, are my shepherd. I will never be in need.

PSALM 23:1 (CEV)

Now to the best known and most beautiful psalm! Matter-of-factly, in simple and straightforward terms, David spells out the result of God being our shepherd: "I will never be in need." The King James Version reads, "I shall not want."

This tremendously powerful statement contains one of the keys to our walk with God, a key that can unlock the whole spiritual life. Please accept it as the absolute truth: with God you have what you need – every day! He gives you enough for the day. With God present, you have sufficient resources to handle every situation. Today you will have enough to do today's tasks, to surmount today's challenges. God is enough for you today. Tomorrow will be the same.

If we can accept in faith that God really is a Good Shepherd who will give us what we need for today, we can have peace. That is what total surrender means.

Good Shepherd, I trust You. You will supply
what I really need in this situation. Amen.

YOU HAVE ENOUGH

He makes me lie down in green pastures. He leads me beside still waters.
PSALM 23:2

The shepherd must make sure that his sheep always have sufficient grazing and ample water. In order for that to happen the biblical shepherd, just as in modern times, had to move his flock around. For the summer they could be at a certain place, but for the winter they had to go around the mountain, for example.

Sometimes they had to go far and stay away for months. The shepherd knew where good grazing was available and where the water holes were. It is the same way with the Good Shepherd's sheep. These verses do not imply that we will always, leisurely, remain at green pastures and still waters. No, life has its seasons, and sometimes we will trek, hot and thirsty, through areas in which we find little comfort. Still, we will always end up, as often as necessary, with sufficient provision for our needs, with rest, and with comfort.

That is the task of the Good Shepherd. Trust Him for that! You can have this peace: "I shall not want" (Ps. 23:1). Yes, your needs will be met.

Good Shepherd, thank You that You will lead me
to green pastures again, to still waters. Amen.

FOLLOW THE TRACKS

He leads me in paths of righteousness for His name's sake.
PSALM 23:3

The phrase "in paths of righteousness" refers literally to "tracks." It can mean a path, figuratively, but there is something beautiful about real tracks: footprints and other indications that someone, or something, walked there.

Tracks are something to be spotted and followed intentionally, more than just a path to be walked. The Bible suggests to us here that someone established that path of righteousness before us. It is He: Christ, the Master, the Righteous One! It is in *His* footsteps that we need to follow, like a child walking in the footsteps of his dad. *He* is the Good Shepherd that walks ahead of His flock, calling us to follow Him.

If we walk where He walks, do as He does, see as He sees, feel as He feels, and react as He would react, *then* we are walking in the paths of righteousness!

Good Shepherd, lead me in Your footsteps.
Make me a good follower. Amen.

IN DEATH'S DARK VALE

Even though I walk through the valley of the shadow
of death, I will fear no evil, for You are with me;
Your rod and Your staff, they comfort me.

PSALM 23:4

David tended sheep. He knew that a shepherd sometimes had to take his flock through dangerous or desolate places in order to get to better grazing. In his time there was always the risk of robbers or wild animals. That's why David understood that his own life sometimes had to move through seasons or situations that were not ideal.

His dark words, "the valley of the shadow of death," may refer to death itself, to Hades. However, he asserts that even there he will not fear, because even there the Good Shepherd will protect him – as a good shepherd does! A shepherd has a rod for fending off enemies and a staff for keeping his sheep near to him. Sometimes we do find ourselves in "death's dark vale." Yes, sometimes we come to the very limits of our life. Sometimes we may wonder, *Will I make it through this?* Do not fear! The Shepherd will be with you all the way!

Here is another perspective: Ultimately, no one "makes it through." Eventually all of us will enter that shadowy valley of death. But yes – *He* is there, too, already there, waiting for us!

Good Shepherd, hold my hand when I am fearful. Amen.

WELCOME, WELCOME TO THE FEAST!

You treat me to a feast, while my enemies watch.
You honor me as Your guest, and You fill my cup until it overflows.
PSALM 23:5 (CEV)

We can look at Psalm 23 as consisting of three parts: life, death, and eternity. It is first about green pastures and still waters, rest for the soul and the paths of righteousness. This is all about life's abundance and God's blessing. Then we get to the "valley of the shadow of death," the "dark vale" through which all of us must pass, but God is also there!

Even there He will protect and guide us. Then the whole tone of the psalm changes – it becomes a jubilation! God receives me as His guest at the heavenly feast. "Thou anointest my head with oil; my cup runneth over" (KJV). Yes, when *all* is over and done, when you have given *all* to finish the race, God is waiting for you at the winning post! Then you will be received as a hero and your victory celebrated!

Then your struggle and worry, your pain will be taken away, and you will enter rest. Be encouraged: that day is coming!

Lord, I praise You for the gift of life –
and for the gift of eternal life. Amen.

GOODNESS AND MERCY

Surely goodness and mercy shall follow me all the days of my life,
and I shall dwell in the house of the Lord forever.

PSALM 23:6

The beautiful last verse of this best known psalm is a summary of life and death. As for the first, David makes the powerful pronouncement that "goodness and mercy" will follow him all the days of his life. What a statement of faith!

Make it your own. Write it in your journal; put it on your mirror; stick it onto the notice board. Repeat it to yourself so that it sinks down into your soul and changes your identity. You are blessed – a beloved of God! Goodness and mercy is your portion, your inheritance! If you have trouble, it is temporary. David then adds that he will "dwell in the house of the Lord forever." He means that he will remain in and near God's temple for the rest of his life. But we have a far greater expectation. The temple of God is in our hearts, in our relationship with Him – and that relationship will endure forever!

Take note: the goodness and mercy that we experience in this life can never compare to the goodness and mercy and love and peace and joy of eternal life with God!

Father, thank You that the door to Your
house is always, always open to me! Amen.

EVERYTHING AND EVERYONE: HIS

The earth is the LORD's and the fullness thereof,
the world and those who dwell therein, for He has founded it
upon the seas and established it upon the rivers.

PSALM 24:1-2

God laid the foundations of the earth in the seas, says David according to his ancient understanding of the world. Still, even with all our scientific information we can concur with David in his assertion that God made everything.

Yes, God is behind the universe – He planned it; He created it into existence; He ordered it to become. God knows the mysteries of the speed of light, of dark matter, of the powers that keep atoms together or drive galaxies apart. God is the physicist, the scientist, the project manager, and the owner/developer of it all – it's all *His*! He also knows every human being, because He made them to be.

Every individual, therefore, belongs to God: believing or unbelieving, whether they are Jewish, Christian, Muslim, Hindu, atheist, or secular. Conversion is to realize this, to return to the rightful owner, the Maker, and to get in line with His plan and purpose. Who knows you better than the One who designed you?

*Thank You, heavenly Creator, for loving
each and every one of Your creations. Amen.*

March

Vindicate me, O LORD, for I have walked in my integrity, and I have trusted in the LORD without wavering.

Prove me, O LORD, and try me; test my heart and my mind.

For Your steadfast love is before my eyes, and I walk in Your faithfulness. I do not sit with men of falsehood, nor do I consort with hypocrites.

I hate the assembly of evildoers, and I will not sit with the wicked.

I wash my hands in innocence and go around Your altar, O LORD, proclaiming thanksgiving aloud, and telling all Your wondrous deeds.

O LORD, I love the habitation of Your house and the place where Your glory dwells.

Do not sweep my soul away with sinners, nor my life with bloodthirsty men, in whose hands are evil devices, and whose right hands are full of bribes.

But as for me, I shall walk in my integrity; redeem me, and be gracious to me. My foot stands on level ground; in the great assembly I will bless the LORD.

PSALM 26

NEVER IN VAIN

O my God, in You I trust; let me not be put to shame;
let not my enemies exult over me.

PSALM 25:2

David pleads here with God for some needed intervention. His enemies are equally eager to see whether his God will save him – they will rejoice if nothing happens! Will David's trust be in vain?

We can identify with David here, because we also live in a critical and cynical world to which we would so much like to prove that God is real. We really want God to prove Himself to them. Take note, however, that God does not need to prove Himself to anyone, and it's not our job to prove Him. More than once Christ turned down the temptation to prove Himself.

God is *only* proven by honest and personal faith. Only by faith can He be known! What's more is that God is not obliged to answer every prayer or rescue every time. God doesn't react just because we ask.

God is God! He knows best and does what's best. We do not need to understand Him, but we need to trust Him. Steadfast trust in God will never be in vain. Keep your faith strong, forget the so-called enemies, and know this: you will be the one to exult. Not them!

Lord, I trust in You. Your plan and Your will is best for my life! Amen.

YOUR WAYS, NOT MY WAYS

Make me to know Your ways, O LORD; teach me Your paths.
Lead me in Your truth and teach me, for You are the God
of my salvation; for You I wait all the day long.
PSALM 25:4-5

In his distress, David urgently asks for God's intervention and salvation – and to please be speedy about it! Don't we know that feeling all too well?

David is very anxious, but then he comes up with something rather mature. He not only asks for deliverance *out* of the situation, he asks for God's will *in* the situation. This is important, because we often think prayer is basically to write our will onto God's agenda. Yes, we use all the spiritual techniques we have in order to get God to do what we ask. Often we forget that God might have His own intention in the process – we mostly assume that God's will in a matter is exactly the same as our will! David, however, *asks* for God's will and paths so that his will can align with God's will more closely.

Yes, perhaps we should stop asking God for what we want and start listening for what God wants. Let's speak less and listen more, because God is God.

Lord, what is Your will for me today? What will honor You now? Amen.

FORGIVE YOUR YOUTH

Remember not the sins of my youth or
my transgressions; according to Your steadfast
love remember me, for the sake of Your goodness, O Lord!

PSALM 25:7

David is ashamed of the sins of his youth. We don't know exactly what he is referring to because his better-known transgressions were committed when he was older.

Whatever it was, now, as an adult, he feels bitterly embarrassed about the things he did. Can't we identify with this? Definitely! We can all think of embarrassing episodes from our youth when we said silly things, burst out in emotion, or made the worst decisions. We just acted so immaturely! Yes, we acted immature because we *were* immature! Do you get it? Immature people will act in immature ways – what else can we expect? Now that we are more mature we, hopefully, act more mature.

Forgive yourself, therefore, for your juvenile ways, because you *were* juvenile. Have some sympathy for your younger self who was so uncertain, awkwardly trying to make an impression. Take it to God – for the last time – and accept His forgiveness. Deal with your past!

Lord, thank You for accepting me just as I am – and as I was!
Your grace completely covers my shame. Amen.

MARCH 4
A SPIRITUAL X-RAY

Prove me, O Lord, and try me; test my heart and my mind.
PSALM 26:2

David opens up his heart toward God and asks Him to "test" him. He wants God to examine his motives and thoughts, his words, his deeds, and to show him whatever there may be that does not please Him.

He literally (in the Hebrew) asks God to inspect his reins (kidneys) and heart, as if under a spiritual X-ray machine. Everything will be revealed by its light! David's invitation to God is a very healthy one. Remember, sin has a built-in tendency to conceal itself. Whenever we do something wrong, we immediately want to cover it up. Our heartache and pain is often repressed, swept under the rug. Our "dark side" is everything that must remain hidden to others, even to ourselves.

To God, however, nothing can remain hidden. That's why we can just as well open our heart up to God and let His bright light shine in! Yes, we can face our darkness, confess it, and deal with it. Living in God's light can only lead to forgiveness, healing, and communion. Why not?

Lord, You know me through and through.
Your love sets me free! Amen.

I AM INNOCENT, I AM FREE

I wash my hands in innocence and go around Your altar, O LORD,
proclaiming thanksgiving aloud, and telling all Your wondrous deeds.

PSALM 26:6-7

It's always wonderful to see how simply, directly, and personally David experienced his relationship with God. When he transgressed, he felt deep guilt and pleaded for forgiveness. Then, upon receiving pardon, he immediately had peace and felt his innocence renewed, as in this psalm.

Here David is convinced that peace has been restored between him and God, and it feels great! He is straightaway thanking and praising God! David has little of the neurotic guilt that we so often endure. Remember that God's forgiveness is unconditional, powerful, and real. We are truly set free and truly free to feel at peace with God. That is the goal of our forgiveness.

Stop then with the endless feelings of guilt. Jesus gave His life so that you can put guilt down now. Walk in the freedom He bought you!

Lord Jesus, thank You for setting me free. I am free indeed! Amen.

WHOM SHALL I FEAR?

The LORD is my light and my salvation; whom shall I fear?
The LORD is the stronghold of my life; of whom shall I be afraid?
PSALM 27:1

In God's perfect will there is no fear. There was no fear in Paradise, and eternity will not know fear. Fear is a part of this life, because it's a by-product of sin.

Where sin is, fear comes, because sin brings along danger, enemies, worry, loss, heartache, etc. These things we know so well! Still, the Word teaches that this life should not be lived with fear. Will we fear people, when the Lord is our salvation? Will we be afraid of eventualities, when God holds the future? Will we fear the Evil One, who has been defeated by our King? No, we will not! In principle we will fear only God – remembering that biblical fear is not being afraid of our Father, but living with righteousness, respect, and trust toward Him.

Remember the following: (1) nothing is allowed over you that you cannot handle; (2) everything that you have to deal with will be incorporated by God for good, whether you understand it or not; (3) our end is with Him, where we never, ever will fear again! Let's now give our fear to God!

Lord Jesus, today I give my fear, worry,
and anxiety to You. I don't want to bear them anymore. Amen.

YOUR FOCUS, YOUR REALITY

One thing have I asked of the Lord, that will I seek after:
that I may dwell in the house of the Lord all the days of my life,
to gaze upon the beauty of the Lord and to inquire in His temple.

PSALM 27:4

David loves God so much that he just wants to stay in God's temple! He feels at home there, and he feels God's goodness there – the first thing he associates with God. Yes, the most wonderful experience in our lives is the experience of God.

Don't believe that faith is merely a matter of confessing correct doctrine. Solid doctrine is important, but faith is just as much a matter of the heart. If we never have any experience of God, if we nowhere find Him personally in our walk of faith, we really do not have enough. There is absolutely no formula for experiencing God, because we can find Him in hundreds of ways: in ecstasy but also in silence, in joy but also in suffering.

We need, however, to learn to experience God. We need to focus on finding Him; we must intentionally become aware of Him. David, for example, stayed in God's house looking for Him, inquiring after Him, gazing upon His beauty. Remember, where your focus is, your reality will be.

Lord, help me to look for You more,
to find You more – all around me! Amen.

GOING HOME

For He will hide me in His shelter in the day of trouble;
He will conceal me under the cover of His tent;
He will lift me high upon a rock.

PSALM 27:5

Small children start their journey toward independence from behind their mothers' legs. There is a period in which a child will only go where he can still see his mother. If danger is perceived, he quickly darts back to her legs!

While growing up our parents' house remained the refuge of our lives. There, in our room, we could feel safe from bullies and school challenges. On our bed we could cry when disappointments hit. After leaving the house, adults often go back "home" when their relationships fail or their finances crash. Even when you're old, you sometimes wish you still had a "home" that you could return to, free from worries and fears.

Do you know something? You have a home! You have a home, because you are a child and you have a Father. You can return anytime to that home, to that loving Father! There you can hide away until you can face the world again. Go back home!

Lord, thank You for having an eternal home
where the door is always open! Amen.

LOVED, CARED FOR, NURTURED

Even if my father and mother should
desert me, You will take care of me.

PSALM 27:10 (CEV)

One thing we should understand clearly: God really can be trusted with our well-being. We are not left alone in the universe, left to the mercy of "whatever." No, we are loved; we are cared for and nurtured; we are respected and valued.

David means that God will literally take care of him should his parents desert him. Jesus emphasized the same truth! Let's accept as a personal truth that we really can live carefree in this world. We often take up too much unneeded worry; we accept too many unnecessary responsibilities. Let them go – give them to God! Yes, release them, surrender them up!

Stop clinging to things that you cannot keep anyway. Forget a bit about your many needs and wants, and focus on God's grace – feel it like the sunshine on your face, and start to share that unconditional love with others.

Lord, I am so attached to my possessions, my needs,
and my wants. I surrender them to You! Amen.

IN THIS LIFE, LORD!

*I believe that I shall look upon the goodness
of the LORD in the land of the living! Wait for the LORD;
be strong, and let your heart take courage; wait for the LORD!*
PSALM 27:13-14

David writes a wonderful psalm about God's provision and care. With God he feels safe and cared for. See how beautiful his conviction is that his faith isn't merely a "pie in the sky when you die".

No, he is sure that he'll see the goodness of the Lord in the "land of the living" – that is to say in this life, in his immediate future! Remember that David's faith was a very practical and tangible one. It was less of a spiritual philosophy and more of an everyday reality. Therefore, he encourages the reader of his poem with certainty: trust in the Lord, be strong, take courage, and wait for the Lord!

Take David's advice as a personal promise. Expect the goodness of the Lord in this life. Trust God for it and wait on it – persevere until you have received it! The bonus is that in the next life you will be filled, saturated with God's goodness. With God you cannot lose!

Lord, I am sure I will see Your goodness in my life – I am sure! Amen.

HEAR ME, TALK TO ME

Hear the voice of my pleas for mercy, when I cry to You for help,
when I lift up my hands toward Your most holy sanctuary.
PSALM 28:2

In this psalm, David is pleading for God to hear and answer him. "Be not deaf to me," he says literally. In biblical times people prayed in the direction of the temple with their hands outstretched before them. Then they would – with open eyes – direct their prayer to God.

God's words and answers make David's inner being come alive, he says, but when he's cut off from God it's as if he's dying inside. How true! Communication with God is the lifeblood of our spiritual life. Doesn't communication provide the structure and content of any relationship? Yes, indeed. No communication means no relationship!

Stay, therefore, in a relationship with God by staying in His Word – and by being receptive to His voice in your heart. There must be *some* form of communication between you and God. Work towards that.

Lord, my relationship with You is so important.
Help me to give priority to my spiritual life. Amen.

MARCH 12

YOU GET WHAT YOU DESERVE ... ?

*Give to them according to their work and according
to the evil of their deeds; give to them according
to the work of their hands; render them their due reward.*

PSALM 28:4

It's always interesting to see how simply people of the Old Testament thought about spiritual matters. In this psalm David pleads with God to intervene, and he supports his request by pointing out his innocence and good works. He deserves God's blessing! On sinners he calls down wrath and punishment, because they should also get their just reward.

Let's not condemn David too quickly, because he reasons from a strict sense of justice. We have a similar belief when we say, "You reap what you sow," which we take as a biblical truth. Doing wrong will sooner or later bear its bitter fruits. Well, that's all that David is asking for! For us as believers, however, the principle does not quite work that way. The bitter fruit of *our* sin was borne by Jesus on the cross. *He* reaped the seeds that *we* sowed (and are still sowing).

Divine retribution hit *Him*, so that we don't get what we deserve. That is what we call grace, and our prayer is that all sinners – like us – experience it!

*Thank You, Lord Jesus, for coming between me
and God's justice, for Your amazing grace! Amen.*

MARCH 13
FAVOR FOR A LIFETIME

For His anger is but for a moment, and His favor is for a lifetime.
Weeping may tarry for the night, but joy comes with the morning.
PSALM 30:5

The Israelites believed that God can become angry, but that His anger never lasts forever. In the end God would always forgive them because of His love. They reminded themselves of His covenant – one that He will never break, not even in His anger. God's goodness will always overtake His anger! It's a beautiful thought, and it proved to be true.

But let's add some perspective:

- God's wrath is never rage – God never loses His temper. No, God's righteous anger is because of His demand for love, justice, and righteousness, and quite rightly so!
- God's emotions are never capricious or fickle. No, God is working according to His plan – and His plan for you will succeed!

In the New Testament we read that God's grace is a reality. His anger was directed at the cross for a moment so that His favor can be ours for a lifetime! Praise Him!

Lord, thank You for Your favor – weeping
will be followed by joy. Amen.

YOUR PURPOSE IS TO LIVE

What profit is there in my death, if I go down to the pit?
Will the dust praise You? Will it tell of Your faithfulness?
PSALM 30:9

David is writing here from an Old Testament perspective, which had little insight into an afterlife. Their concern was for the present. They believed that the dead was not aware enough to praise God; therefore, David wanted to live in order to praise the Lord!

Let's take from this rather complicated subject the following truth: God wants us to *live*, truly and abundantly live. We were created to fully live to His glory. *Live* then! Embrace life completely, with all the good that it offers, as God's gift to you. Never say you shouldn't have lived or no longer want to live. Please never allow such thoughts into your mind – they are *not* God's will for you!

It is true that life – even a full and rewarding life – entails hardship and struggle. Yes that's part of the deal, but ultimately life is *worth* living. Live with God and you will see for yourself.

Thank You, Lord, for an abundant life with You. Amen.

IN LOVING HANDS

Into Your hand I commit my spirit;
You have redeemed me, O LORD, faithful God.

PSALM 31:5

Once again we find David flat against the ground. He is in great distress and sorrow – grief is wasting him away; his eyes cannot cry anymore; his body is collapsing. It feels as if his years are filled with suffering.

He is absolutely desperate and despondent. Still, in this psalm we also hear another note. When David is done pouring his heart out, he declares his trust in God: "I trust in You, O LORD; … You are my God. My times are in Your hand" (Ps. 31:14-15). In verse five he sensitively writes, "Into your hand I commit my spirit" – the very words Jesus repeated on the cross. How wonderful is this image!

Are you down, despairing? Then give your life into God's loving hands. The caring hands of your Father will carry you and guide you – and help you up again.

Thank You, Lord, that my life and my times
are in Your loving hands. Amen.

ONLY ONE WAY

Before I confessed my sins, my bones felt limp,
and I groaned all day long.
PSALM 32:3 (CEV)

Sin is the natural inclination in all of us to be independent of God, to do our own thing. Sin is all about control. To make our own decisions contrary to His leads to wrong choices and the consequences they bring. Even then, it's our inclination not to accept responsibility but to ignore everything and just carry on.

We want to sweep our mistakes under the carpet and forget about them. Unfortunately, sweeping things under the carpet is a poor way of handling our wrongdoings, because they all just stay there – under the carpet! The more we repress and ignore sin, the more it exerts influence in other ways. We start living in hypocrisy, or we project our problems onto others, for example.

Neglected sin becomes an unbearable burden in our heart that can even make us sick. No, with sin there is only one way. It must be dealt with before God, with God. Sin involves God. Only He takes sin away!

Father, I cannot hide anything from You.
Therefore, I need to confess the following … Amen.

AT THE TURNING POINT

So I confessed my sins and told them all to You.
I said, "I'll tell the LORD each one of my sins."
Then You forgave me and took away my guilt.

PSALM 32:5 (CEV)

David is mentioning some sin in his life. His first inclination, like all of us, must have been to ignore or deny his sin. He could have excused himself in many ways: he was weak, he was provoked, he didn't mean for it to happen, others should share in the blame, it wasn't so bad after all, or "look at others, they do worse things!"

All of these might have been true, yet David had transgressed and he knew it, because he had a guilty conscience. In fact, his inner burden only got heavier and heavier. At last, when he couldn't keep it anymore, he confessed to God, "I have sinned before you!" Confession – going before God with the truth of who you are, calling sin by its name – is the turning point for growth.

Confession releases our guilt, clears our conscience, and restores our relationship with God. When we do not reach that turning point, when we cannot confess, the burden just gets heavier.

Father, You know me. I fully confess my sin and my failures.
Forgive me and help me to live a new life! Amen.

YOU ARE MY HIDING PLACE

You are a hiding place for me; You preserve me from trouble;
You surround me with shouts of deliverance.

PSALM 32:7

How beautiful that God does not just supply a hiding place, He becomes a hiding place! Sometimes we just need to close the door behind us and let the world and all its demands go by.

Yes, sometimes we need to stop in the rush of things and give our soul a chance to catch up with our body, as it were. Where can we go when we have nowhere to go? We can go to God! He not only becomes our shelter but also gives us a song in our heart. David says with God we are literally surrounded, encircled with songs of deliverance. Perhaps he was thinking of God's sanctuary – which he often visited – where the choirs of Levites were singing?

For us, when we hide with God it can mean to listen to songs of praise and victory, its truth sinking down into our soul and strengthening us. Perhaps David is referring to the singing of the angels around us, saying, "Your victory is assured!"

Thank You for the songs of victory around me, Lord!
Bring its message home into my heart! Amen.

CAN YOU SEE HOW FULL IT IS?

He loves righteousness and justice;
the earth is full of the steadfast love of the LORD.

PSALM 33:5

The psalmist is calling us to praise God. He says we must take the lyre and the ten-stringed harp (their versions of guitars) and exalt His name! Then he gives us reasons for praising God.

He says, for example, that the earth is filled with God's "steadfast love." The steadfast love of God, His dependable, unshakable love, is God's covenant promise to us. God's covenant obligation is to always love us, unconditionally and steadfastly. He promises it, so we can be absolutely assured of it! The lovingkindness of God is all around us, but we often fail to see it because we're flooded by news filled with violence, disasters, and suffering. Yet, God is on the scene and the earth is full of His love.

He is there where the poor share their bread with others, where the lonely offer comfort, where the despairing still find a reason to hope, and where someone forgives despite the hurt they're feeling. Yes, there you will find God! Look for Him – you'll see for yourself.

Lord, open my eyes for Your work –
and open my heart for others. Amen.

GOD HAS PLANS FOR YOU

> But what the Lord has planned will stand forever.
> His thoughts never change.
>
> PSALM 33:11 (CEV)

This psalm proclaims that God is in full control. He made everything, He knows everyone, and He controls whatever happens. God destroys the schemes of sinners and implements His own plans instead. It's beautiful to read about God's plans.

Yes – God has plans! Ultimately, God's plans prevail, because God is God! He also has a plan for you and me! It's not a fixed, set program that ticks off like a clock, because we retain free will (within our limitations). Rather, it's a built-in blueprint according to which we can develop. Discover God's plan for you by discovering who it is that God made. What is your personality? Your values and strengths? Your background and story? This – who you are – is what God made, and this – who you are – is what God wanted to use!

Flow with His design for your life, grow into His story for you! God's plan for you will succeed, believer, because God is working! Even in the events of today.

Lord, help me to grow into Your plan for my life. Amen.

SHIELDS AND CLOTHS

Our soul waits for the Lord; He is our help and our shield.

PSALM 33:20

What a powerful confession that God is "our help and our shield"! Why so? See it like this: on the one hand God protects us in times of trouble ("our shield"), and on the other hand He helps us in times of trial ("our help").

Take note, though, in this verse, that God is not ashamed to be called our helper. He often calls Himself that! We, on the other hand, avoid being a mere helper, as if it's beneath us. We want to be leaders, masters, bosses! Let's remember that it's a sign of maturity to be free to serve. To refuse to be known as a helper is simply immature. You're only great in the kingdom of God when you can take up your serving cloth joyfully (Matt. 20:26).

To get back to our verse, God will help you to do what must be done. He makes you strong to fight (Ps. 144:1), so be strong today. Say what you must and do what you must – God will be with you! Pray these words from Psalm 33:20-21: "[My] soul waits for the Lord; He is [my] help and [my] shield. For [my] heart is glad in Him, because [I] trust in His holy name."

Let Your steadfast love, O Lord, be upon me, as I hope in You! Amen.

THE ANGEL ALL AROUND YOU

> The angel of the LORD encamps around
> those who fear Him, and delivers them.
>
> PSALM 34:7

It's interesting to note that the Bible says the angel "encamps," or encircles (on all sides), those that serve Him. How is that possible? Well, God is spirit, and He can definitely camp in any or all of the dimensions that He wishes to! The point of scripture here, however, is that those who serve God – or literally "fear" Him – will be protected from all sides.

No vulnerabilities will be left open! Yes, He is around us like the wall around an ancient city. Once again, to fear God is not to be afraid of Him (although God is a fearsome danger to His enemies) but to have reverence for Him, deep respect, and definite obedience. Just as for a father!

He will then protect you against the world – just as a father would – on all sides. Be assured of that today.

Lord, be around me like a wall. Shelter me and save me! Amen.

EXPERIENTIAL PROOF

Oh, taste and see that the LORD is good!
Blessed is the man who takes refuge in Him!

PSALM 34:8

Many today have doubts about God. They want to see scientific proof for God, obtained by observation and testing. They want God to be scientifically verified (or falsified) like a hypothesis.

God, however, can never be proven in this way. In which corner can we push Him to be measured? Under which microscope will He fit under? No, we have already said that God, per definition, can never be proven scientifically. In the past some proofs have been put forward in this regard, for example that creation suggests a creator (the cosmological proof), that mankind's widespread belief in God must point to the fact (the ontological proof), or that man's innate sense of right and wrong must come from somewhere (the moral proof). None of these, though, are true scientific proofs. With this in mind, David's invitation here that we should "taste" God, that we should try Him, is interesting.

We are invited here to observe, to experience God for ourselves! We know that millions of believers have done exactly this and found God to be good. Let's call this the experiential proof.

Lord, I have tasted and I have found You to be good.
You are everything I could want! Amen.

WHY IS GOD LOOKING AT ME?

The eyes of the LORD are toward the righteous
and His ears toward their cry.

PSALM 34:15

In this verse David uses the beautiful imagery of God's "eyes" and "ears." He affirms that God's eyes and ears are on His children. His focus is on them, all of the time.

Let's make it personal: You are squarely in God's attention today! He sees what you do and knows exactly why you do it! Remember, God's focus reaches right into your thoughts and motives. When He sees you, He sees your whole being, your whole history, and your whole future. He hears your conversations – with others and with Him, as well as the internal conversations of your heart. The following is important, though: do not experience God's eyes on you as unwelcome or critical, as many might do. God's attention is not disapproving of us.

No, it is approving and helpful; it's fatherly! God attends to us because He cares. He loves. He wants to help and guide us! God's eyes and ears are all about His readiness to see our heart and to hear our cry. That is what David is saying – read it again. How encouraging!

Thank You, Lord, for Your face shining upon me!
I love You for that. Amen.

THE LORD IS NEAR

The LORD is near to the brokenhearted
and saves the crushed in spirit.
PSALM 34:18

Quite confidently David asserts, as if relating a spiritual law, that Jehovah is near to the brokenhearted, that He saves the "crushed of spirit," as is written in the Hebrew.

Yes, it is true: a broken heart attracts God; a crushed and defeated spirit draws Him as close as He can be! It is indeed a spiritual fact that brokenness brings us into the presence of God – especially brokenness before God. Remember that God's character is to care and to love, to save. Therefore, God will not pass the brokenhearted by. He can never ignore the despairing spirit. He will not break the bruised reed and will not quench the flickering and dying wick (Isa. 42:3).

When you are at your lowest, God is at His nearest! Just turn around and see Him, just put out your hand and touch Him.

Thank You, Lord, for being nearest when I need You the most. Amen.

AFFLICTIONS, YES! BUT ...

Many are the afflictions of the righteous,
but the Lord delivers him out of them all.

PSALM 34:19

David accepts the fact that the righteous experience problems, even suffering. They not only have afflictions, but they have many of them! Yes, the truth is this: we shouldn't expect believers to know only prosperity, because that's simply not true, biblically or factually.

Believers know the ups and the downs of life. Luckily there is a "but" in David's statement, and it is this: the Lord protects us from problems (He keeps them from happening), and He delivers us out of problems. In other words, He removes us or them – before too much damage is done. In fact, a loss on one level might be turned around to become an asset on another level.

That's the type of thing God specializes in! The bottom line is that we can always trust God, whatever the circumstances. Do you experience opposition or affliction – again? God will deliver you – again! You will not be defeated.

*Lord, thank You for being in the storm with me,
for calming the storm around me. Amen.*

HIS LIGHT MAKES LIGHT

For with You is the fountain of life; in Your light do we see light.
PSALM 36:9

If God did not switch on the light of the universe, there would still be only darkness. Light is electromagnetic waves travelling at 300 million meters per second. That's fast! Without light, of course, nothing would be seen – it's like taking a photograph in the dark.

Spiritually speaking it's also true: you and I have no inherent spirituality within us – by default we are dark and sinful. Nothing can happen in our lives unless God's light shines into our darkness. Only when the Holy Spirit broods over the void in our lives can creation occur. Only when God orders His light to be can we start off as Christians – and only in His light can we grow as Christians.

That's why we need to read His Word, listen to His voice, and pay attention to His guidance all around us. Only in His light can we see the light, the psalmist says. Look for His light today!

Thank You, Lord, for Your light in my life.
Now I can know You! Amen.

DELIGHT, DESIRE, ACQUIRE

*Delight yourself in the LORD, and He
will give you the desires of your heart.*
PSALM 37:4

Did you think Christians shouldn't have desires? Shouldn't we perhaps just leave our needs to the Lord? Shouldn't we not covet things? Of course we shouldn't be covetous in the sense of enviously desiring something that belongs to others. And yes, of course we should be content with what we have and be grateful and trusting of God for our needs.

Even so, after all the above is said, we will still have personal desires for more than our basic needs. It is only natural! Take note of the biblical perspective on desires, though, as in this verse: When we delight ourselves in God, in other words when we focus on Him and find our joy in Him, not just in what we want from Him, then we will find ourselves receiving what we want.

Part of the deal is that our wants might change when we delight ourselves in Him. Yes, it might change, and it will change! We will want more of what He wants for us!

*Lord, I desire more of You! If I have You,
I have every blessing I can think of. Amen.*

BETTER IS THE LITTLE

*Better is the little that the righteous
has than the abundance of many wicked.*

PSALM 37:16

This psalm is about the paradox that godless people sometimes are more prosperous than the righteous. David struggles to understand it, just as we do! Still, we know that the world is not fair in this regard, because it's a broken and sinful world.

We also realize that the judgment – God's great equalizer – is still ahead. In this verse David states that a righteous man's life is qualitatively better, even if he is poor, than the life of a godless person. It's the truth, but it forces us to rethink success. The world teaches us that success is to be wealthy, but the Bible teaches differently. Success has to do with the sharing of love in our lives.

Success is also to live with God – especially to experience His love, His peace, and His favor. What riches! Those who miss out on these things are the true losers, the failures – even if they're the richest people on earth. They miss the point of living!

*Lord, thank You for all the love in my life –
thank You for Your love! Amen.*

BREAD THERE'LL BE

I have been young, and now am old, yet I have not seen the righteous forsaken or His children begging for bread.

PSALM 37:25

This psalm is about provision, blessing, and righteousness. Let's elaborate on two statements that David makes here:

- The righteous will not be forsaken. This is an absolute fact, because only One was in His life completely abandoned by God, and that was on the cross. Because of Christ, we can forever be sure of God's presence!
- His children will not be in want for bread. The righteous will have enough. It is true that bread in the Bible often stands for food in general, but David could have chosen here meat, milk, or honey. He is specifically aiming at what you need and is saying that there will be enough, that God will provide, that ultimately you "shall not want" (Ps. 23:1).

God will take care of you – every day!

Good Father, I am in Your hands. Supply my needs, according to Your riches! Amen.

HIGHER GRADE HEARTS

The mouth of the righteous utters wisdom, and his tongue speaks justice.
The law of his God is in his heart; his steps do not slip.
PSALM 37:30-31

There are two grades of obedience – a lower grade and a higher grade. Lower grade obedience is to do the right thing even if you don't feel like it. You do the good deed, go to church, read the Bible, etc. – but reluctantly so, as a duty.

At least the good deed gets done and the ego is learning to submit. Yes, outward compliance is good and necessary. A great start. There is a higher level, though, and that happens when our will changes, when our hearts are renewed by God. The Old Testament looked forward to the day when God would write His law onto our hearts, when our hardened hearts would be made soft, when our hearts would reflect God's heart.

The goal of the righteous is to desire to obey God, to have His law become our joy, to be motivated by true love. Give your heart to God, again – to be transformed!

Change my heart, O Lord. Renew my mind,
my emotion, and my will. Amen.

April

Clap your hands, all peoples! Shout to God with loud
songs of joy!

For the LORD, the Most High, is to be feared, a great king
over all the earth.

He subdued peoples under us, and nations under
our feet.

He chose our heritage for us, the pride of Jacob whom
He loves.

God has gone up with a shout, the LORD with the sound
of a trumpet.

Sing praises to God, sing praises! Sing praises to our
King, sing praises!

For God is the King of all the earth; sing praises
with a psalm!

God reigns over the nations; God sits on His
holy throne.

The princes of the peoples gather as the people of the
God of Abraham. For the shields of the earth belong to
God; He is highly exalted!

PSALM 47

APRIL 1

SEEK SHALOM, SEEK HIM

Do not forsake me, O LORD! O my God, be not far from me!
Make haste to help me, O Lord, my salvation!
PSALM 38:21-22

David is writing here during a very troubling time. He is guilt-ridden because of his sin, he is sick, and his enemies wait on his demise. Even his family avoids him at all costs! He has no peace – no shalom.

The biblical concept of peace (shalom) is more than the mere absence of strife. It has to do with peace inside and out, with God's favor, with wholeness. Shalom includes physical well-being, righteousness, relational harmony, standing in the community, successful endeavors, a long life, etc. David is experiencing none of these things. In fact, what he has is just the opposite! Therefore, he pleads for God's nearness, His presence – take note, David prays not just for peace, health, or validation. He wants God!

Is your life in disarray, thrown upside down? Is everything wrong – nothing right? Then you are in urgent need of God's peace! Do not just ask for peace, though – ask for the Peace-bearer.

Lord, I need You! Be near to me and
bring Your peace and blessing. Amen.

APRIL 2
NO HOPE? HOPE!

And so, Lord, where do I put my hope? My only hope is in You.
PSALM 39:7 (NLT)

David was such a passionate person! He goes from one extreme to the other. He is either rejoicing or in the depths of despair, as (once again) in this psalm. Here he writes about life and death.

Life is fleeting – even his own life is about to end. There is little hope left. That's how he feels! What can David do in his dark state? Where will he find hope? He finds his hope in God! The Message translates Psalm 39:7 as follows: "What am I doing in the meantime, Lord? *Hoping*, that's what I'm doing – hoping!" Let's take a lesson from David here. We so often put our hope in our circumstances. When things turn against us – and circumstances *will* be up and down – we feel without hope. Let's rather find our hope in the Lord, who made us to live a unique life, who loves us and will carry us through everything.

With God, life is *always* meaningful and hopeful, whatever the conditions. Also, with God the situation can change. Yes, quite so! Listen: with God you have *every hope* for a meaningful future!

Lord, reveal Yourself to me again – reveal to me Your purpose! Amen.

BACK ON THE ROCK

He drew me up from the pit of destruction, out of the miry bog, and set my feet upon a rock, making my steps secure.
PSALM 40:2

David is rejoicing! He was in the "pit of destruction," in the "miry bog," but now he is on secure footing again, on the rock! The firm footing we look for in life often has the following meaning for us: God changing our circumstances. This is absolutely possible, because God is almighty.

Ask God for it, and trust Him for His intervention. God changing us in our circumstances. *We* must change as well, not just the circumstances. We need to learn to be stronger, to trust, to persevere, and to become resilient. Let's add that God looks at our circumstances differently than we do. Our own purpose is purely to escape all discomfort, and the sooner the better! Yet, we know that life has its obstacles and that we grow best against resistance.

Challenge leads to discipline, and discipline leads to mastery. How else? That's why hardships are sometimes allowed in our lives. May you soon find solid footing again and become a stronger person, and Christian, in the process!

*Lord, things are so unsure at the moment –
be my rock in this time! Amen.*

LIVING PRAISE

He put a new song in my mouth, a song of praise to our God.
Many will see and fear, and put their trust in the LORD.

PSALM 40:3

David is rejoicing, because God saved him from the danger he was in. Now he has a "new song" in his mouth, meaning that he has new reason to sing – he brings fresh praise!

Isn't it a sign of someone who lives close to God when there's always something new to testify about, to praise God for? Such persons experience more of God, hear more from Him, see more of Him during their day. Take note that such a life isn't just meant for a few super spiritual saints. No, it's meant for every one of us! It's actually just the normal Christian walk.

We should wake up to it, open our eyes to God, and become aware of Him around us. When we live such a life of God's presence and involvement, the world will also see God – in us! Our lives will testify of His love and care and works. More reason for praise!

Lord, I want to live close to You. I, too,
want a new song to sing! Amen.

MY DELIGHT?

I delight to do Your will, O my God; Your law is within my heart.
PSALM 40:8

We often take the truth of this verse and turn it on its head – and then we call ourselves *spiritual*! David says his delight – his one desire – is to do God's will.

We say the same, but we actually try to convince God to do *our* will! We often use God as an asset in our portfolio that we can draw upon when things go bad to save us from difficulties, like a type of insurance policy. Then we feel very disappointed when God doesn't comply with our requests. Some even abandon their faith – if it's not working, why hang on to it? Let's be very honest and turn such a wrong picture the right way up: God is God, and God does what God wants to do! His will is the best for us, even in our pain and even when we cannot understand a thing about it. We need to *trust* Him.

Do we think our spiritual life is all about us? That's wrong! Our spiritual life is all about God and His will for us. He gave His instructions and now expects us to be obedient. Are we as delighted to obey God's will as David was? We should be, but we're often like spoiled children.

Yes, Lord Jesus, You're the Lord, the Master.
I will do as You say. Amen.

APRIL 6
CONSIDERING AND CONSIDERATION

Blessed is the one who considers the poor!
In the day of trouble the LORD delivers him.
PSALM 41:1

Do you see the sow and reap principle in this verse? "Whatever one sows, that will he also reap," the Word says (Gal. 6:7). Some people take this the wrong way. They teach that one can sow in a certain way in order to reap in a certain way – as a method to receive personal blessings.

Such a view is not biblical, though, on several levels. Our walk with God is not primarily about what we can receive from Him but about what we can give Him, which is our life! Our focus should be on the sowing, and then God will take care of the reaping. That's how this biblical principle works. We can begin with the poor, the "weak" as this verse literally says. We can start caring.

Let's do the little we can do in circumstances where the need is overwhelming, all around us. Let's be Jesus to someone. That's what it's all about! Then, one day when we are weak and dependent ourselves, Jesus will be there for us.

Lord Jesus, help me to be there for someone.
You are always there for me! Amen.

FAITH IN YOUR SPIRIT

*By this I know that You delight in me: my enemy
will not shout in triumph over me. But You have upheld me
because of my integrity, and set me in Your presence forever.*

PSALM 41:11-12

In these verses David states five things of which he is sure:

- God delights in me – He loves me
- My enemies will not triumph over me
- God upholds me
- I have integrity in God's eyes – He knows my heart
- I will be in God's presence forever

Take these as personal truths for yourself today, friend – as God's words! Then, let's learn the following important lesson from David: See how beautifully he ends his psalm (as he most often does) with a strong statement of faith. Yes, even when complaining to God, he keeps the relationship intact – he keeps communicating with Him. So, if you pour out your heart before God, don't keep it dangling in the air.

End by boldly confessing your faith in God's provision. Confess statements like the above. Pray them to God! Let them become part of your thinking, your expectation, your faith – your life!

*Yes, Lord! I do trust that everything will end well,
because everything ends with You! Amen.*

WHEN? YES, WHEN?

As a deer pants for flowing streams, so pants my soul for You,
O God. My soul thirsts for God, for the living God.
When shall I come and appear before God?
PSALM 42:1-2

Do you sing "As the Deer" (Marty Nystrom, 1981) in your church? It's a beautiful song! The words in these verses are deep and rich. The deer is not just thirsty, it is panting, breathing heavily and thirstily.

The water that it's looking for is described as "flowing streams" – not just a bit of water, but a deep stream that can fully quench its thirst and save its life. What a perfect metaphor for our longing for God! Our need is similar for the living God, because without Him we will spiritually die. Jesus called out that *He* gives the "rivers of living water" that we so long for (John 7:38). But where will we find Him or His water?

According to the Korahite singers, who wrote this psalm, God can be found in His temple. Today, God's temple is in our hearts (1 Cor. 3:16). From out of our hearts the living water of the Spirit flows! *There* our needs will be met and our thirst quenched. When will you go there and drink of it? Go soon!

Holy Spirit, quench my thirst for God with the waters of life. Amen.

APRIL 9

BOTH FEAR AND FAITH

Why are you cast down, O my soul, and why are you in turmoil within me? Hope in God; for I shall again praise Him, my salvation.

PSALM 42:5

Don't we know this typical human struggle well? Like the psalmist in this verse, we quickly become "cast down" and "in turmoil" when we meet obstacles or challenges.

We become alarmed and anxious so readily; we expect the worst so easily! But then again we are reminded of God. *Aren't we believers? Do we not trust in a mighty God?* We then resolve to trust again, to put our hope in Him. Yes, we know both fear and faith! We experience both the natural world and the supernatural. And we can grow in the struggle. See how it happens in this psalm: we *catch* ourselves doubting, and then we *stop* it. We *reconfirm* that we trust God as our helper, and we *confess* that we'll have reason to praise again. Do you see it?

Know your thoughts, and intervene when they are not productive or edifying anymore. Substitute them with positive and faith building truths! This is the transformation of the mind that the Bible talks about.

*Lord, help me to keep my thoughts on
You: unwavering, trusting, believing. Amen.*

LIGHT AND TRUTH

Send out Your light and Your truth; let them lead me;
let them bring me to Your holy hill and to Your dwelling!
PSALM 43:3

The psalmist shows real spiritual insight here. He doesn't merely invite his reader to seek God or appeal to their need for Him. It's as if he realizes that there is something *behind* our search for God. He asks, therefore, that God's "light" and "truth" fall on him and lead him to God.

Let's try to understand it as follows: If God does not reveal Himself to us, we will never be conscious of Him. Only when His Holy Spirit enlightens us do we become aware of God and of our need for Him. Then, as we start searching for God, His Word most often guides us in *how* to find and serve Him.

Yes, it is the Spirit and the Word that will lead us to God. Do you need God? Do you want more of Him? Ask for His Spirit, and pray for His Word's guidance in your heart.

Lord, send me Your Spirit and Your Word –
let them lead me to You! Amen.

GRAB HOLD OF GOD

Awake! Why are You sleeping, O Lord? Rouse Yourself!
Do not reject us forever! Why do You hide Your face?
Why do You forget our affliction and oppression?

PSALM 44:23-24

Wow, what straightforward words are these – directed to God? "Wake up, God! Why are you sleeping? You're hiding Your face!" Such words embarrass us, don't they? What are we to make of them? Remember, this is not temperamental old David reacting from his personal anguishes. No, this psalm was an established part of the Korahite temple choir's repertoire. It was often sung!

The people of biblical times were direct and upfront, as Mediterranean people still are today. They didn't hide their emotions – it just spilled over! Similarly, their relationship with God was experienced as intensely emotional and deeply personal. Let's learn this from them, then: *full* commitment, *total* involvement, *deep* relationship! We, as modern people, are often emotionally repressed and shy away from deep expression. That's why we often end with a shallow spirituality.

Why are we so halfhearted? Listen – do you have a need? Grab hold of God with everything you have!

Lord, I grab onto You with my whole heart:
with my full understanding, feeling, and will! Amen.

RIGHTEOUSNESS IS GODLINESS

Your throne, O God, is forever and ever.
The scepter of Your kingdom is a scepter of uprightness;
You have loved righteousness and hated wickedness.
PSALM 45:6-7

The king of Israel, perhaps Solomon, is addressed in Psalm 45 as God's son, God's anointed one, ruling on the right hand of God – as the kings of Israel were thought of in the Bible.

This verse underlines the king's divine authority and mandate to dispense divine justice. The hallmark of God's king is his righteousness! Let's underline it doubly for today. We are assured that God loves righteousness and hates wickedness. He demands righteousness, justice, and fairness just as He demands love and faithfulness. God has nothing to do with injustice! Those who undermine justice or treat others unjustly cannot expect God's favor. On the contrary, the prophets charge that they should rather stop with their religion, because it is pointless.

To serve God in righteousness means to fully obey God and to act rightly toward others. Let your hallmark, your integrity, your good name be your uprightness! Righteousness is godliness.

Lord, give me a desire for living righteously and acting fairly. Amen.

NOT LOVABLE - LOVING

The King will desire your beauty.
Since He is your Lord, bow down to Him.
PSALM 45:11

In this verse, the psalm about the king of Israel now turns to his queen. The chosen princess will become his bride. A wonderful wedding is described, filled with beauty, glory, and honor. This psalm has been understood as Messianic since early times, because the king is addressed here in exalted, even divine terms.

Christ is the ultimate King, and we – His church – are His bride! The question we need to ponder is why the King would choose us as His bride. Aren't humans known to be self-centered and contrary – at their best, not very lovable? Indeed, we are! So, what does the King see in us? We truly don't know, but Scripture confirms that the King does desire us for Himself.

Yes, He loves us. He seeks us out. He finds us and commits to us. The better answer to our question would lie not in our lovability but in His love and absolute grace.

Thank You, Lord, for Your love! The glory belongs to You. Amen.

AN UNSTOPPABLE STREAM

There is a river whose streams make glad the city of God,
the holy habitation of the Most High.
PSALM 46:4

A stream of water is often associated with God's habitation. In Paradise, from the temple, and in the New Jerusalem we see the waters flowing. It refreshes and feeds and heals and creates new life.

Also here in this verse we see a stream flowing in the city of God, bringing gladness to its inhabitants. It symbolizes God's steady provision amidst the chaos and insecurity of the world. Jesus taught that the Spirit will become a stream in our hearts, an endless supply of "living water" (John 7:38). See it like this: in your soul there's an unstoppable stream of gladness and of joy, of love, of peace, of rest, and of healing. It's all there! It's the gift of the Holy Spirit, and no one can stop it.

It's sad, however, that we are mostly unaware of it. We mostly struggle on without the Spirit's joy – uncertain, restless, longing for peace. Be filled with the Spirit and what He brings!

Lord, I want to experience the life that is within me. Amen.

BE STILL AND KNOW

Be still, and know that I am God. I will be exalted
among the nations, I will be exalted in the earth!
PSALM 46:10

This psalm is about the chaos and uncertainty of this world. Nations threaten each other, wars loom, storms rage – even the mountains shake! We mustn't be anxious, however. With God we are safe and secure.

He is exalted high above the tumult and clamor of the world. He wants us to realize this truth and relax. The word that is used here for "be still" means to let go, to release, to relax the tension. It means to stop trying, to put it down. Somewhere along the way we have tried enough, stressed enough, worried enough. Somewhere we reached the end of our tether. It's time to give up. Let it go! Be still, says God, and quiet down.

Know that God is on the scene. He is in control! Let God be God, friend. Let Him do the God business. Leave it to Him, whatever happens. Let Him do what He wants to do. Surrender now. Be still.

Lord, there are things that only You can do.
I stand back and leave it to You. Amen.

PRAISE IS YOUR CALLING

Clap your hands, all peoples! Shout to God with loud songs of joy!
PSALM 47:1

This beautiful psalm by the Korahites describes God as the King of the whole earth. He is crowned in glory and *all* peoples should come and worship Him. Remember that the purpose of Israel's election was to be the light of the world, to be a model people. In them, the whole world should have seen a nation serving the true God and been invited to serve Him as well.

The Jews were often reluctant with this commission, but it nonetheless happened when their Messiah came. Through Jesus Christ believers from all nations of the earth are now worshiping the one true God, the God of Israel. The New Testament teaches that we, the non-Jewish believers, have joined with the Jewish believers and have become *one* covenant people.

Praise God, then – clap your hands, rejoice, shout to the King of the earth! Remember, to praise God is also a discipline; therefore this verse is a command, not a request.

God of Israel, I praise You for including me in Your people! Amen.

ABRAHAM IS YOUR FATHER

The princes of the peoples gather as the people
of the God of Abraham. For the shields of the earth
belong to God; He is highly exalted!

PSALM 47:9

In this universalistic psalm, in which all people are described as God's people, the Korahites sing of the day when all nations will worship the true God. All leaders will one day surrender their shields and bend their knees before God! Then all will be one people: the people of the God of Abraham.

How wonderful! One day we will see the final and physical fulfillment of this prophecy, but we already see part of this happening around us. Through Jesus Christ we see people from all tribes, tongues, and nations coming to join the people of God. *We*, too, as non-Jewish believers, have become children of Abraham and now worship the God of Abraham, as our verse states.

Abraham had a remarkable faith journey: he heard God's voice; he went into a covenant with God; he followed God unconditionally throughout his life and kept on trusting Him for His promise. What a hero! Let's follow the example of our father Abraham.

God of Israel, help me to live like Abraham with full commitment! Amen.

THE GOLDEN CITY AWAITS

Great is the LORD and greatly to be praised in the city of our God!
His holy mountain, beautiful in elevation, is the joy of all the earth,
Mount Zion, in the far north, the city of the great King.

PSALM 48:1-2

Jerusalem is still a beautiful city. The required use of the region's yellow sandstone in the architecture creates unity and led to the description of Jerusalem as the "city of gold."

In biblical times, the city was much smaller, but still beautiful: on Mount Zion in the crisp highlands of Judea, the Kidron brook flowing by, the Pool of Siloam supplying ample water surrounded by fields, gardens, and hills. Within the walls were the royal palace and other state buildings, and on the highest peak, of course, God's impressive temple. There, in the Holy of Holies, the presence of God rested. Wonderful! Even so, this beautiful city is only a symbol of the eternal Jerusalem that is coming.

When the King of kings comes to be with His people forever – and He is on His way – the presence of God will fill the earth from side to side, according to the Bible (Rev. 21:23). The whole earth will become one big sanctuary, one big temple. Wait for the New Jerusalem – *then* you'll see true beauty!

Lord Jesus, come! Come be with us. Amen.

APRIL 19
IN THE MIDST OF IT ALL

We have thought on Your steadfast love,
O God, in the midst of Your temple.
PSALM 48:9

The Levitical Korahites formed a choir group who served in the temple permanently. They were privileged to be busy with God's things every day. Remember, for them Jerusalem was the holiest city on earth, the temple was the holiest place in the city, and the Holy of Holies was the holiest place in the temple.

There, on the golden lid, called the atonement cover or mercy seat, the presence of God, His *Shekinah*, rested. What a setting to work in! In this psalm the Korahites tell us what they experience as God's most salient feature. In the midst of all the holy things, they were most aware of God's "steadfast love". This term described God's never-ending love for His people. Steadfast love flows from God like a stream – unilaterally and unconditionally, unaffected by human sinfulness.

Everything that God does is motivated by His steadfast love, even His righteous demands, His judgments, and His punishment. It cannot be any different, because God *is* love! His love cannot and will not waver!

I am encouraged, Lord, by the love that never ceases.
Thank You for loving me regardless of what I do. Amen.

CAN I RANSOM MYSELF?

*You cannot buy back your life or pay off God! It costs
far too much to buy back your life. You can never
pay God enough to stay alive forever and safe from death.*

PSALM 49:7-9 (CEV)

This psalm is about the foolishness of arrogant people. They think that their wealth can buy anything. There are many things, though, that money cannot buy. For example, money can never redeem anyone from death – that price is far too high!

Jesus quotes this verse when He says, "What can a man give in return for his soul?" (Mark 8:37). The answer is clear: you cannot give anything! Therefore, Jesus advises us not to even try. Yes, forget about bargaining with God in this regard. Only One could pay *that* price, and He already paid it on the cross. Only He could afford the price; although it did cost Him His life. What a tremendous payment it was!

In return He asks of you *your* life, not as co-payment but as a dedication to Him who did such a great thing. He really asks for it! Give therefore your life. Or to put it better, give the rest of your life to Jesus.

Lord, thank You for giving me Your life. Now I give You my life. Amen.

APRIL 21
SOULS FROM SHEOL

But God will ransom my soul from
the power of Sheol, for He will receive me.
PSALM 49:15

The people of the Old Testament had a limited view of the next life and eternity. For them everything was about *this* life. They believed that the righteous would have their reward and the sinners their punishment in *this* life.

When you died, you went – according to them – to Sheol (in Greek: Hades), a bleak place where you existed as a mere shadow. The phantoms who lived there either slept or moved about weakly. True, colorful, and vital life was to be had while on earth. Yet, in this psalm we find an expectation that God would save the psalmist's soul from Sheol and "receive" (come and get) him. How beautiful!

The New Testament confirms that Christ has indeed ransomed every believer from death. We will also be received by our Savior, and our lives will continue with Him – vitally and eternally! We'll meet each other before God's throne!

Father, You so loved me that You sent Your only Son
so that I, who believe in Him, shall not perish
but have eternal life (John 3:16). Thank You! Amen.

THE MEANING OF IT

Be not afraid when a man becomes rich, when the glory
of his house increases. For when he dies he will carry
nothing away; his glory will not go down after him.
PSALM 49:16-17

We live in a very materialistic society. Money is our main purpose, to buy and consume is our ideal. Wealth dictates our success or failure in this world. We measure people's worth by their wealth.

The biblical message, however, is the opposite. No one warns about the dangers of money as much as Jesus did. He says "mammon" (money) can easily become an idol (Matt. 6:24, KJV). Money can easily come between us and God. We should take His message to heart, because material wealth is *not* the meaning of life. Money never really satisfies. It cannot be taken into eternity. Money is always, always lost!

According to the Bible, the successful person is not the one who made money but the one who loved. Less well-to-do people with warm hearts and warm relationships are more successful than well-off people in cold and empty houses. Yes, *love* is the meaning of life. Show love – there is so little time!

Lord, give me a life of love. Help me to love! Amen.

APRIL 23

THERE IS ONLY THE ONE

The Mighty One, God the Lord, speaks and summons the earth
from the rising of the sun to its setting.
PSALM 50:1

This psalm starts off interestingly with some of God's names: El, Elohim, and Yahweh. Here *El* is translated as "the Mighty One" (this general word for God rests on the idea of might or strength), *Elohim* means "God" (specifically the God of Israel), and *Yahweh* is "the Lord" (Yahweh being the personal name of the God of Israel).

This repetition underlines and intensifies the fact that Israel's God, Yahweh, is the only true God. Let's remember that! We live in a world of many religions, and we treat each with the utmost respect. That is very important. Still, with all due respect and in much love we hold to our belief that there is only one true God, not many. All gods and all faiths are not equal. There aren't many roads up the same mountain. There is only one true God, the God of Israel, and only one Savior, the Lord Jesus Christ!

There is only one true faith and that is the one confessing the above. With great conviction Christians call on the whole world, from east to west, to accept Christ as Savior. Keep your faith – be strong. And don't forget to love!

Lord, keep me faithful and give me a heart of love. Amen.

APRIL 24

A COVENANT CUT WITH YOU

*Gather to Me My faithful ones, who made
a covenant with Me by sacrifice!*
PSALM 50:5

In this psalm God is on His throne and judging His people. Some remained faithful to the covenant, but others did not. The psalm describes the covenant as made (or literally "cut") "by sacrifice," because a sacrifice was offered at the establishment of the covenant and because the covenant was upheld by regular sacrificing.

God has something to say about their sacrifices, but more about that later. For today, let's underline the following in regards to a covenant with God: we belong to the same covenant! Through Jesus Christ, Israel's Messiah, we are grafted into the tree that is Israel. Most importantly, Christ's sacrifice on the cross validated the covenant that was cut between God and us. Christ is the covenant maker, and by faith we are part of it.

See it like this: as believers you and I stand in a personal covenant with the God of Israel! This covenant entails privileges and responsibilities, which should be taken very seriously.

Lord, help me to remain true to our covenant! Amen.

THE REMAINING SACRIFICE

Offer to God a sacrifice of thanksgiving,
and perform your vows to the Most High.
PSALM 50:14

The Old Testament prescribed a complex sacrificial system. Different sacrifices had to be offered at different times. When the temple was destroyed in 70 AD, though, animal sacrifices came to an end, since these could only be offered in the temple.

Since then, Jewish sacrifice consists of praying, fasting, and tithing. Many rabbis believe that animal sacrifices will resume at the coming of the Messiah and the rebuilding of the temple, but others believe that at that time only the praise-offering will remain. In this psalm God reprimands His people over their sacrifices – not because they lacked in sacrificing, but because they sacrificed with disobedient hearts. For God, it's not so much about slaughtering animals, but about offering hearts and lives to Him.

A heart filled with praise is a heart that's focused on God – clearly the sacrifice that pleases Him! Just remember, Messiah did come, and praise and thanksgiving is indeed the sacrifice that we bring to Him today. Bring it daily!

Lord, every morning I will praise You –
You are a good and gracious God! Amen.

NOW ISN'T THIS WONDERFUL?

Call upon Me in the day of trouble;
I will deliver you, and you shall glorify Me.
PSALMS 50:15

God is taking His people to task. They did sacrifice to Him – in other words they went through the prescribed rituals of their faith – but their hearts were not with Him. He now reminds them that He already owns all the cattle on all the hills and does not have a need for sacrificial animals.

The sacrificial system was merely a vehicle for them to express their heart's devotion and their gratitude to Him. More than all their sacrifices, God asks His people three things: (1) a praise-offering meant from the heart, (2) that they keep the vows made in His name and then, surprisingly, (3) that they call upon Him in their need. He will answer and deliver them, and they will then honor Him for that.

How wonderful is this? The sacrifice God asks for is the chance to be God to them – to prove Himself as the great God that He is! Shall we take God up on His invitation? Yes, we shall. Thank You, Lord!

Lord Jesus, accept my sacrifice of praise
for what You have done! Then I offer You my need.
Deliver me, Lord! Amen.

OLD TESTAMENT GRACE

*Have mercy on me, O God, according to Your steadfast love;
according to Your abundant mercy blot out my transgressions.*

PSALM 51:1

The people of the Old Testament knew the concept of grace well. They believed, for example, that an essential characteristic of their God was His "steadfast love," or lovingkindness.

God's *chesed* – the Hebrew term for it – was the guarantee of the covenant between them. Chesed was God's promise to never stop loving them, to forgive again and again – no matter what! *His* chesed would always follow and overcome their tendency to sin. It's to this "steadfast love" that David is appealing in verse 1, after his sin with Bathsheba and Uriah. God *did* respond in His steadfast love, forgiving David even though David had to face the consequences of his adultery and murder. From the perspective of the New Testament we understand grace even better: because of Christ's atonement, our sin is covered by grace.

Because of *Him,* we experience God's favor. Grace now operates in our lives like a spiritual force. We live by grace; we trust God on the basis of His grace; we stand on His grace by faith. Yes, grace is how we experience God – grace is who God is.

*Lord, thank You for Your steadfast love –
thank You for Your grace! Amen.*

DO YOU REALLY KNOW IT?

Wash me thoroughly from my iniquity, and cleanse me from my sin!
For I know my transgressions, and my sin is ever before me.
PSALM 51:2-3

In this psalm David is under a deep conviction of sin. The prophet Nathan fearlessly came to him and shouted his sins in his face: adulterer, fraudster, liar, murderer! Immediately David was struck in his heart and fell on his knees, pleading for forgiveness.

He says he *knows* what his sins are. What an important start! Our own awareness of sin is often so shallow that we can only think of one or two weak points. Others are satisfied with avoiding the "big" sins. Sin really goes much, much deeper! Sin is not just the wrong things we do, but the right things we never do. Sin is especially our lack of love – the Great Commandment.

Sin is ultimately the fact that we do not reach the potential, the dream that God intended for us. Sin means falling short. Fall on your knees!

Lord, I know my sin and my shortcomings. Forgive me –
I could have been much further! Amen.

YES, I HAVE SINNED

You are really the one I have sinned against;
I have disobeyed You and have done wrong.
So it is right and fair for You to correct and punish me.
PSALM 51:4 (CEV)

David is confessing his sin before the Lord. He had an affair with one of his soldiers' wives and then, to prevent it from coming out, organized for the man to be killed in battle. The matter is extremely serious.

When he says that he sinned against God "only," he doesn't mean that he committed nothing against a fellow man. He means that he realizes that his transgression primarily grieved God – that his sin against another has brought him into direct conflict with God. Sin against a creature immediately brings the Creator into play. What you do against the child will bring the Father to your door! Let's consider the following: sin can never be swept under the rug. We cannot just decide to do better the next time around or turn over a new leaf. No, sin is a matter between God and us, and it must be sorted out with God. It must be acknowledged to God and confessed.

God's light must shine on it. The Holy Spirit must be involved to help you grow away from those things. Live your life in a spiritual way, not in a worldly way.

Lord, there are things that cannot remain the way they are.
Help me with the following … Amen.

CLEANSING AND CONTACTS

Purge me with hyssop, and I shall be clean;
wash me, and I shall be whiter than snow.
PSALM 51:7

Ritual purity is a central concept in the Old Testament law. Purity led to communion with others and worthiness before God. Many, many regulations covered this topic and had much to do with avoiding unclean things: unclean food, unclean people, or unclean items.

If someone was unclean, he had to abstain from contact with others and stay away from the temple. Temporary impurity could be resolved by a ritual or a sacrifice, but some people – like lepers or heathens – were permanently impure. In these verses David – because of his sin – feels deeply unclean and completely cut off from God. He desperately needs God to cleanse him, to "unsin" him as is literally stated.

In the New Testament, however, we live by faith in the cleansing blood of Christ, which permanently brought us into communion with God. We are clean because of Him, but we also want to be clean for Him. To that purpose, it remains useful to remember that impurity is transmitted by contact.

Lord, help me not to become stained by that which is impure. Amen.

May

O God, You are my God; earnestly I seek You; my soul thirsts for You; my flesh faints for You, as in a dry and weary land where there is no water.

So I have looked upon You in the sanctuary, beholding Your power and glory.

Because Your steadfast love is better than life, my lips will praise You.

So I will bless You as long as I live; in Your name I will lift up my hands.

My soul will be satisfied as with fat and rich food, and my mouth will praise You with joyful lips,

when I remember You upon my bed, and meditate on You in the watches of the night;

for You have been my help, and in the shadow of Your wings I will sing for joy.

My soul clings to You; Your right hand upholds me.

But those who seek to destroy my life shall go down into the depths of the earth;

they shall be given over to the power of the sword; they shall be a portion for jackals.

But the king shall rejoice in God; all who swear by Him shall exult, for the mouths of liars will be stopped.

PSALM 63

FIX MY SPIRIT

Create in me a clean heart, O God, and renew a right spirit within me.
PSALM 51:10

David is asking God for a "right" spirit. The word here refers to being right, upright, firm, or affixed. Some translate it as a "steadfast" spirit (NIV). It's as if David's spirit has become loose, unstuck, wavering after his sin with Bathsheba. His inner being is in turmoil. Take note of the following:

- An impulsive and unguarded person easily falls for temptation. When David saw Bathsheba bathing, he immediately desired her. Without thinking of the consequences, he had her brought to him. When her husband became a problem, David again made a foolish and rash decision. Yet the Word praises a steadfast man, one who's planted like a tree at the waterside, who walks a straight path and refuses to be tempted – that's how David wants to be!

- A spirit is also steadfast and at peace when it knows God's favor. David is ill at ease and uncertain because he knows he has lost his peace with God. Therefore, he now longs to have a "right" spirit again.

Let's be known to be steadfast: strong, unwavering, grounded. And let's be right with God!

Lord, give me a strong and steadfast spirit! Amen.

DON'T THROW ME AWAY

*Cast me not away from Your presence,
and take not Your Holy Spirit from me.*
PSALM 51:11

David is deeply convicted of his sin and is pleading for forgiveness. It feels as if God is far away. He therefore begs with God not to reject him – literally not to "throw" him out of His presence.

His fear is that he might lose his kingship, that he might be considered unworthy to rule. He asks God not to withdraw His Spirit from him, since the Holy Spirit was given in the Old Testament onto certain anointed people like kings, prophets, or priests. David, for example, was filled by the Spirit at the moment of his crowning as king. Is he going to lose it all now? From our New Testament perspective, we believe that the Holy Spirit is not easily withdrawn from believers, but we are warned not to "grieve" the Holy Spirit (Eph. 4:30) or even to "quench" Him (1 Thess. 5:19).

One can indeed live a life in which there is, practically speaking, no place for God's Spirit, where He's not welcome. What will the end of such a life be?

*Holy Spirit, be with me! I pray that my behavior
will never grieve You. Amen.*

RATHER, SACRIFICE THIS

The sacrifices of God are a broken spirit;
a broken and contrite heart, O God, You will not despise.

PSALM 51:17

David sinned gravely with Bathsheba and is now suffering the consequences. Nathan calls out his punishment: "The sword shall never depart from your house" (1 Sam. 12:10).

Violence begot violence: the son Bathsheba bore died; David's beloved son Absalom grabbed his throne, drove him from Jerusalem, and was then killed; his other sons were also killed one after the other; and finally, God refused David's request to build Him a temple because of all the blood on his hands. What a price to pay! David's spiritual insight now tells him that no amount of sacrificial offerings can fix this situation. His heart can be the only sacrifice that will suffice. Desperate and broken, with deep remorse over his actions, he offers his whole heart to God again.

Yes, God doesn't want anything from us, but He wants *us*! Eventually, David was restored, and Bat Sheva's (her Hebrew name) son Solomon became king after him – the greatest king Israel ever had. David is right. Brokenness before God avails much!

Lord, my heart, too, is broken about my sin. Amen.

GREAT OR GRATEFUL

You people may be strong and brag about your sins,
but God can be trusted day after day.
PSALM 52:1 (CEV)

David had to flee from King Saul, who wanted to kill him. Doeg the Edomite saw how the priest Ahimelech, not knowing that David was fleeing, supplied him with bread and a weapon.

Ahimelech also prayed with David, thinking he was still the king's right-hand man. When Doeg told Saul about this, Ahimelech and his subordinates were called and charged with treason. Saul instructed his soldiers to kill them all, but none of them dared to kill the priests. No one moved! That's when Doeg took a sword and personally killed eighty-five of those "who wore the linen ephod" (1 Sam. 22:18). Afterward he went around bragging about his heroic deed! This really angered David, who must have felt some responsibility. David knows that bragging is the opposite of what God expects.

Let's remember that greatness before God and greatness before people are two completely different things. Let's try less to be great and more to be grateful. If you want to be great in God's kingdom, learn to be humble, learn to serve, learn to be small. God is great, and that's enough!

Lord, be great in my life – I'll be small! Amen.

A BRIDGE, NOT A HOLE

He will return the evil to my enemies;
in Your faithfulness put an end to them.
PSALM 54:5

Here we have the biblical principle of sowing and reaping again. What you do to others will be returned to you. David's prayer that God must destroy his enemies may sound strange to us, but it fits into this principle when correctly understood.

Take note that it's the enemies' own evil that is returned to them, not God's evil intentions. The effects of sin are part of the sin, following it like a shadow – and sometimes the shadow hangs around long after the sin has passed! God allows it as He allowed sin, together with its consequences, since Adam and Eve. It's part of our freedom to choose.

If you dig holes for others, the consequence will be that there are holes around you – which you will fall into yourself. It's best not to dig holes! Rather, build bridges for others – bridges for you to cross as well. Leave the punishing to God.

Lord, help me to give encouragement, love, and peace.
On the day of need it will return to me. Amen.

MAY 6
HANDLE THE PRESSURE

*I am restless in my complaint and I moan, because of the noise
of the enemy, because of the oppression of the wicked.*

PSALM 55:2-3

David's best friend has betrayed him and has now become a sworn
enemy. David finds it extremely disturbing. He cannot sleep, his
thoughts are racing back and forth, and his heart feels heavy.

The word translated here as "oppression" can also mean pressure,
constraint. The bad news presses onto David, in other words. Pressure is
actually a mechanical term referring to a force that is exercised against
a physical system. If the system cannot adequately handle it, the
tension (or stress) inside the system increases – eventually it can break.
This can also happen to the human system. If undue expectations and
responsibilities are laden onto us, we can feel the stress increasing. If
we cannot bear it, something must give way.

What can you do? Well, the stress must be reduced, the load must
be lightened. There is no other way. Don't just pray – do something
about your stress load. Negotiate with those involved, and rid yourself
of some of the burden. Working off stress by exercising and intentional
relaxation also helps.

Heavenly Father, I feel stressed! Show me how to handle it. Amen.

RUN FROM IT

*Oh, that I had wings like a dove! I would fly away and be at rest;
yes, I would wander far away; I would lodge in the wilderness.*
PSALM 55:6-7

David is feeling stressed and anxious. His friends are now his enemies, and they're out to get him! He spells out his emotional reaction in superb detail: he's restless and fearful, his heart is cringing inside of him, and his body is trembling.

That's exactly how anxiety and fear feels. David says he wishes he could just take off and fly away, just escape to the wilderness where he can find peace and rest. This is typical, isn't it? We have similar desperate ideas of running away from it all, of hiding somewhere. The good news is that we *can* actually run away, spiritually speaking. The desert to which so many prophets and men of God have retreated in order to find Him is available to all of us, because it resides in the heart.

There, deep in the spirit, we find the quiet place where the Holy Spirit lives, where we can have our peace and rest. Remember to regularly go to that place, because it takes practice to find it!

*Lord, help me to find peace amidst the throng
and the noise – help me to find You! Amen.*

ESCAPE THE CROWD

Day and night they go around it on its walls,
and iniquity and trouble are within it; ruin is in its midst;
oppression and fraud do not depart from its marketplace.
PSALM 55:10-11

There's a commotion in the city, with people coming and going – shouts can be heard. David looks at the melee with apprehension, because he cannot trust anyone anymore. It could be that they're plotting against him, because this psalm was probably written in the time that his son Absalom led a rebellion against him.

At that time literally anyone – even a friend or family member – could have been a spy or a traitor. Eventually David had to flee his city. With this in the background, let's say something about modern-day city life. We live alongside millions of people. Faceless masses move by daily, the pavements are alive with pedestrians, and streets flow with never-ending streams of vehicles. Living among such a multitude of people can be stressful.

To be constantly faced with so much need can be draining. We do need to escape it from time to time! Come aside. Recharge. Get a new perspective on the city from the Lord – and on your place in it.

Lord, I need to get away, to be alone – just me and You. Amen.

THREE TIMES DAILY

*But I call to God, and the L*ORD* will save me. Evening and morning and at noon I utter my complaint and moan, and He hears my voice.*
PSALM 55:16–17

David is feeling anxious, but the fact that he can pray about it three times a day helps a lot. He is certain that God hears him! It's possible that David is referring here to the ancient Jewish prayer hours.

According to Judaism, the Morning Prayer (shacharit) was instituted by Abraham, the Afternoon Prayer, after work (minchah), was added by Isaac, and the Evening Prayer (arvith or maariv) was added by Jacob.

In New Testament times a signal was sounded from the temple to indicate these prayer times. Jesus prayed according to these hours, and the disciples as well, according to Acts. Prayer is still our recourse in time of need. We know that prayer is good for us because it calms and strengthens us and brings us new perspective. Still, why are we so badly practiced with it? No wonder we remain so stressed out!

There is no reason why you and I cannot pray to God three times a day. Set the alarm of your cell phone and take just a minute or two. It will change your day!

Lord, help me to make time for praying. Amen.

THROW YOUR CARES AWAY

Cast your burden on the LORD, and He will sustain you;
He will never permit the righteous to be moved.
PSALM 55:22

Some translations render the meaning of this verse in very general terms. For example, "We tell you what worries us, and you won't let us fall" (CEV).

The literal translation here is better, though, because the text's first verb is an active "casting" or simply "throwing." It's an action word! See it like this: we can get to the point where we're so discouraged or frustrated with our problems that we would rather take the lot and throw them in the bin – if it were only possible! Have you ever gotten to that point? Now God is saying that it is possible. We can throw our burdens – the unbearable emotional load of our problems – onto Him. We cannot ignore the problem itself or avoid the responsibility it brings, but without so much of the burden it becomes lighter, more bearable, manageable. Give your burdens to God in prayer one by one. Then make a firm decision not to be anxious about them anymore. Whenever anxious thoughts arise, identify them summarily as unwelcome, and exchange them for strong confessions of faith. It's an active deed: a decision, a release, a refusal, a willful exchange. Be strict with yourself – intentionally build your faith!

Lord Jesus, I now cast the following burdens onto You …
Take them away, Lord. Amen.

FAITH OR FEAR

In God, whose word I praise, in God I trust;
I shall not be afraid. What can flesh do to me?

PSALM 56:4

It's easy to tell someone not to fear, to trust God. It would be the truth, because scripturally fear does stand against belief. Our problem, though, is that it's not as easy as that. We *know* it's true, but we're human and some situations are really worrying! How can we just switch off an emotion like fear? It's not easy, but there is a way to get more of a hold on our emotions. The following will help you:

- Confess your trust in God – say it, write it down, repeat it! It works because our emotions react to our perceptions, and our perceptions can be programmed by the truths of the Bible. Take the truth in this psalm, for example: no man can do anything to you, in fact *nothing can happen* that the loving Father does not allow. God is always in control!

- Learn to relax in God's presence. Take fifteen minutes, get aside, and be still before God. Play worship music, and just breathe deeply and intentionally. Relax in God's presence. Your fear will subside.

Father, I do trust You. Help me with my fears! Amen.

YOUR JAR OF TEARS

*You have kept count of my tossings; put my
tears in Your bottle. Are they not in Your book?*

PSALM 56:8

What a surprising verse! It says that God puts our tears in a bottle. It may refer to the practice of putting the tears for a deceased loved one in a bottle and burying it with them. Here it underlines the fact that God notices our tears and that they matter to Him deeply.

Can we say something about crying today? To cry is natural, normal, and good for us. It releases toxins and stress hormones. Crying relieves stress better and faster than many medicines, yet we are so reluctant to cry. We were taught to contain our emotions – especially men believe that "cowboys don't cry." Let's make it clear that the people of biblical times weren't so inhibited. They cried when they wanted to cry – the men as well!

David often wept, and believed that God counted his tears. Jesus wept, as did many of the faith heroes and spiritual fathers. Learn to release your emotions, release your tears – have a good cry when you need it. Remember, God knows about the heartache you suffer – He weeps with you!

*Thank You, Lord, for knowing my tears.
Every tear is treasured by You. How beautiful You are! Amen.*

GOD IS ON MY SIDE

Then my enemies will turn back in the day
when I call. This I know, that God is for me.

PSALM 56:9

David says here, "God is for me." The New Living Translation states, "God is on my side." It's a powerful statement, but isn't it a bit presumptuous? Isn't God on everyone's side? Does David want to hijack God all for himself?

Remember, Old Testament believers felt that if they kept God's law they were right with God. For them, God would certainly be on the side of the godly – never on the side of the godless! (We, however, are so aware of our inner failures, our sinful thoughts and motives, that we feel that we always have some sin.) Remember also that David had an absolutely personal relationship with God. As shepherd, soldier, singer, and sovereign he always lived closely with God. He spoke with God, heard His voice, and lived with the full knowledge of God's presence and involvement.

For David, success meant God's blessing and failure meant God's displeasure. What do these things mean to us? Well, Christ's death *proves* that God is most definitely on your side – very personally so! He died for *you*. There is really no one who is more on your side than God!

Lord, I live today in the knowledge that You are
wholly and completely for me! Amen.

MAY 14
AWAKE TO JOY!

My heart is steadfast, O God, my heart is steadfast!
I will sing and make melody! Awake, my glory!
Awake, O harp and lyre! I will awake the dawn!
PSALM 57:7-8

Beautiful, poetic words! This psalm refers to a time when David had to run from Saul. He confronted Saul (from a distance) and pleaded his innocence, upon which Saul apologized wholeheartedly and retreated.

What a relief! Now, David feels vindicated, energized, alive! He feels as if he passed a test, since he was in the position to kill Saul but didn't lay a finger on him. For all his mistakes, Saul was God's anointed. He dealt with Saul in the way that God approved of, which gives David a feeling of victory and joy. He rejoices! He feels like singing, like taking his guitar and waking the dawn. See how intensely David lived with God? God was the center of his life, the reason for his joy! We often live without God, only remembering Him when we are in need. Let's awake to truly live for God – it will bring us much joy!

Father, I do love You and I do want to live for You! Amen.

MAY 15

THERE *IS* A GOD LIKE THAT

Mankind will say, "Surely there is a reward
for the righteous; surely there is a God who judges on earth."

PSALM 58:11

In this psalm David sets himself against evil, corrupt, and violent people. He prays that God will judge them and even suggests some punishments! He is asking for blood to flow.

Jesus of course taught us otherwise, but statements like the ones found here come from a deep sense of righteousness and justice. Evil people must not get away with their misdeeds. Do you also wonder about that? Take note: Of course God isn't a God who will let evil people get away with everything. If that were true, the whole system of justice would fall apart. Will our courts let guilty parties just walk out, scot-free? Never! No, the full retribution and punishment of sin has been handed to Christ, and justice was fully served. Those who accept that in faith can have the benefit of full pardon.

So, there *is* a God "who judges on earth" – there is punishment and there is reward. Leave your matters with Him. Let Him judge whom He wants to judge, and let Him show mercy where He wants to show mercy.

Lord, You are the judge, the perfect judge – not me. Amen.

EVIL SURROUNDINGS

Each evening they come back, howling like dogs and prowling about the city. There they are, bellowing with their mouths with swords in their lips - for "Who," they think, "will hear us?"

PSALM 59:6-7

Saul again wanted David out of the way and ordered his house to be surrounded. As David looked out of his windows at night, he could see the dark figures standing watch. He compares them to the packs of dogs that prowled about the city during the night, looking for food.

In Scripture, dogs have mostly negative connotations because they were wild, dangerous, and unclean, like wolves or pigs. They were often associated with sin, evil, or death. For some, David's depiction here has demonic overtones. Perhaps he didn't mean it as such – although they did believe in evil spirits, and Saul did have a problem in that regard – but behind the ominous figures at night, one can see a spiritual onslaught. One can see David as a symbol of righteousness and obedience, while Saul stood for rebellion and rejection. With the enemy encircling him, David seeks refuge with his God. Nothing came of their plans. God protected his child.

Father, deliver me from evil, in Jesus' name! Amen.

A TRAP OF WORDS

*For the sin of their mouths, the words of their lips,
let them be trapped in their pride. For the cursing and lies
that they utter, consume them in wrath.*

PSALM 59:12-13

David is so angry with his enemies here! He's especially upset with what they're saying about him. Their words are all lies and curses, he says.

Therefore, he asks God to trap them with their very own words – which can readily happen when you curse or lie. We can be more attentive to what we say. As children of God, we don't speak like the children of the world. We don't swear or curse. We don't need to scream or scoff. We don't need to use sarcasm, because it's not helpful. We stick to the truth and the truth alone. It's unnecessary to brag, exaggerate, or twist the facts.

Things like these can easily become traps! No, we say what's true and what's beneficial. We build up; we don't break down. Our words express wisdom, love, and kindness. And when we cannot say anything good, we remain quiet. It's not necessary to always answer or even always talk.

*Holy Spirit, help me to speak like a child of God.
Teach me discipline and teach me silence. Amen.*

LET THE SUN COME UP FIRST

But I will sing of Your strength; I will sing aloud of Your steadfast love in the morning. For You have been to me a fortress and a refuge in the day of my distress.

PSALM 59:16

In the night, David sees people lurking around his house. They were sent by Saul, possibly to prevent him from escaping, because Saul distrusted and hated him.

David describes these ominous figures as a pack of dogs that prowl around, growling, showing their teeth. They make him feel anxious, and he pleads to God for protection. Then, in this verse, the new day has dawned and the enemy is nowhere to be seen. The fear and foreboding of the night hour is a mere memory. Isn't this typical?

During the night everything seems so much worse – the darkness so easily produces the worst case scenario! Don't make big decisions in the literal or figurative night. Wait for the day. Let God's light shine on it first.

Lord, when it's dark in my life, give me
faith and patience to see through to the dawn. Amen.

CERTAINTY IN UNCERTAINTY

From the end of the earth I call to You when my heart is faint.
Lead me to the rock that is higher than I, for You
have been my refuge, a strong tower against the enemy.
PSALM 61:2-3

David is calling to God, for he is anxious and fearful. His heart is "faint." He is afraid and worried about the future. He says he's calling to God "from the end of the earth," because that is how he feels – as if God is far, far away.

David has a great need for security, for certainty, and he therefore asks to be led to "the rock that is higher than I." In other words, to something that exceeds his own power, and powerlessness. According to the church fathers, that rock is Jesus Christ. Do you also feel uncertain, anxious, apprehensive about the future?

Do not fear, because Jesus knows your future. He is speaking to you from the future, telling you that He has the future under control. *He* is your safe place, your strength, your Rock – your future! You will not go under.

Lord Jesus, bring quiet to my heart. Give me peace. Be my Rock! Amen.

MAY 20

I SEEK ... HIM

I seek You; my soul thirsts for You; my flesh faints for You,
as in a dry and weary land where there is no water.

PSALM 63:1

A man after God's own heart! David feels a longing, a thirst. All people have such a longing, but David correctly identifies it. His longing is a longing for God!

Most people do not understand their longing. They have a yearning for something they cannot place, a desire for fulfillment, meaning, love. They then try to fulfill it in various ways. Most often we seek our fulfillment in money, because we think that money can buy everything else. Otherwise we seek it in pleasure, excitement, or security. We seek to make a difference, to live meaningfully, to love others, or to leave a legacy.

These are all good things, but as Christians we believe that our deepest longing, that big ol' hole in your heart, is a longing for God. Your thirst is for *Him*!

Lord of my heart, You alone fulfill my deepest need.
With You my life has meaning! Amen.

GOOD THINGS IN THE NIGHTS

*When I remember You upon my bed, and meditate on You
in the watches of the night; for You have been my help,
and in the shadow of Your wings I will sing for joy.*
PSALM 63:6-7

David says he thinks of God when he cannot sleep. He meditates upon Him during the "watches of the night," meaning for extended periods, for example from midnight till daybreak. During the night he rejoices over God's goodness.

He feels blessed, loved, and cared for. Nights can indeed be wonderful. When we're awake at night – and not worrying about it – good things can happen. We can think clearly and calmly. We can work productively. In the past, we could drive safely during the night. We can also do soul work in the night. Use your wakefulness to pray!

Pray for your family and loved ones by name. Pray for your enemies and your problems. Pray for your marriage. Ask the Lord what to pray for. Also, think about God's goodness and grace. Think of how blessed you are. Yes, let your heart rejoice – in the night!

*Lord, in the night I feel close to You.
In the night I want to praise You! Amen.*

MAY 22
MY SOUL FOLLOWS HARD

My soul clings to You; Your right hand upholds me.
PSALM 63:8

The King James Version of the Bible is beautiful when it says my soul "followeth hard after Thee." David is implying that his soul is adhering, clinging – that he is *stuck* on God!

Let's unpack a bit what it means to follow God so intensely. First, we notice that David's soul is not longing after the world but after God. That's important! How does one seek "hard" after God, practically speaking? It means that we find time for Him, that we *want* to pray, that we are eager to learn about God's Word, and that we really want to be obedient. To follow closely means to want to be where God is. We find the converse true as well: God stays near to him, God follows him, God "cleaves" to him!

God's "right hand" holds David near and carries him. So, a very, very close relationship is described. The lesson is this: seek after God, and God will seek after you!

Lord, I do have a longing for You. Help me to find You! Amen.

HEARER AND ANSWERER

Our God, You deserve praise in Zion, where we keep our promises to You. Everyone will come to You because You answer prayer.

PSALM 65:1-2 (CEV)

In this psalm David rejoices about the good rains, the rich and fertile soil, and the abundance of the harvest. God has answered their prayers!

It is indeed wonderful to pray and then experience God's answer. It makes us feel that our prayers are working. Still, it doesn't always go as we expect, because our idea of how prayer should work is often wrong. It's not wrong for our prayers to be answered just like we ask, but we often ask the wrong things. God's perspective is different from ours, and although He hears everything we ask for and knows the way we want prayers answered, he responds the way He wants to respond.

Luckily, in Scripture we read that the Holy Spirit improves our prayers by interceding for us "according to the will of God" (Rom. 8:26-27). *His* prayers (in us) are then answered exactly as asked! From our side, prayer is mainly to lay our life at God's feet and then to simply trust Him with it.

Lord, I boldly ask You and simply trust You. Your will is best! Amen.

HOW BLESSED!

Blessed is the one You choose and bring near,
to dwell in Your courts! We shall be satisfied with
the goodness of Your house, the holiness of Your temple!

PSALM 65:4

David is rejoicing, because God has answered their prayers! Everywhere he looks he sees abundance: good rains, large herds of cattle, wheat fields that are heavy with the harvest. Yes, the one that serves God is blessed. He declares that even those in the farthest lands will see and honor God for it (Ps. 65:8). Let's also have this wonderful mentality of abundance. Aren't we indeed blessed, favored, and loved by God? Yes, we are! Let's develop the attitude then of always seeing the good, of pointing it out.

Of course we know that things are not always rosy, and there isn't always just abundance. We know that, but still as believers we *believe*. We believe that God is in *all* situations, that He controls *every* season, that He *always* has a worthy goal in mind. We can always praise God, because God is always praiseworthy! Even in our need God remains loving, present, and involved. In every situation He can be trusted for His speedy intervention. So learn to praise! Yes, sometimes it's difficult, but remember, praise brings abundance right into our hearts.

Lord, my heart overflows with love and goodness. Amen.

FIRE AND WATER

We went through fire and through water;
yet You have brought us out to a place of abundance.
PSALM 66:12

The poet says in this psalm that God's deeds are "awesome" (verse 3), or "terrible" in the sense of fearsome, frightening (KJV). All people should bow before such a God!

Then his mind wanders to a specific time when Israel endured extreme hardship – wondering perhaps if that contradicts God's power. He might be thinking of their slavery in Egypt – this psalm is read by the Jews during Passover – or of the time the Assyrians besieged Jerusalem for two years. Yes, those were terrible times when they went "through fire and through water." Where was this awesome and powerful God then? Then comes the climax. God saved them from all of that and brought them again into abundance! Their experience teaches us that there *will* be fire and there *will* be water.

Challenges, stress, and heartache are a part of life. Remember, though, that we move through these things – that they come, are endured, and they pass away. They're temporary, in other words; they're passing. This is God's promise! After the crises, there will be abundance again – joy, peace, love. There will!

Heavenly Father, I know that life entails good and bad.
I also know that life ends with You, who are the ultimate good! Amen.

I KNOW, BECAUSE I KNOW HIM

For I cried out to Him for help, praising Him as I spoke.
PSALM 66:17 (NLT)

In this verse the poet tells us of two actions: first he cried to God, and then he followed it up with praise. The verse literally says that his praise was waiting "under [his] tongue" to be expressed as he prayed.

From out of his prayer, his praise directly flowed. He did not praise because God had instantaneously answered him. No, his praise flowed out before God could answer. It was purely an act of faith. He praised God just because he knew God! He knew his God could be trusted with his petition, his needs, his life. He praised God in advance for His intervention, but also just for who God is. What a lesson! To know God is to love Him and to trust Him, because our experience with Him teaches us that.

So get to know God. In closure, do you have a need, a cry in your heart? Pray to your God and praise Him straightforwardly for it, for He is already busy in your life. Yes, He is present and He is deeply involved.

*Lord, I leave my need with You now. I trust You,
because I know You. Amen.*

BLESSED TO BLESS

The earth has yielded its increase; God, our God, shall bless us.
God shall bless us; let all the ends of the earth fear Him!
PSALM 67:6-7

The psalmist begins Psalm 67 with words that remind us of Israel's priestly blessing: "May God be gracious to us and make His face to shine upon us." It's beautiful! He then asks all nations to acknowledge the God of Israel as the true God and to come and worship Him.

This is more or less the topic of the whole psalm: that God blesses us, and that we are (or have to be) a blessing to the world. We are blessed to bless, in other words. This is exactly the purpose of God's covenant. God tells Abraham that He will bless him, bless his descendants, and bless the whole world – through him! It helps us understand why God blesses at all: He doesn't just want to bless us, He wants to bless others through us! He doesn't just love us, He loves the world – and wants to love them through us!

We are, as Israel of old, God's example in the world, God's testimony. Our testimony in the world is therefore extremely important, especially our love. We represent the Lord. It's vital that we should be a blessing to others today!

Lord, I am so blessed. Show me today
where and how I can bless others. Amen.

MAY 28
PREPARE AND REJOICE!

Sing to God, sing praises to His name; lift up a song to Him who rides through the deserts; His name is the LORD; exult before Him!
PSALM 68:4

In this psalm the coming of the Lord (here named *Jah*) is described. Where He comes, the enemy is defeated – every knee bows before Him! As Christians we see this in Jesus' coming.

Remember, He is already on His way. When Christ comes, we as His children have definite tasks. We need to prepare for Him. What does that mean? Well, we prepare by getting our lives in order so that we can meet with Him confidently. Also, we need to declare to the world that our God is coming, so that they can also be prepared. Finally, we can start to celebrate. Yes! We can start rejoicing because our salvation is near, because everything will end well with Him, because we will be loved forever!

Rejoicing prepares our hearts and prepares the way for His coming, spiritually speaking. It is a powerful act of faith to rejoice – it makes us spiritually stronger, and that's a fact.

Lord, I am excited over You and Your coming.
I will begin singing Your praises! Amen.

FIND YOUR FAMILY

*Our God, from Your sacred home You take care of orphans
and protect widows. You find families for those who are lonely.*
PSALM 68:5-6 (CEV)

How wonderful! God finds a family for the lonely. Family are those who will accept and love you no matter what. Even if you made bad choices – or if they did, for that matter – family remains family, and they help each other.

Similarly, we also have a spiritual family with a spiritual home and spiritual brothers and sisters. They are those with whom we share the spiritual journey. Together with them we can worship, pray, minister, serve, and grow – or just hang out! Everyone needs such a family! Go and find, or rediscover, your spiritual family. What? Do you say that you've been in a church, but then you were hurt there? I truly believe you, but remember, this is how family works.

They're not perfect, but they remain family. Life is always better *with* brothers and sisters than without. The spiritual life was designed by God to be done in community, not alone.

Lord, I do have a need for spiritual friends – and just for friends. Amen.

THOUSANDS OF ANGELS

*The chariots of God are twice ten thousand, thousands upon thousands;
the Lord is among them; Sinai is now in the sanctuary.*
PSALM 68:17

This psalm is about God's greatness and victory. By faith David sees God's heavenly host – His armies, "thousands upon thousands" of angels and chariots, brilliant and glorious! He sees by faith how they escort God to His new residence, Zion, the temple mount in Jerusalem. It's a triumphant parade complete with captive enemies, gifts, and a lot of celebration. This knowledge makes David feel safe. It makes him want to rejoice! Let's open our eyes of faith a bit. Let's see the myriads of angels, ready to perform God's will.

Their existence and work is a biblical fact, after all. Let's feel safe in the knowledge that they are with us, guarding and helping us. Yes, know by faith that heavenly beings are with you now – strong, intelligent, holy, spiritual beings that are one hundred percent for you! Do you feel like rejoicing? Oh, you should!

*Lord, I am indeed encouraged by my knowledge
of Your angels around me! Amen.*

GOD IS IN TODAY

Blessed be the Lord, who daily bears us up; God is our salvation.
PSALM 68:19

It's beautiful how David motivates his praise for God. In this verse he states two reasons for blessing the Lord:

- *God carries us daily.* The statement is not week by week or year by year; although, of course, days become weeks and weeks become years. That's true, but Jesus said we should live much more in the now, in *today* and less in the future. We don't know what the future holds, and it's therefore meaningless to worry about it. Today, though, God will carry you.

- *God is our salvation.* Remember that those in the Old Testament didn't see salvation as pertaining so much to eternity, but as pertaining to the present. In this life God will save us from many things and will bless us physically and spiritually, with a way out, with solutions, with strength, with His help.

Yes, God's salvation is a very real salvation. It starts now and extends right into eternity!

Lord, You are my salvation, my help,
my blessing, my portion. I praise You for that! Amen.

June

Make haste, O God, to deliver me! O LORD, make haste to help me!

Let them be put to shame and confusion who seek my life!

Let them be turned back and brought to dishonor who delight in my hurt!

Let them turn back because of their shame who say, "Aha, Aha!"

May all who seek You rejoice and be glad in You! May those who love Your salvation say evermore, "God is great!"

But I am poor and needy; hasten to me, O God! You are my help and my deliverer; O LORD, do not delay!

PSALM 70

JUNE 1
LOSE CONTROL

I sink in deep mire, where there is no foothold;
I have come into deep waters, and the flood sweeps over me.
PSALM 69:2

David is desperately calling out to God in this psalm. He feels as if a strong stream has taken hold of him. The water is already at his neck, and his feet are losing their grip. It's terrifying!

Yes, how terrible to feel that you are losing control in your circumstances. Sometimes things just happen and take you along: Management makes a decision; the results are in, and they're not good. Or economic or political changes affect you negatively. Remember, if there is something that you can do about such things, you should surely do it. Do not hesitate, and do not delay. In many circumstances, things can be turned around. Be bold, knock on doors, go and speak with someone. Then again, there are things about which you can do nothing – absolutely nothing!

Don't despair, though. Resist the feeling that you're going to sink. You will not! Faithfully and willfully surrender your circumstances to God. Trust Him who is still in control! He will carry you through.

Almighty God, circumstances are against me,
but You are strong! Amen.

NOT THEM, LORD

Let not those who hope in You be put to shame through me,
O Lord God of hosts; let not those who seek You
be brought to dishonor through me, O God of Israel.

PSALM 69:6

In this psalm David realizes that his sins are catching up with him. Still, he is very mature about it. See in this verse how he pleads with God that his poor example will not be a stumbling block to others.

Yes, through it all, he is concerned about them! We, on the other hand, would sooner try to deny our mistakes and the implications that they may have on others. Let's remember that Christians live in the limelight. People are watching us! When we fail as Christians, unbelievers feel vindicated while believers are disappointed. That is sad, isn't it? Have you recently failed God and others with your behavior?

You can still repair your tarnished testimony – to a degree. Go and apologize honestly. Tell those affected that your behavior was wrong and that you want to do better. Let them see that you're genuine. Turn it into a good testimony! God will help you.

Lord, help me to draw others to You, and not to push them away! Amen.

NOT TOO FAR?

It is for Your sake alone that I am insulted and blush with shame.
I am like a stranger to my relatives and like a foreigner to my own family.
PSALM 69:7-8 (CEV)

David mentions something that we also sometimes encounter. He says his desire to serve God fully is not understood by his family and friends. It causes uneasiness between them, distance.

In our day, we have freedom of religion, and many are nominally Christian, but the moment you really want to live differently, it causes problems. Then people say you're taking things too far, that you've become unbalanced, that you're overly spiritual, and so on. Let's be very honest: Christians must live wisely in this world. It's of no use to fret because unbelievers look at us and are completely put off. No, that would miss the point completely.

Let's live inspiring lives that are filled with love, joy, peace, and faith. That is what others must see. Our walk with God entails choices that will be unpopular with others. That's just how it's going to be – we will be pleasing God *first*.

Lord, help me to live wisely in this world,
and help me to put You first in all things. Amen.

PRAY IT AND PRAISE IT

May all who seek You rejoice and be glad in You!
May those who love Your salvation say evermore, "God is great!"
PSALM 70:4

David is seeking God's help, as in most of his psalms. Let's have a closer look at his approach, though. It usually consists of two parts. First he describes his dire circumstances and urgent requests to God – often in some detail.

To pour out your heart to God has the advantage of externalizing and objectifying your problem. It is talked *out* and, as such, becomes more understandable and manageable. Prayer is therapy! Try writing out your prayers, and you'll see.

Second David praises God for his intervention, as in this verse. Most of his psalms end in this way. Take note that David offers praise before his prayers are answered. He praises not because God already answered but – as an act of faith – because God *will* answer.

You and I can also learn to praise God, to trust God, to surrender to God, to find peace in God before any prayer has been answered – in faith! Faith works before God works. Faith changes things, and it changes us!

Lord, teach me to praise You regardless of anything else. Amen.

FROM MY CHILDHOOD

For You, O Lord, are my hope, my trust, O Lord, from
my youth. Upon You I have leaned from before my
birth; You are He who took me from my mother's womb.
PSALM 71:5-6

In this verse the poet takes his relationship with God right to the beginning. He says he trusted in God from his youth. Sometimes we tend to belittle childhood conversions as not sincere or valid, but that's a totally wrong assessment – Jesus considered children's intentions absolutely valid!

The poet takes it further, to his birth, when he says that God took him from his "mother's womb." He then takes it back even further when he says that God was his support "from before my birth." Wow!

Let's take this line of thought right back to the very beginning: for all eternity God has known us, planned for us, and loved us! Yes, we have been in God's heart since forever! God is our true Source, our true Father.

Yes, Lord, You have been a trustworthy God
my whole life through. Help me to love You back! Amen.

TO MY CHILDREN

So even to old age and gray hairs, O God,
do not forsake me, until I proclaim Your might
to another generation, Your power to all those to come.
PSALM 71:18

The poet looked back at his life and saw that God was good. Now he is looking forward, and he's asking God to grant him grace till the end.

Of course God will be with him – and with you and me – right till the very last breath. See, however, how thoughtfully the poet presents his request for God's assistance. He still wants to tell the next generation about *Him*. Yes, it's beautiful! Remember that the next generation won't automatically be Christian. It isn't hereditary! In fact, Christianity is always just one generation away from extinction. We need to actively teach the next generation our faith.

It's a scriptural command that you speak about God "when you sit at home and when you are on the road, when you are going to bed and when you are getting up" (Deut. 11:19, NIV). Yes, indeed! My child must hear it from me – and see me living it. That's still a part of your life's goal.

Lord, help me to tell my children about You.
And make me the living example of what I teach. Amen.

GENERATION TO GENERATION

May they fear You while the sun endures,
and as long as the moon, throughout all generations!
PSALM 72:5

Solomon is praying for God to protect the king, so that righteousness and peace can reign in the land and God be served "throughout all generations."

Let's explore this last idea a bit further. The current generation got their faith from their parents but have embraced it as their own. You, for example, are in a personal relationship with God: you speak with Him and experience His works. Your child is watching all this: she sees you praying, living in faith, and speaking about God. Later on she will decide whether she wants that faith, which she saw in you, as her own.

Your example, and others', is extremely important in this regard! When she does take it up as her personal faith, she will for herself seek God and live according to her beliefs – then later on her own children's eyes will watch her being a Christian. That's how it works. Our faith is not so much taught as caught, as they say.

Lord, let me live in such a way that my children
will want to accept You as their God! Amen.

JUNE 8
WRONG ASSUMPTIONS

But as for me, my feet had almost stumbled,
my steps had nearly slipped. For I was envious
of the arrogant when I saw the prosperity of the wicked.
PSALM 73:2-3

Asaph says that he almost doubted God, for it seemed to him as if wicked people are more prosperous in this life than the God-fearing. Why serve God, then? Have you also wondered about this? We'll get back to that, but first let's point out some wrong assumptions, biblically speaking, in this whole matter:

- It is wrong to think believers are supposed to be the more prosperous, materially speaking – that our faith is supposed to directly benefit us financially.
- It is wrong to think money should be the standard of success in this life. Why money – why not love, joy, relationships, meaning?
- It is wrong to think that unbelievers are "doing better," by any standard, than believers.

Yes, actually the whole argument is not valid, but we still tend to think in these terms! Remind yourself that you are *indeed* blessed and loved by God. If you can accept this as truth, it will change your life!

Lord Jesus, help me not to lose perspective when it comes to money. Let me remember what You said about mammon (Matt. 6:24). Amen.

THE TURNING POINT

> But when I thought how to understand this,
> it seemed to me a wearisome task, until I went into
> the sanctuary of God; then I discerned their end.
>
> PSALM 73:16-17

Asaph got stuck in his faith. He is wondering whether it's worth serving God. It seems to him that the godless are well off, while the God-fearing are struggling! How can that be?

In these verses he gets to a turning point, however. He says it remained a burden to him "until I went into the sanctuary of God." Now then, there's the answer! Meeting with God about the problem makes all the difference. In fact, a true encounter with God changes your whole perspective, your attitude, your goals, your life's meaning – everything! Do you identify with Asaph? Does it burden your faith to live among unbelievers? Do you wonder whether they might be right not to believe after all? Do you?

Go, then, again to your God, in His sanctuary, whether it be in your quiet time, your worship, at church, or wherever. That is something unbelievers can never do – and it will make all the difference!

Lord, I do have such a longing for You! Amen.

THE OTHER WAY AROUND

When my soul was embittered, when I was pricked in heart,
I was brutish and ignorant; I was like a beast toward You.

PSALM 73:21-22

Asaph was bitter over the many godless and sinful people who apparently did so well. He asked, "Why isn't God punishing them? Why am I still serving God when I keep struggling? Is it fair?"

Afterward, though, he realized his mistake: He wanted God to judge *now* and set everything right *now*. He wanted God to give what he asked for *now* – he wanted heaven now! Unfortunately, it's not heaven yet – it's still earth, and things do not work that way here. In fact, they work the other way around: God puts His hand on your shoulder and drafts you into His service. He wants you to follow *Him* and serve *Him*. He is asking certain things from you and is now waiting on your answer! He promises much blessing for you, but ultimately it's not about your comfort or wealth. You are not the center of all.

Ultimately, it's about God's plan and God's glory. So, let's get past our own will and declare ourselves available for His will. Get in line with Him. Do not concern yourself too much about everything that hasn't been set right as yet. It will be set right, but in due course.

*Lord, forgive me. I sometimes think
it's all about me. It's all about You! Amen.*

AS FOR ME

But for me it is good to be near God; I have made the Lord God
my refuge, that I may tell of all Your works.
PSALM 73:28

Asaph is done being bitter and envious over the prosperity of unbelievers, even though he is struggling himself. He had struggled
emotionally but now has worked through it. Ultimately, one conclusion remains with him, which he states as follows: "Whom have I in
heaven but You? And there is nothing on earth that I desire besides
You" (Ps. 73:25).

How beautiful! Then he says these words: "But for me it is good
to be near God" (v. 28). We can *so* identify! We, too, have anxious and
doubtful thoughts and ask questions that no one can answer. We also
sometimes struggle with our faith. In the end, though, we know in our
hearts it's better to be with God than without God.

We cannot and do not want to live without Him! No, we want to be
near to Him, because He means everything to us. Doubts may come
and go, but our hearts will always return to God.

Lord, thank You that I can always return to You, and
always find my rest in You! Amen.

COME LORD, COME LOOK

Direct Your steps to the perpetual ruins;
the enemy has destroyed everything in the sanctuary!
PSALM 74:3

This psalm was written after the people were taken from their land, and their cities and temple were demolished. It's sad that they now wanted to "show" God the ruins of the temple: "See Lord, how the beautiful carvings were smashed up. See here, where the walls stood."

They also "tell" God that His name is now mocked by the heathen. "What will You do about it, Lord?" It's not as if God didn't know these things. It was *He* who warned them about them in the first place. However, they remained disobedient, so God allowed their captivity for the full term. Does this leave you with the feeling that prayer doesn't work? Doesn't God do what God wants to do? Why pray then? Let's put it like this: We're human and we will pray! Like the priests of old, we cannot help but share our hearts with the Almighty.

Even though He knows it all, we want to tell Him our wishes, fears, needs, and joys – and that's just perfect, because prayer is the way we live with God. Prayer connects our feeble life with His immortal life. Just to be sure, prayer *does* make a difference. He said it Himself (Jer. 29:12).

Lord, I cannot help but pray. Hear my heart,
see my life. Be with me! Amen.

JUDGMENT WILL COME

At the set time that I appoint I will judge with equity.
PSALM 75:2

God is the one who judges. We shouldn't assume that role for ourselves – it's *His* work; He is the Judge! Asaph adds here that God's judgment is always completely fair.

Yes, good deeds will be rewarded, and bad deeds will be punished – full justice will be served! Still, when we look around us, we often see a lot of injustice. Why do bad people seem to get away with their misdeeds? Why do so many innocent people suffer and so many good deeds go unheeded? Where is the justice in this world? Is God still here? Well yes, He surely is! The reason we don't see full justice now is because the judgment has not yet taken place.

Remember, judgment day is still ahead, right at the end. Then the sheep and the goats will be separated, and everything will be fully and finally set right! We're not there yet, so be patient. Until then, God wants us to personally and communally grow in justice, fairness, and righteousness. Justice is a very important matter to God.

Lord, I leave the judgment to You.
Only You can exact justice with absolute fairness. Amen.

BOTH, YOU KNOW

It is God who executes judgment,
putting down one and lifting up another.
PSALM 75:7

It is arrogant to boast that you're a "self-made person," that your success is to be attributed wholly to yourself, because most often this is just not the case.

Research has shown that success seldom arises from a vacuum – it mostly stands on the family's knowledge, experience, money, or connections, on the privilege of having had a good education or on opportunities that came your way. What others would call good fortune, we as believers would call grace, or God's favor. Let's not be arrogant, the poet says. Let's be humble. It's up to God who rises and who falls! Of course we should work hard to attain something, because from our side that's the way to success.

However, we should also pray, because not everything is in our hands. Both of these aspects are important: praying *and* working! Remember that we cannot work what we should have prayed, or pray what we should have worked. There's a distinction.

Lord, thank You for Your grace and blessing.
My hard work is nothing without that! Amen.

JUNE 15
A HAND ON YOUR SHOULDER

In Judah God is known; His name is great in Israel.
His abode has been established in Salem, His dwelling place in Zion.
PSALM 76:1-2

Asaph, in this psalm, is rejoicing over the Lord, who rules His people from the temple in Zion. He says God is "known" in Judah, with the grammar suggesting that God has made Himself to be known in Judah.

It's a biblical truth that we would have known nothing of God if He hadn't revealed Himself to us. We only know Him insofar as He has made Himself known. This happens to us in a very personal way. We carry on with our lives – without God – until we realize that a hand, His hand, is resting on our shoulder. It happens in many ways: by hearing the Word, by our circumstances forcing us to think, by an inner discontent that will not go away. At first we might not relate these things to God – we'll probably only try harder to find fulfillment in what we do.

Eventually, however, as fulfillment eludes us, we may realize that it's Him, it's His hand we feel on our lives, it's Him speaking to our hearts! It's God! Yes, God is speaking to You indeed, friend – even through this message He is calling out to You! Will you listen?

Heavenly Father, these things that are happening,
is it You? What are You saying? Amen.

RECEIVE SO MUCH MORE

The earth feared and was still, when God arose to
establish judgment, to save all the humble of the earth.

PSALM 76:8-9

For Asaph, God is the God of the whole earth. One day God will come to judge all men. That will also be the day, Asaph states here, that God saves the "humble."

It's a biblical fact that God is particularly on the side of the humble, the helpless, the suffering. Yes, He has a heart for such people! When we stand with those who suffer as well, we find ourselves standing with God. Still, the Bible's emphasis is not on helplessness or need, as such. It's on realizing your dependence on God, on *trusting Him* in your need. True humility is humility before the Lord. It is faith. Such people are blessed, Jesus said, for they will inherit the kingdom of God (Matt. 5:3-10).

Remember, it's by the measure of our expectation that we can experience Him. Blessed are those with a great need, for they can receive so much more!

Lord, I have such a need for You. I trust You with my life! Amen.

ON YOUR BED - YOU, HIM

*When I think of You, I feel restless and weak. Because of You,
Lord God, I can't sleep. I am restless and can't even talk.*
PSALM 77:3-4 (CEV)

The psalms are deeply emotional songs. They describe fear, anger, frustration, and jealousy – but also love, joy, and exhilaration over God. That is why we so readily identify with them!

In this psalm Asaph is lying on his bed, vexed with the question of God's presence. Where is the God who does wonders? Why are there so many testimonies of His work, but he continues to struggle? Yes, where is God? Asaph tosses and turns and thinks and prays, but receives no answer. The psalm itself does not provide an answer, either – it merely ends with God who is great. Don't think there isn't a deep lesson in this, though. See how Asaph directs his questions *at God*, how Asaph thinks on his bed *about God*, how Asaph has a great need *for God*.

Asaph is in a relationship *with* God! God is very much present in his life! It's not so much about God's answers – which we would not fully comprehend, anyway – it's about living with God. We don't need answers as much as we need Him.

*Lord, there are many things that I cannot understand.
You are with me, though, and that is enough. Amen.*

JUNE 18
GREAT ENOUGH

I will ponder all Your work, and meditate on Your mighty deeds.
Your way, O God, is holy. What god is great like our God?
PSALM 77:12-13

Asaph is greatly troubled and pleads with God for an answer. He prays and prays, but nothing happens. That's how this psalm begins.

In the second part, Asaph asks a lot of questions. Where is the God who does wonders? Why isn't He answering? What about His steadfast love? Did He forget to be gracious? Then, in the last part of the psalm, Asaph merely reflects on God's greatness. God, for example, opened the Red Sea for His people to trek through – a mighty deed! That's how this psalm ends – as if Asaph is just leaving his problem with the Mighty God. He can deal with it, and He can be trusted with it.

How it's going to happen Asaph doesn't know, but that's not important. The God who could take His people through the sea can take an individual through his problems! We can also leave our troubles with the Great God, with the Almighty. He is great enough for it.

Lord, You know me, and You know my challenges.
I trust You with them all. Amen.

GOD *KNOWS* US

He restrained his anger often and did not stir up
all His wrath. He remembered that they were but
flesh, a wind that passes and comes not again.
PSALM 78:38-39

In this psalm Asaph looks back over Israel's history and is reminded again of how disobedient and rebellious they were. They almost never kept the covenant conditions!

Time and again they experienced God's punishment, but they never learned. Asaph states, however – he weaves it into the structure – that God *knows* His people. He knows they are "flesh" (merely flesh and blood, in other words), that they're merely *human*: imperfect, broken, sinful, wonderful humans. He knows that they're frail, that their lives are fleeting like a "wind that passes." God knows it! He made them so, as humans, and He loves them so, as humans. God does not resent our humanity, because He knows we can never be anything else. He accepts our brokenness, even our sinfulness. What He does resent, however, is that we do not come to Him for healing, forgiveness, completion. Human lives were made to be shared with God. Oh, that's our true sin!

Lord, I am human, typically human.
But I do want to live with You! Amen.

JUNE 20
SHINE ON ME

Give ear, O Shepherd of Israel, You who lead Joseph like a flock.
You who are enthroned upon the cherubim, shine forth.

PSALM 80:1

The poet is asking God to return them from their exile. In this verse he asks God, who is "enthroned upon the cherubim," to "shine forth."

His reference is to the *Shekinah*, God's presence, His radiance, which shone as a visible light between the two cherubim of the Ark of the Covenant. At the time that this psalm was written, the phrase was merely an expression, since the physical temple was in ruins and the ark lost. For the psalmist, it's as if God Himself was gone, as if His face was not shining on them anymore in blessing.

It's as if his world has become dark and cold with God far away. Do you feel the same way sometimes? Do you long for God's presence again? If this is your prayer, it's just a question of time – God will shine His face on you again!

Lift up Your face upon me, Lord, and bless me.
Make Your face to shine upon me again, and give me peace. Amen.

JUNE 21

HE IS BUSY WITH US

Have regard for this vine, the stock that Your right hand planted, and for the son whom You made strong for Yourself.
PSALM 80:14-15

Asaph says that Israel is like a vine stock brought from Egypt by God and replanted in Canaan. Now, however, the vineyard has been ravaged by enemies. He pleads with God to return and tend to His work once again.

It's understandable that Asaph feels like this, but of course God never really left His vineyard at all. He tends to His people as His full-time task. The fact that they had to go into exile did not change that. The vineyard was not abandoned. The Bible is clear that they had to stay there for seventy years, but after that – at God's appointed time – He brought them back and had a new temple built. He brought forth the Messiah, allowed the temple to be demolished, had them dispersed, brought them back again – and he is *still busy* with them.

God *is* tending His vineyard! Let's not doubt or question that. Rather, let's try to discern what God is busy with, and then flow with His work in our lives. Yes, let's be co-workers with God. That's our task!

Lord, what are You busy with in my life?
How can I join Your work – what can I do? Amen.

TURN ME 'ROUND, LORD!

Restore us, O Lord God of hosts!
Let Your face shine, that we may be saved!
PSALM 80:19

Look at the typical pattern that Asaph uses in these verses. It goes more or less like this: let Your hand be on us, then we shall not turn back from You; give us life, then we will call upon Your name; restore us, and we will be saved.

Do you see? God does something, and then the people respond to it. Asaph realized, probably when the people were in exile, that they cannot serve God, and definitely cannot save themselves, on their own. If God doesn't work, they can do nothing! That's why he pleads with God in this closing verse to restore, or to turn, them. Then they will be turned around to God, converted, restored!

What does this mean for us? It means we cannot *make* God's work, but we can pray for God's work. We cannot make His wind to blow, but we can stand in His wind and go where it moves us. Pray for God to work!

Lord, shine over me, work in me, give me life.
Then I will be where I need to be! Amen.

JUNE 23

GO AND CELEBRATE!

Blow the trumpet at the new moon, at the full moon, on our feast day.
For it is a statute for Israel, a rule of the God of Jacob.
PSALM 81:3-4

Asaph calls up the people, the Levites and the priests: the feast, probably of Tabernacles (*Sukkot*), is about to begin! The Feast of Tabernacles
is a joyful harvest festival that also celebrates the Jews' deliverance
from Egypt.

It happens only five days after the most solemn and holy Day of
Atonement (*Yom Kippur*), so the change in tone is considerable. Anyway,
when the shofar is blown, the people must join with joyful hearts. You
know, there is a time to fast and a time to feast. Both are important, and
both are God's command. It's not spiritual to merely pray and fast.

Some Christians cannot relax and cannot enjoy or celebrate at
all – they feel it's unfitting, sinful. That's wrong! God's children must
absolutely be able to enjoy life, to laugh without reservation, and to
celebrate exuberantly. To celebrate life is a gift from God that we may
not refuse. So, do not be ungrateful – there are so many reasons to
celebrate!

*Lord, thank You that I may enjoy the life You've given,
that You grant me true happiness! Amen!*

JUNE 24
OPEN UP WIDE

I am the LORD your God, who brought you up out of the
land of Egypt. Open your mouth wide, and I will fill it.
PSALM 81:10

At the time of the Feast of Tabernacles, Asaph is thinking again of the
covenant the Lord made with them at Sinai: if they served God fully,
God would fully provide their needs.

In our verse, we read a particularly poignant and meaningful perspective on the covenant from God's own mouth: "I am the LORD your
God, … Open your mouth wide, and I will fill it." It's beautiful! The
reference of course is to baby birds who open their beaks wide for their
parents to put food in. This image of fledglings illustrates our complete
dependence on God and emphasizes that we should look up to Him
with great expectation and trust.

Take note, though, God does not just *give*. We should also actively
receive. God provides, but faith is to ask for it, to expect it, to patiently
wait for it, and then to take it from His hand. Develop your faith while
you wait.

Father, I have such a great expectation from You.
Provide in my need, in Jesus' name! Amen.

MILK AND HONEY

But I would feed you with the finest bread
and with the best honey until you were full.

PSALM 81:16 (CEV)

In this psalm the people are called to the Feast of Tabernacles. Israel was delivered from Egypt, but due to their stubbornness could not inherit the Promised Land immediately. They first had to wander through the desert for forty years.

The Feast of Tabernacles celebrates how God provided for them there, in every way. Still, their true goal was Canaan, the "land of milk and honey" (Exod. 3:8). God's ultimate intention with them wasn't the desert, but the promised blessing and abundance! This is God's goal for us as well, but we are often like the Israelites, spiritually wandering in the desert. Let's put it like this: a desert life isn't a life without struggles, but a life without God. It's when we stumble along where our own will takes us. It's where we really try to be in control.

That can never lead to God's promises! In this verse God says that the "finest bread" and the "best honey" is found with *Him* – nowhere else. He affords us provision and sustenance, milk and honey! Listen, if you cannot find your Canaan in Him, you will never find Canaan anywhere.

Lord, You are the living water, the bread of life.
You satisfy and fulfill! Amen.

SHOW ME YOUR LOVE

Give justice to the weak and the fatherless; maintain the right
of the afflicted and the destitute. Rescue the weak and the needy;
deliver them from the hand of the wicked.

PSALM 82:3-4

Sometimes we get so involved with church or get so *spiritual* that we forget the purpose of it all. We become completely focused on our relationship with Jesus, on studying the Word, praying, praising God, ministering with our gifts, and so on.

Some have become so proficient in these things that they're quite intimidating! We can easily become sidelined, however, when our whole spiritual life starts to revolve around *me*: me and my blessing, me and my ministry, me and my walk with God. It can also happen that we consider ourselves ahead of others, spiritually speaking. We are more spiritual than others, aren't we, and know so much more about the spiritual life than others do. Really? Take note that true spirituality leads to transformation, a change of heart.

In fact, spirituality translates into love. Love is the fruit, the result! There is no other way. And remember, love is a practical and visible thing. It has to do with helping the weak, the parentless, the destitute. Read the verse again. The world says, "Don't show me your spirituality – show me your love!"

Lord, help me bear the fruit of the spiritual walk – love! Amen.

MY SOUL LONGS

How lovely is Your dwelling place, O LORD of hosts!
My soul longs, yes, faints for the courts of the Lord;
my heart and flesh sing for joy to the living God.

PSALM 84:1-2

The Korahites are singing in this psalm about their love for God's temple. Such beautiful words! Nowadays, not many have such love for the house of the Lord. In fact, the church finds itself in a crisis.

Some stay away because they are lukewarm, but others stay away because the church is lukewarm! They would rather look after their own spiritual needs, thank you very much. Others are disappointed in the church or its members. Many see the church as hypocritical, judgmental, or just irrelevant. It's true that the church is suffering a crisis of credibility, and it's true that the church urgently needs to address its problems. Still, the church, for all of its failures, remains God's instrument – Christ's body!

Change your attitude. Go to church with an expectation, then you will find worth there. Go in order to give, not just to receive, then it will be meaningful. *Be* the church that you want to see! Yes, be there, be a living member of the body – be the church! Church is always *us*, it's never *them*. It's *us* who have problems!

Lord, I pray for the church. It's my church,
because I am part of You. I am the church! Amen.

EVEN THE SPARROW

*Even the sparrow finds a home, and the swallow a nest
for herself, where she may lay her young, at Your altars,
O LORD of hosts, my King and my God.*

PSALM 84:3

The temple in Jerusalem was always bustling. Remember, it was basically a huge slaughterhouse: Levites were continually killing and slaughtering the many sacrificial animals that were brought by worshipers.

The priests then poured the blood against the altar, offered the specified portions to God, and said a prayer over them. People also stood in the temple courts praying audibly, not to mention the bleating and bellowing of the animals. Yes, it must have been quite noisy, although the temple building itself would have been quiet, serene – a holy place. The poet, however, notices the birds' nests underneath the eaves of the roofs and gates of the buildings. There, amidst the noise and commotion, they found their home.

The poet so identifies with them! In the whole churning machine that was the temple, amidst the sacred and the ordinary happening there, he felt completely at home, because his God was there! You know, God's sanctuary is in our heart. Amidst the hustle and bustle of the day we can find quiet, because *He's* there!

*Lord, thank You that the noise of the outside
can never extinguish Your presence on the inside. Amen.*

SPRINGS START FLOWING

You bless all who depend on You for their strength and all who deeply desire to visit Your temple. When they reach Dry Valley, springs start flowing, and the autumn rain fills it with pools of water.

PSALM 84:5-6 (CEV)

How beautiful is the song of the Korahites here! Blessed are those, they say, who depend on God for strength, not on themselves. Such people have "highways to Zion" in their hearts, meaning that they often think of going to Jerusalem again.

They long for the city of God, because they long for God! There – with Him – they will renew their strength. If they go through dry spells in their lives, they will find inner springs opening up to carry them through, early rains that will suddenly fall to bring relief. The application is self-evident: the sanctuary of God is not in Jerusalem anymore, but in our hearts, where the Spirit of God dwells.

Blessed are you when you find God there! He will become a fountain in your heart – as Jesus promised – that will carry you through the most difficult of times. *His* strength will become *your* strength. Yes, find that strength!

Lord, I so need Your strength. Open up Your fountains in me! Amen.

HOUSES WITHOUT GOD

One day in Your temple is better than a thousand anywhere else.
I would rather serve in Your house, than live in the homes of the wicked.

PSALM 84:10 (CEV)

The poet says one day in God's temple is better than a thousand ordinary days! He says he would rather stand on the doorstep of the house of God than live in the homes of the godless.

Today, there are many homes where God isn't welcome, where His name is never mentioned. Sometimes believers live in such a house. Perhaps the mother serves God, but the father does not – or their children are rebellious. Other times, again, a child is the only believer in a house, faithfully praying for her parents. Let's make Joshua's decision our own: "As for me and my house, we will serve the LORD" (Josh. 24:15).

Do not hesitate to give God His place in your home. Talk about Him. Pray when you want to pray. Let your family see that you read the Bible. Do not let your home become a cold and indifferent house without God. No, make it a house of God!

Lord, be welcome in our home. We want to serve You! Amen.

July

On the holy mount stands the city He founded;
    the L<small>ORD</small> loves the gates of Zion more than all the
dwelling places of Jacob.
    Glorious things of you are spoken, O city of God.
    Among those who know me I mention Rahab and
Babylon; behold, Philistia and Tyre, with Cush –
"This one was born there," they say.
    And of Zion it shall be said,
    "This one and that one were born in her;"
    for the Most High Himself will establish her.
    The L<small>ORD</small> records as He registers the peoples,
"This one was born there."
    Singers and dancers alike say, "All my springs are in You."

P<small>SALM</small> 87

JULY 1

MY SUN AND SHIELD

For the LORD God is a sun and shield;
the LORD bestows favor and honor. No good thing
does He withhold from those who walk uprightly.

PSALM 84:11

The Korahites, who wrote this song about the temple – "How lovely is Your dwelling place" (Ps. 84:1) – now end it with a beautiful blessing: "The LORD God is a sun and shield; the LORD will give grace and glory; no good thing will He withhold from them that walk uprightly" (KJV).

This is the psalm's conclusion. Remember, in this psalm it's not so much about love for the outward temple, but love and longing for the God who can be found in the temple. Such a longing is always rewarded with a blessing! Do you also long for God – do you seek after Him? Remember, when we seek we will find (Matt. 7:7); when we draw near to God, He will draw near to us (James 4:8).

Yes, when we take a step in His direction, He will take two steps in ours! Oh, and when you have found God, you have found the greatest blessing this universe can offer! In Him all the good things of this life can be found.

"Lord of hosts, blessed is the one who trusts in You" (Ps. 84:12). Amen.

REVIVE ME

Will You not revive us again, that Your people
may rejoice in You? Show us Your steadfast love,
O LORD, and grant us Your salvation.
PSALM 85:6-7

In this psalm the Korahites feel as if God is far away. Where is the God that used to live with His people? Why does it feel as if everything is cold and distant between them?

That's why they pray for God to revive them again – for Him to restore their joy. Revival can only be experienced by someone who was once alive for God but lost that zeal along the way. It can so easily happen! We start off with excitement for God, but then life takes its course. Obligations and disappointments quench much of the spiritual life we once had. Some become cynical or even lose their faith altogether.

It's true that youthful zeal can be misdirected or unsustainable, but even so, don't we miss the passion, the joy, the presence of God, and the reality of the faith we once had? Pray that God will revive those things in you again!

Yes, Lord, revive me! Restore the passion I had for You. Amen.

SALVATION IS NEAR

Surely His salvation is near to those who fear Him,
that glory may dwell in our land.

PSALM 85:9

Take this as a personal promise: *surely* salvation is near those who fear God. What a wonderful and great assurance, which always remains true. Salvation is near, because God is near!

He is your salvation, not some or other hoped for event, blind luck, or influential person to whom you may be looking. Let's put it this way: For us as Christians help is always near, just around the corner – always imminent! Faith knows that it can happen at any time. That's how faith operates.

It remains expectant, trusting, longing, waiting! Remember, our relationship with God rests on faith. It's our way of living. Live therefore with strong faith, with great expectations! Confess your faith, wait for God in faith, receive what He gives in faith. Do not hesitate or retreat – salvation is near!

Lord, I do believe, but help my unbelief (Mark 9:24)! Amen.

ONE DAY, TODAY

Steadfast love and faithfulness meet;
righteousness and peace kiss each other.
PSALM 85:10

In a beautiful and poetic way the Korahites are singing about the day when God will intervene on earth. Then, they say, love and faithfulness will come together, and righteousness and peace will embrace and kiss. Take note:

- Love is when I accept others as they are, when I have deep regard, respect, and concern for them.
- Faithfulness is when I do what I promise, when others can truly depend on me. It is trustworthiness, loyalty, and honesty.
- Righteousness is when I do what is right toward God and toward others. It is when fairness prevails, especially toward the vulnerable.
- Peace is when I am in harmony with God, myself, and my world. It is to experience God's blessing on me, to see His grace and favor in me and around me.
- One day, this is how things *will* be. In the meantime, though, this is how things can be! May the kingship of God increase in your heart and work these fruits in your life – may you have these blessings today.

Lord, establish Your kingdom in my life. Amen.

JULY 5

THE TIME IS NOW

*Yes, the LORD will give what is good, and our land
will yield its increase. Righteousness will go before Him
and make His footsteps a way.*

PSALM 85:12-13

In this psalm the Korahites are looking forward to the day when the Lord will return to His people. They sing of the peace and love, faithfulness and righteousness that will reign in that time. It will be a time of prosperity and blessing.

It's beautiful to note that these promises are meant for us today! Look at this verse again: the "righteousness" that is predicted here has since ancient times been seen as the Messiah, the Righteous One. He would come first, before God's final intervention, and He did come! Jesus the Messiah (translated from Hebrew into Greek as "Christ") introduced the "Messianic Age," even though that age is still to be concluded. Now is the expected new age, the time of the Spirit, the year of jubilee! We already live in it – we already experience new and heavenly things! Live, therefore, the new life. Live Spirit driven.

Work for the expansion of the kingdom and for the coming in of the nations. Share in the peace, joy, and prosperity that this time brings. Live boldly, with great faith and strength! Get up! Receive God's favor: expect it, take it, and share it! The time is now!

I will stand up, Lord, and be counted for You! Amen!

CONTRACTUAL BENEFITS

Protect me and save me because You are my God.
I am Your faithful servant, and I trust You.
PSALM 86:2 (CEV)

See how David identifies the two persons involved in his petition: (1) "You are my God," and (2) "I am Your faithful servant." These concepts evoke the terminology of the covenant between Israel and God, which in the Old Testament is often formulated as, I will be your God; you will be my people.

David applies the covenant personally, because as an individual he feels part of it. God will be his God! That's why he prays with boldness. He feels he has kept his part of the agreement – he is "faithful" (literally "godly" which means-devout, pious) and can therefore appeal to God's part of the agreement, which stipulates that God will provide for him and protect him.

Remember, as believers we are part of the exact same covenant. We, too, are in a legal agreement with the Almighty! Isn't that wonderful? Commit yourself 100 percent to Him, as He has committed Himself 100 percent to you. The covenant was signed in blood, remember!

Lord, Your covenant is very important to me.
Help me to keep to my side of it, in Jesus' name! Amen.

ALL THE NATIONS

*Among those who know me I mention
Rahab and Babylon; behold, Philistia and Tyre,
with Cush – "This one was born there," they say.*
PSALM 87:4

The Korahites are singing in the temple a song about the temple. They say that one day all nations will worship the true God there, in Zion. On that day God will adopt those nations as His children as well. Remember, God loves all nations equally – not just His covenant people, Israel! He wants all to serve Him.

Although non-Israelites joined into the covenant in the Old Testament, the Jews expected multitudes from other nations to join them in the Messianic Era. And they have! Since Jesus, the Messiah, non-Jewish nations are turning to the God of Israel en masse. Eight percent of Chinese, for example, are currently Christians, as are thirty percent of Koreans. In fact, 2.7 million people are turning to God – through Jesus Christ – from other faiths annually.

The greatest Christian outreach ever is currently underway! Every Christian should be involved. All the nations must hear that God loves them!

Lord, how can I be involved in letting the nations know? Amen.

JULY 8
IN THE PIT

You have put me in the depths of the pit,
in the regions dark and deep.
PSALM 88:6

Oh dear, from the mountaintop to the pit of despair! This psalm is probably the darkest in the entire Bible. Heman, David's court singer, describes his condition in detail: "Your wrath lies heavy upon me, and You overwhelm me with all Your waves. ... My eye grows dim through sorrow" (Ps. 88:7-9) – and much more!

Only those who know depression will realize the gravity of what he feels. All color disappears from life: nothing can be enjoyed, nothing is worth the effort, and for nothing can I summon the energy. Do you know the condition? Do consult a doctor or a knowledgeable counselor – it will really help!

Can I also add the following: depression is a common condition and well known in the Bible; God knows about you and is with you – whether you feel it or not; and you can work through episodes of depression in a meaningful way. You can learn to manage it with God's help. Do what Heman did: talk, talk, talk with God about it!

When all is darkness, Lord, shine Your light!
In Your light I will see the Light. Amen.

MORE THAN YOU KNOW

The heavens are Yours; the earth also is Yours;
the world and all that is in it, You have founded them.
The north and the south, You have created them.

PSALM 89:11-12

Ethan was a great sage who lived about a millennium before Christ. In this psalm he describes the greatness of God as seen through his particular (and primitive) knowledge of nature.

Oh, Ethan, if you could only realize that your God is much, much greater than you could ever know! If you could only know that your galaxy contains 300 billion stars – and that there are billions of other galaxies containing billions of stars arranged around unbelievably large amounts of open space. If you could only have an inkling of the forces that keep these together, of time, of probability, of the possibility of different dimensions.

And we still know so little! Ethan, all these things are simple and elemental physical phenomena: The most complex creation of all, the most intricate and valuable design made by God is man – you and me – and as you know, God has declared His unending love for us.

What a great God, and what a great love, Ethan! In that respect you're so right!

Lord, thank You for Your great love! Amen.

THE TWO CIRCLES

You have renounced the covenant with Your servant;
You have defiled his crown in the dust.
PSALM 89:39

Ethan the sage is struggling to understand God. God made a covenant with His people and with their king: they would forever be His people and would forever have a Davidic king to rule them. However, now His people have been overrun by enemies, and their throne stands empty! What now? In this psalm Ethan deliberates these questions. The covenant has two circles:

- The inner circle has to do with conditions and benefits. If the people are obedient, then God will protect them. They were not obedient, though, and that's why Ethan sees what he sees.
- The outer circle – encompassing the previous one – is the circle of God's grace. It covers the disobedience of the inner circle, meaning that even given their disobedience God will not forsake them. In the end God did save them from their crisis, and today the Davidic Messiah, Jesus Christ, is the King of the Jews forever. The promises remain true!

Ultimately, the whole covenant depends on God. It's a covenant of grace. Just receive it gratefully.

Thank You, Lord, for saving me by grace.
Now I want to please You with my life! Amen.

FROM ETERNITY TO ETERNITY

Lord, You have been our dwelling place in all generations.
Before the mountains were brought forth, or ever You had formed
the earth and the world, from everlasting to everlasting You are God.
PSALM 90:1-2

In the midst of many troubles, Moses feels heartened by the fact that God exists from eternity to eternity. Although the earth and mountains were seen in those times as symbols of absolute immovability, Moses says they are small and insignificant compared to the greatness of God.

Against the awesome backdrop of God's greatness man is even more diminutive, fleeting, and fragile. Remember that God also created time and can look upon it as on a mountain range. Yesterday, today, and tomorrow are merely different peaks upon which His gaze rests. For God, our future is as exactly well-known as our past! Still – and this is the wonder of His greatness – God enters into our own time and comes to live our little lives with us.

As we live moment by moment, day by day, wondering and deciding, God is with us. When we're worried about the future, though, He is not worried, because He already knows precisely how our future will end: in glory, with *Him*!

Thank You, Lord, for being my beginning and my end! Amen.

LIKE A THOUSAND YEARS

*For a thousand years in Your sight are but as yesterday
when it is past, or as a watch in the night.*

PSALM 90:4

We often think, wrongly so, that God lives *in* time as we do. No, God exists *over* time, because He created it when He created space and everything in it. God looks upon yesterday, today, and tomorrow as if they are mere points on a graph.

Moses realizes this when he says in this verse that a thousand years for God is like yesterday: concluded, done, already half-forgotten and unreal. Like a "watch in the night," which is slept through in an instant. Although for us a thousand years is an extremely long time, for God it's a mere moment. On the other hand, God can also change everything in an instant, because a second for Him is like a year to work in.

The lesson is this: Let's not be so concerned about time and about timing, because God isn't! Whatever He does, God is always *on time*! Just keep on trusting Him.

*Eternal God, in Your eyes my life is already concluded
in You: finished, accomplished, won! Amen.*

LIVE THE SEVENTY!

*The years of our life are seventy, or even
by reason of strength eighty; yet their span is
but toil and trouble; they are soon gone, and we fly away.*
PSALM 90:10

In this psalm Moses feels particularly small before God. He notes how short life is, about seventy or eighty years. The years fly by like thoughts! He says we are like grass, strong and green in the morning but cut down in the evening, already dying away.

The lesson for Moses is this: life is God's greatest gift to us. Let's take it from God's hand, then, with appreciation and decide to make the best of it! Live purposefully through the hard times, but also fully enjoy the good times, the victories. Live freely, deeply, and with passion. Do what you relish. Laugh a lot! Give yourself completely. Love without holding back.

Celebrate as much as you can! While we must avoid sin, self-centeredness, and hard-heartedness as much as possible, we must never, ever avoid life. Never retreat from living fully, especially out of fear. Overcome your fears and take part in life. It's a gift!

Lord, thank You for the gift of life – teach me how to live! Amen.

TEACH US TO LIVE

So teach us to number our days
that we may get a heart of wisdom.
PSALM 90:12

Remember, Moses saw God's majesty with his own eyes! Therefore, he was deeply under the impression of how small and fragile man really is. He stresses that we only live for seventy or eighty years, which flash by like a dream, and he prays in this verse that we will use our years to obtain wisdom.

What he is asking for here is that life itself be our teacher, that life be the course that we follow in order to achieve the goals that God has in mind for us. How else are we going to learn life if not from living life? Live therefore with an open and inquiring mind, eager to grasp whatever you can learn. Develop depth. Above all, don't be afraid to fail, because failure is necessary for learning. We will fail and we must fail! Learn to fail productively, though.

Do not take it too personally. Understand the lessons to be learned and adapt your behavior accordingly. Eventually you will obtain what the Bible calls wisdom – a worthy goal!

Master, teach me wisdom. Use my life and teach me how to live. Amen.

SATISFY US IN THE MORNING

*Satisfy us in the morning with Your steadfast love,
that we may rejoice and be glad all our days.*
PSALM 90:14

Moses states that man is small before his Creator and that his days are few, beset with many challenges. He is praying, therefore, that God will always be with them. Here he specifically asks for God's "steadfast love," for His lovingkindness to "satisfy [them] in the morning."

What beautiful words – read them again – describing our need for God as a hunger to be satisfied! More specifically, our need is for God's steadfast love – His sworn covenant-love, in other words. We merely ask for what God has already promised! Consider this: Will God do what He promised? Most assuredly He will, because He is God! His promises are completely certain – a solid foundation to build upon.

We will experience His steadfast love, no matter what! Like Moses, we can wait upon it "in the morning" – and be satisfied by it. Then, as Moses states, we will rejoice and be glad in it every day!

Lord, satisfy me with Your love as I wait upon You in the morning. Amen.

SADDENED, GLADDENED

Make us glad for as many days as You have afflicted us,
and for as many years as we have seen evil.
PSALM 90:15

Moses knew God's greatness as few people did. He saw Him personally! As leader of the recalcitrant Israelites, he also knew God's anger like few others. Especially in the desert with its many hardships, the Israelites had trouble with their obedience.

Still, Moses takes the liberty here to ask if God will give them as many good days as He had allowed bad. What he asks is for God's forgiveness to overtake their sin, for His grace to cover their guilt – for His steadfast love to conquer all weakness and failure. Moses asks for these things because he really knew God – he knew God's graciousness and forgiveness, His abiding love!

So, what Moses, the man who knew God personally, is suggesting to us so many thousands of years later is this: God is good and God is gracious. Things will turn around! Gladness will overtake your sadness.

Heavenly Father, I pray for Your grace in my life. I so need it! Amen.

THE BEAUTY OF THE LORD

*Let Your work be shown to Your servants, and Your
glorious power to their children. Let the favor of the
Lord our God be upon us, and establish the work of
our hands upon us; yes, establish the work of our hands!*

PSALM 90:16-17

This is undoubtedly one of the most profound verses in the Bible.
Moses is spelling out his, and our, deepest longing in words that are
rich with meaning and strikingly poetic.

It is impossible for us to explain or understand its full meaning, but
do ask the Holy Spirit for a personal explanation. Take an unhurried
quiet time and meditate upon each of these phrases:

- Let Your work be shown. Let it appear to me, Your servant, Lord.
- Let Your glory, Your magnificence, be shown (manifest, become
  visible) to my children.
- Let Your favor (literally "beauty"), Lord my God, be over me this day.
- Establish the work of my hands upon me – yes, establish it!

What do these words mean to you? God will open it up in your
heart!

*Yes, Lord! Let Your beauty be over me like a mantle.
Let everyone see You in me! Amen.*

THE SHADOW OF THE ALMIGHTY

*He who dwells in the shelter of the Most High
will abide in the shadow of the Almighty.*
PSALM 91:1

This psalm is one of the best known and most beautiful in the whole Bible! This first verse introduces God in two ways:

- The "Most High" (El Elyon) is God-above-all, especially God-above-all-gods. The one who finds shelter with Him is truly safe, because nothing and no one can get to that high hideout!
- The "Almighty" (El Shaddai) is the omnipotent God, God-who-can-do-all. The one who remains in His shadow – in other words right beside Him – is also truly safe!

The lesson is simple. Are you tired, weary? Filled with despair, worry? Did life get to you? Did someone hurt you? Well then, come! Come to the secret place, come hide away with the Most High. Yes, come sit, come rest with the Almighty, who can fix anything. How? Just close the door behind you – you'll find Him there, right where you are!

*Lord, I now turn to You. I now come to You
for my rest. Amen.*

MY REFUGE, MY FORTRESS

I will say to the LORD, "My refuge and my fortress,
my God, in whom I trust."
PSALM 91:2

The unknown poet of these beautiful verses first introduces God as the Most High and then as the Almighty. He asserts that the one who finds refuge with that God will surely be safe. In the next verse the mood changes and becomes personal and intimate.

He says the one that seeks God – and the subject is now "I" – will call Him by His personal name, Yahweh (here translated as the "LORD"); he will say my God, in whom I trust. Do you see? The language becomes that of a personal God and a personal relationship. It's the language of personal faith. It also answers the question: Where do I find the shelter of the Most High, and the shadow of the Almighty?

Well, you will find that refuge in a personal relationship with God. It's in your conversation with Him, in His Word speaking to you; it's in your attention to His voice, in your reaction to His instruction. There you will know that your God is the Highest, the Mighty One. Look for Him there!

Lord, my need is for more of You in my life,
more relationship – more, Lord! Amen.

BENEATH HIS WINGS

He will spread His wings over you and keep you secure.
His faithfulness is like a shield or a city wall.

PSALM 91:4 (CEV)

This striking psalm is about God's protection. See how beautifully it is portrayed. When we need protection:

- We will be under God's wings. The image is that of an eagle protecting its young by extending her wings over them, or of a hen to whose wings the scared chicks quickly run.
- God's faithfulness will be around us like a shield or a city wall. Soldiers of this time of course had a shield in their left hand to ward of attacks. Their cities were walled in, providing safety.

We know that in this life there will be attacks, there will be onslaughts. It is a fact of life. When you perceive, then, the shadow of a raptor over you or if you find yourself suddenly under attack, flee to God! Raise your shield! God's faithfulness will stand between you and any enemy, any attack. With Him you *will* be safe!

Thank You, Almighty God! Under Your wings I feel truly safe. Amen.

REPROGRAM YOURSELF

*A thousand may fall at your side, ten thousand
at your right hand, but it will not come near you.*

PSALM 91:7

This psalm is about the fact that God protects us. We needn't fear the "terror of the night," nor the "arrow that flies by day," nor "pestilence" or "destruction" (Ps. 91:5-6). To not fear is an important but difficult topic.

Fear comes naturally! Remember, fear is a basic instinct programmed into us for the sake of our survival. Fear keeps us from danger, because arrows and pestilences can hurt us. However, fruitless and unnecessary fear is counterproductive. We therefore need to work productively with our fear, and we do it through faith.

If we reprogram ourselves with truths such as in this psalm, we take away fear's sting because fear responds to a perceived threat. See it like this: When this psalmist confirms that he will not fear, he is reprogramming his soul with God's truths. Yes, let the truth about God's protection take hold of your soul! As it sinks into your spirit and changes who you are, your fear will decrease – your faith will increase!

Thank You, Lord, that I need not fear. Teach me not to fear! Amen.

THE SUPERNATURAL AROUND US

*For He will command His angels concerning
you to guard you in all your ways. On their hands
they will bear you up, lest you strike your foot against a stone.*
PSALM 91:11-12

We don't just live this natural life. According to Scripture, the supernatural is also part of our lives. It must be, because we believe in a supernatural God who intervenes on this earth and in this life!

In this verse we again encounter God's angels, who are extensively mentioned in the Old and New Testaments. The angels are appointed to guard over us, amongst other duties, for which we can be very grateful. In just the next verse we encounter other supernatural beings, too, referred to as *lions, adders,* and *serpents* to be trampled underfoot.

In the New Testament these symbols clearly refer to the Evil One and his spirits. How do we deal with him? Well, we keep him under our feet as an act of faith. We rule *over him* in Jesus' name!

*Lord God, help me to live wisely.
Command Your angels over me, deliver me from evil! Amen.*

DO YOU LOVE ME?

Because he holds fast to Me in love, I will deliver him;
I will protect him, because he knows My name.
PSALM 91:14

Can you see that the promises of this verse are meant for only a certain group of people? In this verse, the promises are for those who *love* God. Although the Lord loves all people, not all people love Him!

Take note, though: We often water down our love for God into something that is no more than a spiritual idea, something that has no practical effect on our hearts, lives, or world whatsoever. That's not love! We know love to be a powerful force. It burns in our hearts and changes our attitudes; it focuses our lives on our beloved. Love as a very practical thing is the love that God wants from us as His first commandment: to love *Him* above all.

After Peter's relationship with Jesus went awry, Jesus' first question to Peter was, "Do you love Me?" (John 21:15). That is also the question that Jesus asks us. Remember, it's for *those* whom His promises are meant!

I love You, Lord, but help me to love You even more! Amen.

THREE ANSWERS

When he calls to Me, I will answer him;
I will be with him in trouble; I will rescue him and honor him.

PSALM 91:15

This beautiful psalm about God's protection and provision ends with these powerful promises about Him answering our prayers. God hears all prayers of all people, but here He says that He *specifically* listens to His children's prayers.

Elsewhere the Bible says, "The eyes of the Lord are on the righteous, and His ears are open to their prayer" (1 Pet. 3:12). Do you say that you *are* a child of God, but your prayers are not answered? Well, God heard and even answered them all, but often we're not happy with the answer we receive! God's answer usually comes in one of the following ways:

- Yes – you see a breakthrough and have much reason to thank God!
- No – the loving Father decided otherwise because of reasons that you don't know, but you need to trust Him.
- Later – the Father is still working together things in your life for good, and you must keep on praying, asking, trusting, and waiting.

Remember, in *all things* God can be trusted – and should be praised because of His goodness!

Father, I will keep on trusting You. Help me to trust! Amen.

SING THE SABBATH SONG

It is good to give thanks to the LORD, to sing praises
to Your name, O Most High; to declare Your steadfast
love in the morning, and Your faithfulness by night.

PSALM 92:1-2

The Jewish Sabbath commemorates God's act of creation and His redemption of Israel from Egypt. It acts as a foretaste of the coming Messianic Age, *Olam Haba*.

Each entails first work and, after that, rest. The Sabbath, as symbol of Israel's covenant with God, is still celebrated weekly by Jews with beautiful ceremony and much joy. Although we as Christians do not keep the Sabbath as such – not being Jewish and the Old Covenant having been fulfilled in the New – we understand what it's about, because everything that the Sabbath stood for has been fulfilled in Jesus the Messiah. *He* is man's rest from his works, the Redeemer, and the reason for our joy! On the Lord's Day (Sunday) we celebrate His rest.

So, if believers of the Old Testament had reason for joy, believers of the New Testament have much more! *They* expected and anticipated, but *we* have received. That's reason for singing a Sabbath song!

I will sing a song unto You, O Lord, for You fulfill every promise. Amen.

JULY 26
FORGET THEIR PROSPERITY

Though the wicked sprout and spread like grass,
they will be pulled up by their roots.
PSALM 92:7 (CEV)

The psalmist is singing a beautiful song about God's greatness. In this verse he's struggling with the fact that godless people often prosper but feels vindicated by the conclusion that God will wipe them out.

We already dealt with the topic of the success of the godless, so let's add here just the following: forget the godless and forget their prosperity. What we mean is that there will always be those who have more than us. Many will have newer cars or bigger houses. If we fixate on that, we will always feel inferior. Leave them to God, who will judge all people fairly. Let's rather focus on those who have less than us.

There are so many in whose eyes *we* are the fortunate, the ones having abundance and prosperity. Be grateful for what you have, therefore – and willing to share with those who struggle. Do you see how your perspective changes the whole matter?

Thank You, Lord, for my prosperity!
Make me generous with what I have received. Amen.

GROWING UP IN THE TEMPLE

They are planted in the house of the LORD;
they flourish in the courts of our God.
PSALM 92:13

The author of this beautiful song is emboldened by the fact that his God is with him. God has given him strength so that he can now look fearlessly onto his enemies. While the enemies will be defeated, the righteous will flourish and grow "like a cedar" (Ps. 92:12).

Where do these righteous people get their strength? Well, "they are planted in the house of the LORD; they flourish in the courts of God." Yes, they are rooted there, in God's house – they flourish there! Churches sometimes struggle to find their place in a changing society, but one thing is certain: the church lays a solid foundation for our faith and the faith of our children. Those who have that base effectively taught, practically applied, and demonstrated by spiritual mentors have a tremendous advantage.

Many try at home to care for their own faith and their children's in a haphazard way, but that can never be as solid. No, take your child to church! Let him grow up and flourish there.

Lord, I pray for my children. I want them
to step into a strong, personal faith. Amen.

DRAW DEEPLY

They will be like trees that stay healthy and fruitful,
even when they are old.

PSALM 92:14 (CEV)

The righteous can expect God's blessing. It's always true, because God always blesses! To be blessed is our default position in God. In the Old Testament, God's blessing was seen in things like ample rain, good harvests, many children, material wealth, the respect of the community, good health, and a long life.

To see your grandchildren and great-grandchildren was also seen as a great blessing. Here the psalmist says the righteous will keep their vigor and productivity in their old age. It's true that we receive these blessings in varying amounts because we live in an imperfect world, but let's have more faith.

Ask God for these blessings, receive them by faith, and live them! May God bless and reward your expectant heart.

Father, You are a good God. I so want to draw deeply
from Your fountain of blessing. Amen.

HIGH, HIGH ABOVE

*The floods have lifted up, O LORD, the floods have
lifted up their voice; the floods lift up their roaring.
Mightier than the thunders of many waters, mightier
than the waves of the sea, the LORD on high is mighty!*
PSALM 93:3-4

This short psalm has an interesting structure. It starts and ends with the indestructibility of the earth and the security of God on His throne. Then, in the middle we find these verses about the raging and thundering waters.

See how poetically the threat is intensified: Floods become "many waters" and then the "the waves of the sea;" the waters are "lifted up." Then they lift up their "voice," and then they lift up their "roaring." Remember that the dark and restless waters were seen in the Bible as a symbol of peril and chaos. What does it all mean? Well, there will be difficulties in life, even onslaughts. When difficulties happen they take center stage of our attention.

Everything starts to revolve around the problem. However, if we look away for a bit, if we just look around – and up – we'll see God's might encompassing all our weaknesses, His throne towering high, high above our problems. Listen! You are actually completely safe.

*Thank You, Lord, for being with me,
for being in full control! Amen.*

IN GOD'S CLASS

Blessed is the man whom You discipline, O LORD,
and whom You teach out of Your law.

PSALM 94:12

The psalmist is describing God as a teacher, a lecturer. Those who are taught by God can really be considered blessed, according to this verse. They are specially favored. Wouldn't it be wonderful if the Lord could lecture a class at the local university?

That would be a full classroom! Still, God *is* teaching us – classroom or no classroom – and if we show up to be taught, we will definitely be blessed for it. See God's teaching as a very personal matter. There are things that you need to learn, and God wants to teach them to you: who you are, what your purpose is, and God's will for your life among other lessons.

The material that God wants to use is His Word (here, literally His "law," but the concept extends to the whole of Scripture). Decide, then, to take His class and come equipped with your Bible, notebook, and pen – and a teachable heart. Oh, you will receive such a blessing!

Teach me, Lord! Teach me all I need to know. Amen.

STEADFAST OR SLIPPING

When I thought, "My foot slips," Your steadfast love, O LORD,
held me up. When the cares of my heart are many,
Your consolations cheer my soul.

PSALM 94:18-19

The psalmist is upset, disturbed. The ungodliness and sin around him is becoming too much. He also feels that he, who truly wants to serve God, is standing alone – he's struggling on without God!

Where is his God? Remember that we said we may wrestle with God and reason with Him as long as we do it *in* the relationship. We often find exactly that happening in the psalms! In such psalms we usually find a turning point, though, at which the psalmist declares that God *will* intervene, that He *is* faithful. Here it is the same. Due to his struggles and problems, the psalmist feels his spiritual feet slipping – but then, suddenly, he finds himself held up by God's faithfulness, by His steadfast love.

That restores peace to his soul! So share your anxiety or frustration with God, but at a point draw the line. Realize that God is still near and still in control. Confess that belief! That will put you on firmer ground.

Lord, for me there's only one way of living. With You! Amen.

August

Make a joyful noise to the Lord, all the earth!
 Serve the Lord with gladness!
Come into His presence with singing!
 Know that the Lord, He is God! It is He who made us,
and we are His; we are His people, and the sheep
of His pasture.
 Enter His gates with thanksgiving, and His courts with
praise! Give thanks to Him; bless His name!
 For the Lord is good; His steadfast love endures forever,
and His faithfulness to all generations.

Psalm 100

AUGUST 1
DO YOU SEE IT?

In His hand are the depths of the earth;
the heights of the mountains are His also. The sea is His,
for He made it, and His hands formed the dry land.
PSALM 95:4-5

What a beautiful psalm of praise! The reader is called upon to worship the Creator, who made everything good. The Bible teaches us that all men can see God's hand in nature – to *not* see or recognize it is wrong, a sin. Do *you* see it?

Learn to intensely enjoy and appreciate the beauty of the environment around you: the majesty of snow-tipped mountains, the lushness of dark forests, a babbling brook in a deep valley. The wide expanses of the grasslands and the stark formations of the desert have their own beauty. Think of the waves crashing on the beach, the clouds rolling over, bringing rain and lightning. These are all God's works! Recognize God in the mild and golden autumn days, in sweet spring evenings laden with fragrances and colors.

Exclaim, then, with the poet, "God is great!" Have you lost God somewhere along the way? Then reorient yourself in nature. Get outside, especially early in the morning. Take in the fresh air, and look around. The Creator who made everything is working all things for good in your life.

My God, when I think of all You have made, my soul sings! Amen!

PRAISE BECAUSE HE IS GOD

> For great is the LORD, and greatly to be praised;
> He is to be feared above all gods.
>
> PSALM 96:4

This psalm is from the beginning to end one great call to praise. The psalmist says God *must* be praised because He's great above all gods. We usually think that God must be praised for the blessings He bestows on us, but above all God must be praised for who God *is*.

Praise befits Him, for He is *God*! Remember that God does not need our praise. He is not so petty as to demand validation from men – or otherwise He'll get angry! Definitely not. No, *we* need praise! Praise brings *us* into the right relationship with Him.

It confirms Him as God and us as – well, *not* God. It teaches us to live with faith, because when we praise we confess – in good and bad times – that we have a great God in our lives. Learn to praise as a spiritual discipline!

Lord, I praise You because You're God. Be, then, God in my life! Amen.

A SPECIAL PLACE

Let the heavens be glad, and let the earth rejoice; let the sea roar,
and all that fills it; let the field exult, and everything in it!
Then shall all the trees of the forest sing for joy.

PSALM 96:11-12

All of creation is called up here to praise God, from top to bottom: the heavens and the heavenly beings, the earth, the sea and its creatures, the fields, and all the animals – even the trees of the forest! Everything and everyone must rejoice in the Creator!

In ancient times everything was given a place in a detailed, all-encompassing chain of being: minerals were at the bottom, then came the plants, the animals, humans, angels, and of course, right on top, God. Every division also had many subdivisions – putting the *useful* items above unuseful ones. Although we see things differently today, it's true that with God everything and everyone has a necessary place – because God put them there!

Remember, *you* also have an essential place in the giant mechanism of creation, like a cog without which the whole thing won't turn. Without you, this world just wouldn't be right! God deemed you indispensable for this world and for those around you – otherwise you wouldn't be here! You make a vital difference. Be *you*, then, for heaven's sake!

Thank You, Lord, that You have a plan for my life.
Help me to grow into Your goals for me! Amen.

ONLY GOD CAN JUDGE ...

For He comes, for He comes to judge the earth. He will judge the world in righteousness, and the peoples in His faithfulness.

PSALM 96:13

It's interesting how the people of the Old Testament expected God to come to earth and set things right. Believers always expect God's coming – and God *is* coming!

God *will* come to judge, because God *is* the Judge. Judging is God's business, although we so eagerly want to judge as well! Yet, Scripture is clear that judgment – and condemnation – belongs to God alone. The reason is that only He has all the information about a person's heart. We only have certain information and a particular perspective, which means that our judgment can never be truly comprehensive or fair.

Let's just refrain from condemning people left and right. Especially, let's never write people off, because God never writes them off – He keeps on working in the worst of men. To change hearts and lives is His specialty! Let's rather just treat everyone with love and respect.

Lord, help me not to judge or condemn. Help me to love! Amen.

SHROUDED IN MYSTERY

*Clouds and thick darkness are all around Him;
righteousness and justice are the foundation of His throne.*
PSALM 97:2

This beautiful psalm looks forward to the day of God's return. His appearance is described in dramatic detail, including the fact that He will be surrounded by "clouds and thick darkness." What can it mean that God is enclosed with darkness?

Well, when Scripture speaks of God's darkness, it symbolizes His mystery. It reminds us of the fact that the human mind can never encompass God or understand or explain His greatness. God is forever more than what I can understand of Him. Bigger than my God image, in other words. I must understand that I do not have final answers about God, because that would just be arrogant.

I must be willing to settle for partial understanding, for mystery, for awe – for faith! That's how man must approach God. There is, however, this redeeming factor: God revealed Himself in Jesus Christ. God is like Christ. That helps us a lot!

*Lord, I can never fully know You, but You fully know me.
I do know, however, that You are good! Amen.*

AUGUST 6
HATE AND ANGER

O you who love the Lord, hate evil! He preserves the lives
of His saints; He delivers them from the hand of the wicked.
PSALM 97:10

Must we hate or not – that is the question! Well, we know that we should not hate people, since Christ proved on the cross that God loves all. No, we are only allowed to love people. What about hating sin, as this verse says? Consider this: Jesus' reaction to sin is not best described as hate. We actually never find the emotion of hate with Him.

Hate is never the fruit of the Spirit. We therefore do not hate, period. However, we remain acutely aware of the many things wrong in this world. Just think of the crime and corruption around us, the many injustices against innocent and powerless people, the things done to children or animals that are too cruel even to mention. Can we be indifferent towards such things?

Never! No, our sense of justice causes us to immediately react with indignation, with anger – with holy wrath! It makes us want to jump up and put things right, doesn't it? Now *that* is an emotion that we find with Jesus! Just look at the whip in His hand (John 2:15).

Lord Jesus, let me be driven by Your righteousness.
Help me to make this world a bit more whole. Amen.

EMOTIONS CAN BE MOVED

Make a joyful noise to the Lord, all the earth;
break forth into joyous song and sing praises!
PSALM 98:4

Can you see that this verse does not contain a friendly request? No, it's a straight forward command that all must praise God with joy and singing! It requires mere obedience.

Perhaps you might say that you don't *feel* like praising, and that it's important to stay true to one's emotions. It's indeed true that we need to be in touch with our emotions and not live a false life, yet Scripture often prescribes certain emotions to us as well. We, for example, have injunctions to love, to not hate, to not be jealous, to not fear or despair, to forgive others – all these are emotions.

Let's put it like this: While we do have genuine feelings and need to acknowledge them, we cannot be controlled by those feelings. They're not in charge of us! We can move, emotionally, to a better place. God will help us – *He's* in charge!

Lord, move my emotions to those that will glorify You. Amen.

HE IS HOLY, MAKE ME HOLY

Exalt the LORD our God; worship at His footstool! Holy is He!
PSALM 99:5

In this psalm we read three times that God is holy. Holiness is an attribute of God – just think of the seraphim before God's throne who call out day and night, "Holy, holy, holy!" (Isa. 6:3).

Holiness means to be completely separated, and in that sense God is completely different from us: utterly perfect, whole, good – against our own imperfection, brokenness, and sin. Theologians often call God the "Wholly Other," which describes His greatness, mystery, and awe. What are we to make then of Scripture's injunction that we, mere men, are to become holy? Is that even possible? Let's emphasize this: holiness can never be something we work from our own strength. It's not about trying harder. Holiness is an attribute of God alone and can only be had *from* God alone!

It will happen when we turn our lives more and more onto Him – like a flower to the sun – and allow Him to reflect His light off us into the darkness. What the world will then see from us is never *our* holiness, but always *His* holiness. Spend more time with God, and holiness will happen by itself!

Lord, as I gaze upon Your holiness, make me holy! Amen.

HOLY TOUCHING UNHOLY

O Lord our God, You answered them; You were a forgiving God
to them, but an avenger of their wrongdoings.
PSALM 99:8

This psalm is about a holy God and how He interacts with sinful men. It's a very important topic, because the Old Testament prohibited contact between holy things and profane things – between clean and unclean. Contact with unclean things make clean things unclean, after which a sacrifice would be required to restore its ritual purity.

That is why the priests working in the temple had to sacrifice daily for their own and others' sinfulness and impurity. God is holy! How can it be, then, that a holy God works and interacts with sinful man? Well, God brought His own sacrifice, making it possible for holy to touch unholy!

In fact, through God's sacrifice, Jesus Christ, even the unholiest man on earth can be reconciled with the Most Holy God. We who are in Christ share in Christ's holiness, and in that sense we're also holy. We are saints. Our holiness-in-Him must, however, steadily become holiness-in-our-lives. That will happen in a life that is turned towards Him.

Thank You, Lord, for making me holy.
Shine through me, flow through me! Amen.

GOD LOVES PEOPLE!

Make a joyful noise to the Lord, all the earth!
PSALM 100:1

This beautiful and well-known psalm forms the end of a cycle in which the whole world is called up to serve God. God wants to be the God of *every person*! Can we realize how much God loves people?

He enjoys making them in never-ending variations – no two are alike! Just think of the Lapp and Inuit people (Eskimos) of the Northern Arctic, the original Indians of North and South America, the many African peoples (some very, very ancient), the different European nations, the numerous numerals Arab, Indian, and Chinese people groups, the other inhabitants of the East and of the islands, all the way to the Maori of New Zealand.

Every group and every individual is different. God evidently loves diversity! We are often hesitant about others' differences. We often find our safety in the familiar. If we, however, can learn to love all people as *persons* loved by God, it will add to God's dream that one day there will be believers gathered around His throne from all tribes, tongues, and nations!

Lord, give me a love for people because You love people! Amen.

ONLY WITH GLADNESS

Serve the LORD with gladness! Come into His presence with singing!
PSALM 100:2

We must get away from any perception of an overly-serious or heavy religion. There is a stereotype of dour and joyless Christians who aren't allowed to do anything that gives ordinary people pleasure. Who would want to join *their* ranks? Not me! Take note:

- We cannot save ourselves by keeping the law or doing good deeds – or keep ourselves saved in this way. It's impossible. Forget it!
- We are saved by God's grace in spite of our sin, which we'll do till the end of our days. God blotted it out, because Jesus was fully punished for it and for my future sin.
- We are now freer and gladder than anyone else on earth, because *nothing* (especially not our sin) can separate us from the love of God.
- Serving God means living our life with Him joyfully and freely, steadily growing through the guidance of His Spirit.

    If we as Christians live bound by legalism or fear, we are mis-understanding the whole gospel. Remember, hard and joyless religion really does not please God – it pleases no one!

Lord, take the yoke of heavy religion from my shoulders,
and give me Your yoke that is easy and light. Amen.

THE ARTIST STANDING BACK

Know that the LORD, He is God! It is He who made us,
and we are His; we are His people, and the sheep of His pasture.
PSALM 100:3

He made us. We are His. God who masterly made everything also takes complete ownership of His creation. He made it, and therefore it's His! We ascribe high worth to each person because the Almighty skillfully fashioned them, personally!

Also, each person belongs to Him! Think of God as an artist who feels proud of what He made and remains concerned over His art-works. Isn't it so sad that God's authorship and ownership is so widely denied today? Many would rather attribute our exquisite and intricate universe to an unbelievably small factor of chance than to consider the possibility of an intelligent being behind it all.

For us, though, there was an artist who made everything perfect, and then stood back – as artists do – to declare it "good," magnificent (Gen. 1:31)! Yes, God made *you* personally. He made you *good,* and *you* are His!

Thank You, Lord, for Your beautiful works.
Thank You also for making me beautiful in every way! Amen.

AUGUST 13

DOES MY CHILD BELIEVE?

*For the LORD is good; His steadfast love endures forever,
and His faithfulness to all generations.*

PSALM 100:5

We said that Christianity is always one generation away from extinction – the next generation must be converted to the faith one person at a time! Each Christian must come by himself and believe for himself. What a responsibility!

Even so, it's fortunately not just *our* responsibility to convert the next generation – God's faithfulness will do it. It's His love and grace, His salvation that flows from one generation to the next, the psalmist says. Are you worried about your children's faith? Do you pray that they will choose God? Do you? Then do not worry! God's love and faithfulness will flow to them, will knock on their hearts, calling them, urging them to remember the God of their fathers.

When they discover the superficiality and emptiness of what the world offers, they will turn to God. Remember, you and I were the "next generation" for whom our parents prayed. And we came, didn't we? We turned to God. They will come as well – God is faithful!

Lord, I pray for my children. Draw them to You! Amen.

SOMETHING IN THE HEART

I will sing of steadfast love and justice;
to You, O Lord, I will make music.
PSALM 101:1

David is singing again! His heart is making him take up his harp. As with all artists, he wants to express his emotions through his art. He feels moved to compose a song about how he feels, to play and sing!

Other artists would want to write about their feelings or capture them as a painting, a dance, or a drama. Through the centuries people have produced artworks for the church, knitted jerseys for the children, manned soup kitchens in the winter, or helped repair the church's roof – because they felt something in their hearts! Our questions therefore are: What do you feel in your heart for God? How do you want to express it?

Do you want to sing, to make something, to make a difference, to help somewhere? Be your unique self, and convey your love for God in your unique way. Are you still stuck at the first question? Make it a matter between you and God, and find the answer.

Lord, I am moved by You in my heart. How can I act on it? Amen.

YOU BECOME WHAT YOU FOCUS ON

I will not set before my eyes anything that is worthless. I hate the work of those who fall away; it shall not cling to me.
PSALM 101:3

David is writing here as the king of Israel. He spells out what kind of a king he wants to be. First he wants a sincere walk with God. Then he wants to be a good and just king. He will not pursue unworthy goals.

Literally, he says he will "not set anything worthless before his eyes," meaning he will not *focus* on things that are not worthwhile. On the contrary, he wants to prevent things like that from clinging to him, in other words from gaining a hold on him. It reminds us of the fact that we become what we focus on. That on which you spend your time and effort becomes your habit, your lifestyle – it becomes who you are!

Please don't be drawn into unworthy goals, habits, or company – don't let it cling to your soul and define who you're becoming. No, focus on worthy goals! Focus especially on God; make God your goal. Now, that's worthwhile!

Lord, let my eyes only see what is good and worthy.
Let my eyes only look at You. Amen.

A BETTER PLACE

*I will find trustworthy people to serve as my advisors,
and only an honest person will serve as an official.*
PSALM 101:6 (CEV)

In this psalm David is writing that he wants to be an upright king, wise and fair. He wants to do things right! He says corrupt people will not have a hold on him, his courts will uphold justice, and his officials will treat people with respect.

Wow! If *our* government could be that good! This description gives a clear view, however, of what the Bible presents as good government. Corruption and disregard for the rules should not be accepted from leaders! Where wrongdoings are discovered, citizens should confront leaders as a spiritual duty since it's God's will that clean and efficient government work for the benefit of all, especially the vulnerable. Things must be done right, because God demands righteousness! Let's become involved, then, and work for a government that is efficient, transparent, and caring.

Look after your attitude, though. We are Christians, and our behavior should honor God. Speak with respect about your opposition, absolutely keep to the truth, and steer away from stereotyping or generalizing, which usually is just untrue.

Lord, what role can I play to make this country a better place? Amen.

POUR YOUR PROBLEM OUT

Hear my prayer, O LORD; let my cry come to You!
PSALM 102:1

The psalmist, distressed and weak, is pouring out his complaint before God. We know the situation! When we find ourselves in a crisis, we cannot help but pour out to God whatever we feel – *all* the fears and worry, the confusion, the anguish! That's a good thing, though. In fact, it's very important. Take note:

- Pouring out your emotions to God is therapeutic, healing. It's cleansing and cathartic. If you want, or need, to cry your heart out to God, that would be good! It has proven benefits – even for men!
- Talking out your problems with God brings new perspective. It externalizes the problem, bringing it to the outside to be looked at, and objectivizes it, making it an object to be analyzed and handled. This helps you to understand and deal with your problem!

Where are you going in your crisis? Go to the Lord! Close the door behind you, and pour out your heart before your Father!

Lord, I have such a need to share my heart with You! Amen.

BAD, WORSE, WORST

I am like a desert owl of the wilderness,
like an owl of the waste places; I lie awake;
I am like a lonely sparrow on the housetop.
PSALM 102:6-7

The psalmist is pouring out his heart before God. He's very ill and in pain, his body emaciated. Even worse, his own people have turned their backs on him because they don't know how to respond to his troubles.

Remember, in biblical times people often felt that sickness was the result of sin. Now he feels depressed and alone – like a lonely desert bird or an owl that inhabits empty ruins. He feels like a sparrow on a roof, looking down as others carry on with their lives. The absolute worst for him is the feeling that God has left him, forgotten about him. Sadly, he bemoans the fact that his God has thrown him away.

Physically, psychologically, and spiritually he is in pain, in distress. Yes, one can get to such a point, and sickness can take you there: a point where you only feel dark desolation. Some who read this might recognize this point from their own experience. Listen, then. There is hope!

Lord, I also feel lonely and lost. Be with me, Jesus! Amen.

THERE COMES A DAY

You will arise and have pity on Zion;
it is the time to favor her; the appointed time has come.
PSALM 102:13

This psalm is about a person going through a very dark time. His body is ill, he is mentally exhausted, and he feels spiritually worn out and abandoned – by men and by God. He describes his distress in great detail! Then the mood changes – as so often happens in the psalms – and we suddenly find the language of faith.

"You will arise!" He feels that God's time, "the appointed time," has come. How wonderful that there *is* such a time! Yes, on a day the current season will be over and the next one will begin. It often happens unexpectedly – something just happens and then the new time is here. Faithfully wait on the next season as you faithfully do what this season asks of you.

Ask yourself questions like these: What is the purpose of this season of my life? How can I work together with God so that the purpose of this season can be accomplished? How can I live in this season so that God will be honored?

Lord, what is the purpose of this season
in my life? How should I live in it? Amen.

AUGUST 20
IT WILL PASS AWAY

They will perish, but You will remain; they will all wear out like a garment. You will change them like a robe, and they will pass away.
PSALM 102:26

The psalmist, who had been in a very dark place, has now fully put his faith and trust in God. He realizes that God is so much bigger than people, their problems, and their feelings.

Everything on earth is so transient – the days go by like the people walking by your window. That which we experience as acute and important becomes insignificant once we view it from a higher perspective. Millions of people are born and die, nations come into being and are wiped out again as the centuries roll on. Even the earth and the heavens will perish, the psalmist says. The earth is actually already being worn out like a garment!

The lesson is that we shouldn't hope for this life alone. Although we must take and enjoy life as the greatest gift that God has given us, our hope is in Him! Only with Him can we meaningfully live these years – and then eternity in His presence! Aim there!

Lord, thank You for living my life with me.
Thank You, also, that I will live my eternal life with You! Amen.

AUGUST 21
FAITH AND THE FUTURE

The children of Your servants shall dwell secure;
their offspring shall be established before You.
PSALM 102:28

The psalmist is worried about his country. The people have been captured, Jerusalem has been ravaged, the temple has been torn down, and the land laid to waste. Will there ever be a future in their country again? Will their children serve the God of Israel?

We often have the same kind of worries about our own futures. Then he realizes that God can be trusted. He confesses his belief that their children "shall dwell secure" and serve the God of their fathers. *God* will see to their children! Let's take a leaf from his book about our own future. Think about it. What type of Christians are we when we have no hope or no faith? What faith do we demonstrate to the next generation when we tell them there is no future, that everything is going downhill?

It's no faith at all! There *is* a future for us, and there *is* a future for our children. In fact, there is a good and blessed future, because God is in that future! He will look after us and after our children. Tell them *that*!

Father, forgive me when I speak without faith.
I do believe in the future You have for us! Amen.

ALL THAT IS WITHIN ME

Bless the LORD, O my soul, and all that is within me, bless His holy name!
PSALM 103:1

David is the composer of this beautiful and classical psalm. He wants to bless God with his soul and all that is within him! He is speaking poetically, of course, but even so we may wonder what the *all* could be that is within us? From our perspective, we could perhaps describe the whole man as follows:

- Our body. Yes, we can praise God with our bodies. When we offer our bodies to Him as a "living sacrifice" (Rom. 12:1), we are growing in obedience.
- Our soul. Our psyche consists of our mind, emotions, and will. When we want to think what God thinks, feel what He feels, and want what He wants, we are being led by the Spirit.
- Our spirit is our deepest being, our *heart*. The spirit is where God alone knows us, where the motives of our psyche lie hidden. When we ask God to completely fill us with His Spirit, He will transform us from the center outward.

This is *all* of us! Give, then, your *all* to Him – body, soul, and spirit. All for Jesus!

*Lord, I want to offer all that I am – body, soul, and spirit –
to You as a sacrifice of praise. Amen.*

THESE ARE YOUR BENEFITS

Bless the LORD, O my soul, and forget not all His benefits.
PSALM 103:2

David is praising God for the "benefits" He bestows on him. Then he lists those benefits in verses 3-5:

- It is He who "forgives all your iniquity" – God forgives us all our wrongdoings,
- who "heals all your diseases" – He heals your body in Jesus' name,
- who "redeems your life from the pit" – He saves your soul for eternity,
- who "crowns you with steadfast love and mercy" – yes, He covers you with love!
- He "satisfies you with good" – He blesses you abundantly,
- so that "your youth is renewed like the eagle's" – God gives you strength for living.

Yes, God gives forgiveness, wholeness, salvation, abundance, and strength! With these benefits we can take on life with confidence! It's really all we need.

Thank You, Lord, that everything I need is in You.
I lack nothing! Amen.

AUGUST 24
SLOW TO ANGER

The LORD is merciful and gracious,
slow to anger and abounding in steadfast love.
PSALM 103:8

How beautiful is this description of the Lord as "merciful, gracious, slow to anger" and "plenteous in mercy," as the King James Version states! The portrayal of God as "slow to anger" goes against a popular but false notion that God is essentially displeased with man, even wrathful, ready to punish the littlest transgression.

On the contrary! The same Old Testament from which such views are deduced often testifies of God's goodness and grace, of His "lovingkindness" that is "new every morning" (Lam. 3:22-23). God's kindness and love are much greater than His wrath! On the other hand, though, we should not miss the fact that God does indeed get angry! What angers God?

We read in the Word that injustice angers God (Prov. 11:1), as does hatred and rebellion – especially after a time, because God is "slow to anger." There comes a point, though, when God says *enough*, when he demands obedience, justice, goodness, righteousness. And that's a good thing!

Lord, thank You for Your patience and grace!
Help me to stay obedient to Your will. Amen.

AUGUST 25
SO FAR AND SO COMPLETELY

As far as the east is from the west,
so far does He remove our transgressions from us.
PSALM 103:12

The Bible presents us with two undeniable facts: man is sinful, and God is gracious. Concerning sin, we must understand that, for us, being sinful is part of being human.

Our brokenness is part and parcel of our humanity! We cannot escape it, but we can handle our brokenness in a way that will honor God. Then, concerning grace, God knows and accepts that we are sinful. He has dealt with our sin in His own way. By virtue of the cross, God forgives us our sin – not just current sin, but all our sin past, present, and future. Our whole sinfulness! The full weight of our sin has been removed by Jesus, and it's *gone* "as far as the east is from the west"!

Our sinfulness no longer stands between God and us! It does hamper our spiritual growth, though. We therefore need to work at it. Know your weak points. Keep them on the agenda openly and be as obedient as you can, and grow away from those things! The Holy Spirit will give you the strength.

Thank You, Lord, for dealing with my sins.
Thank You for removing them completely. Amen.

AUGUST 26
GOD IS A DAD

As a father shows compassion to his children,
so the LORD shows compassion to those who fear Him.
PSALM 103:13

In Scripture God is described by many images, comparisons, and metaphors. For example, God is like a king, a judge, a shepherd, a lion, and a rock. Every image highlights an aspect of God.

The image that says the most about God, however, is that of God as a father. In fact, throughout the New Testament, God is called "the Father" – God is like a father and God *is* a father. The Father! What does a father do? Well, a father brings forth his children, to start with, and then protects and nurtures them. A father educates his children – which can happen outside of their comfort zone! – and demonstrates how to live life by his example.

A father allows his children to stand on their own two feet but remains involved and near, ready to catch them when they should fall. Such a father is God! Our lesson is this: the heavenly Father can be fully trusted, because He is the best dad there is!

Thank You, Abba Father, that I can trust You fully
in every aspect of my life! Amen.

YOU: IN RAW MATERIALS

For He knows our frame; He remembers that we are dust.
PSALM 103:14

God knows us so well, David says. He knows our failings and our frailty. He "remembers" that we are "dust" – because it was He who made us from dust in the first place! Yes, physically we're made from the ordinary raw materials of the earth: oxygen, hydrogen, nitrogen, carbon.

Also in the mix are small amounts of iron, copper, sulfur, and tiny amounts of other elements. As chemicals, we are really worth little. We consist of about fifty liters of water, a small bag of charcoal, enough fat for ten bars of soap (although this can vary!), a kilo of chalk, enough iron for one nail, phosphorus to cover some matches, and that's it!

As a human being, though – a living person with needs, fears, and dreams – as a unique creation, each individual is immeasurably valuable to God. Yes, the Creator deeply loves us – whom He made so artfully – and desires a relationship with us. It's exactly our frailty and dependency that draws Him to us. Say yes to His love!

It's wonderful, Father, that You consider
a struggling and needy person like me as precious. Amen.

BLOOM WHERE YOU GROW

*As for man, his days are like grass; he flourishes like a flower
of the field; for the wind passes over it, and it is gone,
and its place knows it no more.*
PSALM 103:15-16

David says that God knows our frailty. Man's life is like a flower that opens, blooms for a little while, withers, and falls off. Does such a flower have any purpose, any meaning?

Absolutely! That plant grabs at its one chance to live, to survive, to procreate, and for that purpose it produces the best flower that it can – against all odds! It *will* bloom if it only can – even on the rocks. If it then dies off and centuries roll by and no one ever knew that such a plant existed, what does it matter? It did what it was made to do. It succeeded!

Similarly, you and I received a divine task to live. Accept therefore your assignment, and live with purpose, with meaning, with everything in you! *That* is God's will. Don't let the promise of eternity detract you from first living this life fully. Bloom where you grow!

*Lord, help me to find Your will in these short years
of my life. Fulfill my purpose. Amen.*

AUGUST 29
DAY 1 - GOD BRINGS LIGHT

Bless the Lord, O my soul! O Lord my God, You are very great!
You are clothed with splendor and majesty,
covering Yourself with light as with a garment.

PSALM 104:1-2

This psalm is a beautiful Creation Song that proceeds through the seven creation days. In this verse, the psalmist starts by praising God for His splendor and majesty and states that God is covered with light, as if it were a garment. This brings us to the first creation day, where God said, "Let there be light" (Gen. 1:3).

This first light has nothing to do with sunlight or starlight, because these entities were made later. No, this light is the first light ever – the first rays to pierce the dark chaos. This light is the origin and source of all energy, starting off the creation process. According to Jewish tradition this light is nothing less than God Himself who enters and penetrates the nothingness. He is the light. He dwells in an unapproachable light.

He is clothed in a raiment of light, according to our verse. Let's bring it home: In what seems to be the darkness of your life there is a light shining. That light can drive out the darkness and bring brightness and light into every corner of your life! Invite that light in!

Shine, Jesus, shine! Shine Your light in me!
Dispel the darkness. Amen.

DAY 2 - GOD MAKES A SPACE

Covering Yourself with light as with a garment,
stretching out the heavens like a tent. He lays the beams
of His chambers on the waters; He makes the clouds His chariot.

PSALM 104:2-3

In this Creation Song the psalmist is working through the seven creation days. Today we'll look at the second day, in which God created the "heavens," as it's called here.

For the ancient man this heaven was what they saw when they looked up at the sky: blue by day and black by night. For them it was like a dome under which all the natural phenomena took place – the sunshine, wind, rain, thunder, and lightning. This heaven – also called the firmament or expanse – was stretched out like a tent over us constituting our home, man's dwelling place. Over this dome and the waters above it, which they believed in, was God's dwelling. From there, far above the heavens, God rules over His creation.

Let's take the following from this: In God's creation there is a place for all. Plants, animals, and humans have a good and necessary place. The natural phenomena have a place; the sun and moon have their places. Creation is under control, because God is in control! If we look up, we'll see Him!

Lord, thank You that You are in control.
These winds and storms are all under control. I needn't fear. Amen.

AUGUST 31

DAY 3 - GOD SEPARATES ALL THINGS

You covered the earth with the ocean that rose
above the mountains. Then Your voice thundered!
And the water flowed down the mountains and
through the valleys to the place You prepared.
PSALM 104:6-8 (CEV)

In this psalm about Creation we have come to the third creation day. According to Scripture, and science, earth was initially covered by water. On the third day, however, God separated the ocean from the land.

He fixed the boundaries of the sea, which they also saw as a symbol of chaos and peril, so that the land could become a safe dwelling place. Did you notice that God for the first three days mainly separated things? He first separated light from darkness, then the waters above from the waters below, and then the waters from the land. God first had to put the basics in place before the rest could follow! Can we take a lesson from this? Isn't it so that our goals and outcomes get jumbled when we've lost track of our departure points, our core values? Going "back to basics" is often a good idea spiritually. Ask yourself questions like these: Do I want to serve God or not? Do I stand for what is right or not? What do I accept, and what do I reject – where do I draw the line? Only if you have satisfactory answers for these can you proceed.

Lord, help me get the basics in place,
especially my relationship with You! Amen.

September

My heart is steadfast, O God! I will sing and make melody with all my being!

Awake, O harp and lyre! I will awake the dawn!

I will give thanks to You, O Lᴏʀᴅ, among the peoples; I will sing praises to You among the nations.

For Your steadfast love is great above the heavens; Your faithfulness reaches to the clouds.

Be exalted, O God, above the heavens! Let Your glory be over all the earth!

That Your beloved ones may be delivered, give salvation by Your right hand and answer me!

God has promised in His holiness: "With exultation I will divide up Shechem and portion out the Valley of Succoth.

Gilead is Mine; Manasseh is Mine; Ephraim is My helmet, Judah My scepter.

Moab is My washbasin; upon Edom I cast My shoe; over Philistia I shout in triumph."

Who will bring me to the fortified city? Who will lead me to Edom?

Have You not rejected us, O God? You do not go out, O God, with our armies.

Oh grant us help against the foe, for vain is the salvation of man!

With God we shall do valiantly; it is He who will tread down our foes.

PSALM 108

DAY 4 - THE SEASONS

He made the moon to mark the seasons;
the sun knows its time for setting.
PSALM 104:19

In this psalm the psalmist is now touching on the fourth creation day, on which God made the sun and moon. The sun and moon's role is stated here, as in Genesis, as to establish times and seasons: day and night, the tides, the seasons of the year.

It's natural for us to live in these literal times and seasons, but we also find ourselves in figurative times and seasons. Think of Ecclesiastes. The writer says that there is a time to be born and a time to die, a time to break and a time to build, a time for war and a time for peace – and many other times in which we find ourselves (Eccles. 3:1-8). The wise will know which time it is, what the purpose of each season is, and how to appropriately manage each.

The wisdom to work in God's seasons comes with maturity and experience, but it can be asked from God as well, who generously gives wisdom, according to the Word (James 1:5). If we ask God's will for our seasons, He will definitely guide us – and we'll be able to live with so much more purpose!

Lord, I want to do the things You have purposed me
to do in this season. Please guide me. Amen.

DAY 5 - GOD CONQUERS THE EVIL ONE

Here is the sea, great and wide, which teems with creatures innumerable,
living things both small and great. There go the ships,
and Leviathan, which You formed to play in it.

PSALM 104:25-26

This psalm moves through the seven creation days, more or less. In these verses the psalmist refers to the sea creatures, whom God made together with the birds on the fifth day. It is absolutely interesting to see how he describes the Leviathan, the legendary sea monster of ancient times.

He says Leviathan "plays" in the water – literally the text could also mean God plays with Leviathan! Remember, in the Bible Leviathan is always a symbol of chaos, threat, and opposition. It is linked to the Evil One and the Antichrist, who is also described as a beast "rising from the sea" (Rev. 13:1).

Here, however, Leviathan is a plaything, or at least playing! God is so strongly on the scene that Leviathan is no threat at all. Yes, with God we needn't fear Leviathan, Belial, or any evil thing. God, who has conquered and submitted all enemies, is *present*! What is your greatest fear? For God it is a small thing.

Lord, thank You that You are bigger than any threat. Amen.

DAY 6 - GOD GIVES LIFE

When You send forth Your Spirit, they are created,
and You renew the face of the ground.
PSALM 104:30

This creation psalm now touches on the events of the sixth day, when God made the land animals and man. The psalmist says that God sends out His Spirit and then they're created. The word for "spirit" (ruach) can also mean "breath."

Genesis 2:7 states that God sent His breath into the man – "the breath of life" – and then he lived; he became a "living soul," the Bible says. Yes, the Old Testament literally says God gives us our breath and then – one day – God takes our breath away! There is life as long as God says there is life. That is why we must consider life very valuable, especially human life. *My* life, specifically, is God's will and God's gift. That means that I must embrace life.

I must *want* to live, and I must *live* intentionally and abundantly! I cannot just exist. Even in the brokenness of this life we must choose to really *live*. God wants us to! It's a decision that we must regularly make.

I choose to live, Lord – to live with abundance! Amen.

DAY 7 - GOD RESTS, I PRAISE

I will sing to the LORD as long as I live;
I will sing praise to my God while I have being.
PSALM 104:33

We now come to the end of this beautiful psalm. In these verses the sixth and seventh creation days flow into each other and point to what happened after the creation event.

The creation account ends with a call to praise, which is the logical conclusion to the fact that God made everything so perfectly. Let's remember that the whole world was made for us! God created it day by day, as in a fold-out picture, with *us* in mind – and then, when the whole scene was set up, He placed *us* right in the middle of it! Then God rested from His work, but not before He mandated man to take charge of creation on His behalf.

Of course, now we must turn to God to thank Him! Let's thank Him in the words of the psalmist: "Bless the LORD, O my soul, … bless His holy name!" (Ps. 103:1). Praise the Lord!

Lord, help me to live in this wonderful world
so that You will be glorified. Amen.

SEEK GOD'S FACE

Seek the LORD, and His strength; seek His face evermore.
PSALM 105:4 (KJV)

In this verse the righteous are called upon to seek God's presence – or literally, God's "face." It makes us think of the priestly blessing, in which God promises to lift up His face upon us: "The LORD make His face to shine upon you and be gracious to you; the LORD lift up His countenance upon you and give you peace" (Num. 6:25-26).

Of course, God's face is a symbol of God Himself, of His presence. What we deduce, however, from these two occurrences is that there are two sides to God's blessing: *He* promises to shine His face over us, but *we* need to seek His face, continually. Yes, we cannot just expect or wait for God's blessing.

We must seek it out, receive it, live in it – intentionally! How do we receive it? Well, it's received in God's presence, in relationship with Him! In His presence we'll find enough blessing to take us through the day.

Lord, Your presence in my life is the biggest blessing I know! Amen.

ETERNAL RELATIONSHIP

He remembers His covenant forever, the word
that He commanded, for a thousand generations.
PSALM 105:8

The psalmist refers us to history as motivation to serve God full out. He points us to the covenant between God and Abraham and how it extended to Isaac, Jacob, Joseph, Moses, and the whole of Israel.

Here he underlines especially that the covenant was established by God "forever … for a thousand generations." Remember, as Christians we are part of that same covenant! Does the word *covenant* perhaps not communicate well with you – does it mean little or elicit a wrongly negative connotation? It is merely an agreement, a formal relationship. God assumes full responsibility for the relationship but also requires of us certain things. He assures us that this relationship is crucial for us and will bless us with many benefits.

Please place a very high value on God's life-giving relationship with you! I once met a man who wore a ring with a cross engraved on its stone. He said it was to remind him that he is covenanted with God. That's so beautiful!

Lord, Your covenant with me is all-important –
it keeps me alive spiritually. Thank You! Amen.

YOUR SHARE IS TO TAKE IT

*The covenant that He made with Abraham, His sworn promise
to Isaac, which He confirmed to Jacob as a statute,
to Israel as an everlasting covenant.*
PSALM 105:9-10

We still need to say something more about the covenant – the agreement or relationship – between God and man. This covenant entails mutual responsibilities and benefits, but take note:

- It is not an agreement between equals. That would simply be impossible between God and man. The covenant is more of a unilateral contract, like a grant or a will. God grants man certain things, but He also stipulates the terms of acceptance.
- The covenant's validity does not depend on any *quid pro quo* from man's side. It finds its validity in the merit of Christ and the grace that the cross has worked for us. It never lapses, in other words.

How can we describe the covenant? A beggar holds out his hand, and someone fills it with gold. *That* is the covenant! Our share is to hold out our hand, to take the grace that is offered us, and to be eternally grateful.

*Thank You, Lord! I am indeed grateful for the greatest gift ever!
How can I show my gratitude? Amen.*

THE CRISIS HAS A PURPOSE

*When He summoned a famine on the land and broke all supply of bread,
He had sent a man ahead of them, Joseph, who was sold as a slave.*

PSALM 105:16-17

Joseph took food to his brothers in the field, but they seized him and sold him to travelling merchants who were on their way to Egypt. Afterward they told their father, Jacob, a lie about a wild animal killing his son and showed him a bloodied robe.

The news devastated poor Jacob! We can now ask: Where was God in this situation? Why didn't He stop the atrocious deed? Why did a righteous man have to suffer, but the wrongdoers got away scot-free? What about Jacob's blessing? That's how we would have reacted, wouldn't we? From God's perspective everything happened as it should, though.

A great famine was coming, so God sent Joseph in advance to Egypt to guarantee the survival of His people. For many years this purpose was not clear, but afterward it all fell into place. Let's trust God more! Let's accept that God is at work. Let's accept that the crisis has a purpose – whether the purpose is known to us now is less important.

*Lord, I do not understand what is happening,
but I trust that You are in control! Amen.*

IN THE DESERT?

They asked, and He brought quail, and gave them bread
from heaven in abundance. He opened the rock,
and water gushed out; it flowed through the desert like a river.
PSALM 105:40-41

The unknown psalmist of this history psalm is teaching us lessons from Israel's trek through the desert. When the sun burned hot, God was a cloud over them.

When they were hungry, He gave them quails and manna. When they were thirsty, He made water stream from a rock. Remember, these things were not *always* there and available, but *when they were needed*, they were there. We also experience the desert times in our lives. Desert times are hard times, but difficulties focus us back to our priorities, values, and goals – and they bring us back to God! If our eyes are open to it, we will see God's grace operating even then. There will be small mercies, the right word at the right time, sustenance needed for another day, or a much needed rest.

Do you notice what God is doing? He is helping you through! Soon the landscape will change – life will be green and lush again, there will be still waters. Desert times pass!

Thank You, Lord, for small mercies, and thank You for Your grace,
carrying me through! Amen.

RATHER, BE STILL

*Praise the LORD! Oh give thanks to the LORD, for He is good,
for His steadfast love endures forever! Who can utter
the mighty deeds of the LORD, or declare all His praise?*

PSALM 106:1-2

Look at the paradox in these verses: we *must* praise God, but we *cannot* praise God fully. It's an absolute fact that God is much greater than we can ever realize, that my human mind can never fathom or comprehend the depths of God! How should we approach such an awesome God, then? Take note:

- We can praise Him for His greatness and awesomeness!
- Let's learn to not say too much about God. Let's not *explain* Him too much. Sometimes we just need to acknowledge that there are things that we cannot understand. Many of our explanations and predictions about God are simply wrong – or one-sided at best.
- Let's also learn to be still in the presence of the Mighty One. Shall we stop for a little while with our constant, self-centered, and superficial prayers and learn to just sit, worshipfully before the Holy One?

No wonder the spiritual fathers said the more we speak about God the more flippant we become. Let's rather be wholly quiet, because *God is on His throne*!

*Lord, You are bigger than my words –
but I will praise You forever for Your love! Amen.*

SEPTEMBER 11
REMEMBER ME, LORD!

Remember me, O LORD, when You show favor
to Your people; help me when You save them.
PSALM 106:4

The psalmist is thinking of God's love for His people and is asking here for that love to also extend to him. He wants to be included on the day of salvation! Although God loves all people, not all people are saved (John 1:11-13).

God's unstoppable will includes my own free will. His immeasurable love asks to be loved back; His great invitation expects an unreserved "yes" – when He extends His hand, God wants us to take it. He knocks on the door, but we must open it! God will not force or push anyone. He wants to work with our complete and whole-hearted acceptance. You and I must *want* it, *ask* for it, and *take* it in faith.

God's promise is, however, that any honest yearning after Him will surely find Him, that the faintest "yes, Lord" will bring His love into action – that if you draw to Him, He will draw to you! God is not making it difficult. No, He wants you to come. He is ready and waiting for you. Just say the words like those of the psalmist: "Remember me, Lord, include me in Your salvation!"

Yes, Lord, I come! I so need You in my life. Amen.

SEPTEMBER 12
IT'S THEM, IT'S US, IT'S ME

Both we and our fathers have sinned;
we have committed iniquity; we have done wickedness.
PSALM 106:6

Take note how the psalmist is identifying with the sins of his people. He speaks on behalf of all of Israel when he says: "We have sinned. We have done wrong" (NLT).

What a mature way of praying! Our own prayers most often just comprise of a list of personal problems and then – *Amen*! Mature prayer is praying for others' problems! We can pray even more maturely by praying on *behalf* of others – not with the notion that we are spiritual and they are not (and that we do what they should have done), but with the realization that *their* sin is *our* sin. When we realize that they are us – our family, our congregation, our leaders, our country, our common humanity – then we get to the point of true humility.

At that point we know that we are basically the same sinful human beings saved purely by grace, and we plead for God's mercy toward *all* of us. Now *that* is true intercession!

Lord, I want to intercede for others. We have done wrong, Lord! Amen.

HOW THE SNARE WORKS

They mixed with the nations and learned to do as they did.
They served their idols, which became a snare to them.
PSALM 106:35–36

The psalmist is paging through the history of Israel, taking lessons from it. In these verses he tells how God's people once intermixed with the heathen nations around them, against God's command. That led them to serve the heathens' idols, even sacrificing their children to them.

That's why God withdrew from them. There is indeed a lesson for us in this! There are things from which we, as Christians, must stay away. The most important of these are the occult practices of the enemy: divination and fortune telling, sorcery and magic spells, and all mediumistic things. God clearly forbade these things, which are snares of the enemy, binding us spiritually.

Remember, the more you do wrong, the easier it becomes. It starts off being interesting, then becomes acceptable, then commonplace, then a habit, and then an addiction. That's how the snare works. Just stay away!

Lord, let me walk in the light and not in the darkness! Amen.

SEPTEMBER 14

IN AND THROUGH DIFFICULTIES

Oh give thanks to the LORD, for He is good,
for His steadfast love endures forever! Let the redeemed
of the LORD say so, whom He has redeemed from trouble.

PSALM 107:1-2

In this psalm God is *praised* for delivering them from exile! Yes, their Babylonian captivity – a painful and crucial time for them as a nation – came and went. God was faithful! Let's take the following lessons from it:

- Our need is for God – In our difficulties we might believe that we have a need for money, work, or healing. Still, in our problems we first need God so that with *Him* we can work through them.
- The power of prayer – Difficult times bring us to our knees, in prayer! Remember, prayer changes things. Start with a prayer journal, and you will be surprised to see what God did as you flip back through the pages.
- This will pass – in our difficulties, we need to practice faith. That means that we dutifully keep on doing what we need to do while we faithfully wait for God to do what only He can do.

May these truths renew your strength today. Difficult times are seasons – and seasons pass!

*Lord, I fully trust in You. Help me to patiently wait
for Your help. Help me to keep a strong faith! Amen.*

STEER THE BOAT!

He made the storm be still, and the waves of the sea
were hushed. ... He brought them to their desired haven.
PSALM 107:29-30

Just as God saved His people from captivity, He saves many people from all kinds of danger. The psalmist is describing here how God saved sailors from a storm on the sea: tremendous waves lifted their boat up to heaven and then let it down crashing into the depths. Their "courage melted" (Ps. 107:26).

Then they called unto God and the waves were hushed. A quiet wind brought them to their destination. Let's apply these images in a very practical way. You and I are on a voyage as well. We are travelling to the harbor of our destination, the purpose for which our souls were created. It is the place where everything that God put in us will bear fruit – where we will experience deep satisfaction and meaning.

Life's storms, however, can keep us from reaching that purpose. At times our whole life is just about weathering the storms – so much so that we forget about the destination altogether! Keep your eyes on the goal, and keep on pushing toward your purpose. With God you *can* become what you must become!

Lord, bring me to my life's destination! Amen.

LEARN TO WALK

He turns rivers into a desert, springs of water
into thirsty ground. He turns a desert into pools of water,
a parched land into springs of water.
PSALM 107:33, 35

Can you see the turnabout in these verses? God turns rivers into a desert, and then desert into rivers. He can do it either way depending on His plan or what is needed.

With God, things often happen differently. Sometimes He doesn't provide streams in the desert, or takes away the stream and creates a desert. Remember, He is not just the Lamb, He is also the Lion; He is not just our Father, He is also our Judge. Different people often grow in different directions. For example, some need to curtail their anger, but others still need to learn to get angry at that which is wrong. We evidently cannot predict God simplistically or put Him in the box of our small understanding.

But now, if God does what He wants (He does, you know), how shall we live? Well, let's not predict too much of what God will do. Let's remain open to His loving decisions. Let's trust Him completely, because He is trustworthy! Let's learn to *walk* with God – on a day by day basis.

Lord, teach me to daily walk with You. Amen.

GIVE THE CURSE TO GOD

But You, O God my Lord, deal on my behalf for Your name's sake;
because Your steadfast love is good, deliver me!
PSALM 109:21

David is terribly upset, because he has been falsely accused. Some people said that he has no love, that he persecutes innocents, that he never blesses anyone.

That's not all. Some had him cursed in the ancient way (they had magicians and conjurers for that purpose) with curses like the following: "May his days be few; may another take his office … May his children wander about and beg, … may the creditor seize all that he has" (Ps. 109:8-11) – and many more!

David doesn't know what to do with these lies. He feels vulnerable, but he has God. The Lord knows his heart and knows that these allegations are untrue. Therefore, he just hands them over to God. We also sometimes find ourselves the target of others' opinions which can be completely untrue.

Defend yourself in meaningful ways if necessary, but remember some things are better just left with God. Let Him deal with it!

Lord, thank You for knowing me and knowing the truth.
The truth will prevail! Amen.

THE CURSE WILL NOT HOLD

*Let them curse, but You will bless! They arise
and are put to shame, but Your servant will be glad!*

PSALM 109:28

David had been cursed by his enemies. In biblical times you could go to sorcerers and charmers to have someone cursed. They then would pronounce spells, incantations, or charms in order to harm someone. We find a whole list of curses against David in this psalm! God forbade the practice, but it was commonly done.

However, David believed that such curses would not come about because God's blessing would protect him. Proverbs 26:2 says that a curse will not take hold onto a righteous person. It will fly away like a bird! Also think of the time when Balaam wanted to curse Israel, but every time he opened his mouth a blessing came out (Num. 23).

When Balak asked what was happening, Balaam explained: "There is no enchantment against Jacob, no divination against Israel" (v. 23). He could not curse what God had blessed! Take God's blessing as a fact over your life – and never fear the Evil One or others' evil intentions. God is on your side!

Lord, thank You for Your protection in every way. Amen.

THE CURSE RETURNS

May my accusers be clothed with dishonor;
may they be wrapped in their own shame as in a cloak!
PSALM 109:29

David had to deal with the curses leveled at him by his enemies. They were baseless and false. Therefore, he just handed them over to God, trusting in *His* protection.

Still, in these verses he cannot help but return the curses, asking for the things his enemies wish on him to happen to them! We feel uncomfortable with such wishes, because Jesus evidently taught us differently. He said we should bless those who curse us (Luke 6:28)! Still, we can believe that a curse returns – and a blessing as well. It's just the principle of sowing and reaping.

If you curse others left and right in hate and bitterness, you cannot reap happiness and love, can you? If, on the other hand, you bless others with love and forgiveness, you will most assuredly reap its blessing later. Bless others, in Jesus' name!

Lord, help me not to wish others harm,
but to pray for them in love – even my enemies. Amen.

THE KING WHO TAKES CONTROL

The LORD says to my Lord: "Sit at My right hand,
until I make Your enemies Your footstool."
PSALM 110:1

This psalm is about the king of Israel, who was appointed by God to rule. To the extent that the king stays at God's "right hand" he would remain God's "right hand man."

Even in the New Testament this psalm is understood Messianically, in other words as referring to Christ. Wasn't *He* called the "king of the Jews"? Indeed, we believe that Jesus conquered every enemy through His cross and resurrection and now sits at the right hand of the Father. Let's accept Jesus' kingship as a biblical, but also very personal, fact. He wants to be king of my life!

We often want to accept Christ as Savior, but the King isn't satisfied to just act as an insurance policy in our lives. Oh no, when King Jesus moves in, He wants to take over. He wants *full control*! Let's not misunderstand. With Christ, it's all or nothing.

Lord, be my Savior, but also be Lord of my life! Amen.

THE PRIEST WHO PRAYS

The LORD has sworn and will not change His mind,
"You are a priest forever after the order of Melchizedek."

PSALM 110:4

According to the psalmist the king of Israel is also a special type of priest in "the order of Melchizedek." Melchizedek was a Canaanite priest-king who blessed Abraham centuries before in the name of the Almighty.

In the New Testament, this psalm and the priesthood of Melchizedek has been applied directly to Jesus Christ. *He* is our high priest forever! What does it mean, though, in practical terms? It means that Jesus, on the cross, paid the full fine for all your transgressions (past, present, and future), that your account has been redeemed in full. It also means that Jesus is at the moment interceding for you at the throne of God. Did you fail?

Jesus is praying for you! Were you hurt by someone? Jesus is praying for you. Do you have fears? Jesus is praying! Do you have dreams? He is praying for those as well. Jesus is praying for you, and Jesus' prayers are *answered*!

*Lord Jesus, thank You that You are praying
for me today! It makes me feel safe. Amen.*

GOD'S GREAT (AND SMALL) DEEDS

Full of splendor and majesty is His work, and His righteousness
endures forever. He has caused His wondrous works
to be remembered; the LORD is gracious and merciful.

PSALM 111:3-4

In these verses the deeds of the Lord are praised. It's interesting that we can group God's deeds here as follows:

- God's *great* deeds are "full of splendor and majesty." They are the things that change everything: when your life is spared, when you find a soulmate, when your children are born, when doors open that change your life's direction. These things make you feel small before God. They make you want to praise him!

- God's *small* deeds are those in which His grace and mercy are shown. They're less conspicuous, but just as wonderful. They are the things that make you realize that God is still faithful, that He's still carrying you, blessing you, providing for you daily. They make you deeply grateful and secure. They give you peace.

  It's easy to see God in the big things, but He is just as present in the small things: the everyday grace, the silent blessings, the moments of mercy.

Lord, open my eyes and let me see Your works, great and small! Amen.

SEPTEMBER 23

TRUE WISDOM IS WITH HIM

The fear of the LORD is the beginning of wisdom;
all those who practice it have a good
understanding. His praise endures forever!
PSALM 111:10

The Bible stands on the fact that true wisdom originates with God. Nowadays that is not so readily believed. On the contrary, much of contemporary "wisdom" starts off by denying God and deciding that man will find his own way. Knowledge and science have been largely disconnected from God and are now standing on their own feet.

Yes, the ideas and values of popular culture are most often leading people away from God. Consider this, however: Earthly wisdom can only produce knowledge and experience about life. About the *purpose* of life, it can add little! Therefore, it remains a fact that true wisdom starts with God – with an actual relationship with God, with "the fear of the Lord."

In a relationship with Him we receive *His* wisdom and insight, *His* purpose for living, and especially *His* direction for our lives. Be wise in the Lord!

Lord, teach me how to live! Amen.

JOY IN THE COMMANDMENTS

*Praise the LORD! Blessed is the man who fears the LORD,
who greatly delights in His commandments!*
PSALM 112:1

God does not just want us to obey His commandments. No, He wants us to *want* to obey His commandments. There's a difference! He wants us to find joy in doing His will, to "delight in obeying His commands" (NLT).

The Jewish faith, therefore, puts an emphasis on the joy of keeping the Torah, thanking God for His law, and following it whole-heartedly and eagerly. It is beautiful, for example, to see the people in Jerusalem spilling out of their homes at the start of the Sabbath to dance with joy in the streets.

As Christians we are not under the law, but also not without the law. The law teaches us God's will, and the Holy Spirit empowers us to grow in God's will freely and joyfully. When we find it heavy to serve God, we are misunderstanding the gospel: serving God is not a burden, it's a pleasure! The gospel is good news. It's liberty!

Lord, it's my greatest joy to serve You – it's wonderful! Amen.

THE GENERATION OF THE UPRIGHT

His offspring will be mighty in the land;
the generation of the upright will be blessed.
PSALM 112:2

God's blessing is passed on through generations. The Lord wants to bless your children, but He wants to bless them through *you*. It works like this: If you truly serve God, your children will benefit from it because your life will bear the fruit of love, respect, fairness, and grace.

You will have handled your past so that unresolved issues are not projected onto them. On the contrary, your children will have had a healthy upbringing with solid values, strong moral principles, and positive boundaries. Then, since they have been blessed by you, they will be able to rear emotionally healthy children themselves. Do you see how God's blessing flows down the generations? On the other hand, where God is not served, children can grow up with skewed values. Uncertainty and lack of direction may cause them to look for fulfillment in the wrong places – and miss out on God's blessing!

We know that believing parents are not necessarily good parents, but if we grow spiritually, it will most assuredly translate into better parenting. It's a fact – your children *will* be blessed by your relationship with God!

Lord, bless my children and their children.
Channel Your blessing through me! Amen.

SHORT LIFE, LONG INFLUENCE

Wealth and riches are in his house,
and his righteousness endures forever.
PSALM 112:3

The psalmist is saying here that a righteous man's deeds endure forever. Remember, in biblical terms, man's life is fleeting. It's like a lamp that's soon quenched, like grass that's cut off at the end of the day, like smoke drifting by our window. If this is so, how can we produce something enduring? We can!

Take note:

- The Lord said we should store up treasures in heaven (Matt. 6:20). Invest therefore in your relationship with God, in His Kingdom, in the things that have eternal value.
- You can raise up generations for God on earth. Start with your own children. Build up their faith, instill the kingdom of God in their lives! Then they will be able to pass that on to even the next generation.
- You cannot take anything with you into eternity, except for people. So, take along your children by way of speaking – and your friends, your family! Pray for them and let your life and words testify of God so that they will want to serve Him as well.

Make the decision that your life will have enduring value!

Lord, do Your work in me and through me! Amen.

THE BLESSING OF GRACE

Light dawns in the darkness for the upright;
he is gracious, merciful, and righteous.

PSALM 112:4

In these verses the psalmist says that the righteous are generous, gracious, and merciful. Of course it's a blessing to receive grace, but it's an even bigger blessing to offer grace – the latter person is in a much better position than the former. Do you see?

Let's just underline a bit how grace operates in and through our lives: God, the Gracious and Merciful One, extends *His* mercy to us. We gratefully accept His mercy and then pass it forward to others by overlooking imperfections, forgiving people, and offering love even to those who do not deserve it. That's what grace is! We share liberally and generously, which shouldn't be difficult because we just share what we have received!

It's *God's* grace that we're working with, never ours. We merely act as the channels for it. Let's have a grace-filled day!

Father, You have shown me such mercy –
now extend Your mercy to others through me. Amen.

DO RIGHT, BE RIGHTEOUS

It is well with the man who deals generously and lends;
who conducts his affairs with justice.

PSALM 112:5

This psalm lists the blessings of a righteous man, and this verse reminds us that a righteous man deals justly with others. Righteousness is a fundamental requirement of believers, and it should therefore be our honor to live *rightly* toward God and others: to be God-fearing, to be honest, to be just and fair, to be law-abiding, to speak what is right.

You cannot proclaim to be a Christian, but then not be trustworthy in your deeds or words, unfair, or otherwise unbecoming as a child of God. That's embarrassing to our faith and to God! No, let's live openly and transparently. Let's speak the truth even if it's to our detriment.

Let's not exaggerate or slant what happened – just say exactly and plainly how things were, or are. Let's guard our integrity and good name, because we're children of the Almighty. Remember, He *only* stands with what is right and true, *never* with what is wrong or deceitful.

Lord, I want to stand with You – by standing
with what is right and true! Amen.

BUILD YOUR MONUMENT THERE

For the righteous will never be moved; he will be remembered forever.

PSALM 112:6

The righteous "will be remembered forever," the psalmist says. According to Scripture it's a blessing to have a long life, to make an impact, and to leave a meaningful legacy. It's a fact that we influence those who come after us, and it's also a fact that we can decide what that influence will be! How sad that some people remember their parents with pain, especially when they found them to be unfair, harsh, or unreliable.

Sometimes the parents were just absent. Some tell you, for example, "I never had a relationship with my father." Others tell of an agonizing childhood involving negligence, rejection, addiction, or violence. Our question is, how will you be remembered? Work on your legacy. Let your children remember your unconditional love, your unwavering support, your fair and consistent guidance.

Bless them with your approval – show them your love! Also, introduce your children to Christ. Remember, children do not ask of their parents to be perfect but to be good, trustworthy, and present. Build your monument in their memories! It's more important to invest in relationships than to invest in money, because relationships are forever and riches do not last.

Lord, bless my legacy in my children's hearts,
and help me to earn their respect. Amen.

LIVE UNFETTERED

He has distributed freely; he has given to the poor;
his righteousness endures forever; his horn is exalted in honor.

PSALM 112:9

Here the psalmist asserts that a righteous person is a generous giver. While Jesus said it's more blessed to give than to receive (Acts 20:35), many Christians believe the purpose of their walk with God is to receive blessings – which they often construe as material blessings.

We even try to claim or obtain such blessings by a variety of spiritual techniques. Yet, the purpose of our faith is to *be* a blessing! It's our sinful nature, or flesh, that only wants to receive, yet the Spirit helps us to give. Isn't the whole spiritual life an exercise in giving? We *give* our hearts and lives to God, we *give* up our own concerns for His, we *give* love, we *give* forgiveness, and we *give* our service!

It's only in the giving that we receive; it's in blessing others that we are blessed ourselves. It's in loving that we find love! Travel light, live unfettered, give generously, share freely! That's the way to live.

Lord, teach me to give. I have more than enough! Amen.

October

Praise the LORD! Praise, O servants of the LORD,
praise the name of the LORD!

Blessed be the name of the LORD from this time forth
and forevermore!

From the rising of the sun to its setting,
the name of the LORD is to be praised!

The LORD is high above all nations,
and His glory above the heavens!

Who is like the LORD our God, who is seated on high,
who looks far down on the heavens and the earth?

He raises the poor from the dust and lifts the needy
from the ash heap,

to make them sit with princes, with the princes of
His people.

He gives the barren woman a home, making her the
joyous mother of children. Praise the LORD!

PSALM 113

SING THE SONG OF ALL CREATION

From the rising of the sun to its setting,
the name of the LORD is to be praised!

PSALM 113:3

What a beautiful verse! The ancients believed that the heavens were like a tremendous dome that was placed over the earth, blue by day and black by night. Underneath this firmament the sun, moon, and stars went about their courses.

The sun coming up in the east and setting in the west circumscribed the whole of creation – and all are called here to praise God! Our contemporary view of east and west still includes all that exists. Take note that all of creation is already praising the Creator. The forces of evil that exist and the effects of man's sin, of course, produce false notes in the otherwise beautiful symphony.

But Jesus is coming, and all will be made right! Let's turn to the Creator, and let's do what we're called to do – honor our Maker!

Beautiful Creator, I want to praise You the whole day through! Amen.

YOU ARE WORTHY

He raises the poor from the dust and lifts the needy
from the ash heap, to make them sit with princes,
with the princes of His people.

PSALM 113:7-8

This psalm testifies about God's greatness. Here we see how God "raises" the poor and needy right across the social spectrum! Those who are sitting in the dust or on the ash heap will eventually sit down with princes at their banquet.

The reference here is to people who were shoved to the margins of society, who were thrown away, who had little status or dignity in the world. Dust and ashes were symbols of sorrow and loss. The reference could also be to those who were sad, who removed themselves from society to mourn. Whatever the case may be, the psalmist assures us that God joins those who suffer and those in sorrow. He sits down with them, where they are, and restores their dignity.

Have you been sidelined in life? Have you suffered loss? Do you feel useless or worthless? Jesus is with you! Jesus is there and things will *change*!

Lord Jesus, thank You that You're with me today! Amen.

OCTOBER 3
A HOME FOR YOU

He gives the barren woman a home,
making her the joyous mother of children. Praise the LORD!

PSALM 113:9

This verse states that God can give a childless woman a "home," in other words a family, children. This can literally happen and has happened countless times! There is, however, also a more general meaning: God gives the homeless, the lonely, a home.

Everyone wants to belong somewhere. We all long for a place where we are known, accepted, and loved. Part of God's solution is His church! Churches *must* be hospitable places where everyone, believing or unbelieving, are welcome. Look past your congregation's many mistakes and get involved again. Be the solution that you want to see! You can start at the place of your gifts. Do you say you have already tried that, but still couldn't find community or belonging at your church?

Then you may need to look further, because loving relationships are *fundamental* to being part of a church. Often smaller congregations offer more opportunities and closer community, but megachurches might have a friendly small group in your area. Pray about it, and *find* that spiritual home!

Lord, thank You for the house of the Lord, where I can feel at home.
Thank You for brothers and sisters! Amen.

BREAK THE ROCK

Tremble, O earth, at the presence of the Lord,
at the presence of the God of Jacob, who turns the rock
into a pool of water, the flint into a spring of water.

PSALM 114:7-8

In this short psalm the psalmist is referring us to Israel's trek from Egypt to Canaan. In the desert when they had no water, Moses struck a rock and enough water streamed out for all. Yes, God turned hard rock into flowing, life-giving water – as the psalm says. God can also do that to hardened hearts!

Some people are hard-hearted because they were hurt in the past. Others, though, were brought up to not show emotion or even feel too much. Some have ended up cold and cynical – embittered. The Lord, however, can break open such a heart! In fact, the promise of the new covenant is that hearts of stone will become hearts of flesh.

The Holy Spirit *can* flow from even the hardest heart to quench, heal, refresh, and create new life. Yes, it can happen! Keep on praying for hard hearts!

Lord, I first pray for myself, because I, too, find hardness and cynicism in my own heart. Break my heart, Lord! Amen.

GIVE AWAY YOUR GLORY

Not to us, O Lord, not to us, but to Your name give glory,
for the sake of Your steadfast love and Your faithfulness!

PSALM 115:1

We all like to receive attention and honor, to be acknowledged and thanked – to feel that we are important! However, it's not good for the soul to receive too much honor and glory. Our ego cannot handle it and quickly feels overly important.

We forget that it was grace that brought us to this place! "Not to us," says the Word here, "but to Your name" glory should be given. If we are praised, we may sincerely accept it, by all means – it's natural and important. Yes, show your gratitude, but also add (where appropriate) that God is to be thanked. Give as much honor to Him as you can! Then acknowledge the input of others.

Remember the attitude of a good leader: When a project doesn't go well, accept personal responsibility; if it goes well, say it was the team; if it goes very well, tell them, "You were fantastic, thank you!" Learn to deflect glory. To receive honor doesn't necessarily make you great – to give honor makes you greater!

Lord, help me to be mature with honor and acknowledgement.
Thank You for the grace that makes everything possible! Amen.

DON'T BUILD HIGH PLACES

Our God is in the heavens; He does all that He pleases.
Their idols are silver and gold, the work of human hands.
PSALM 115:3-4

Our psalmist is denouncing the idols of his time. They are merely the work of men, he says, made of gold and silver. They have mouths, eyes, hands, and feet, but they cannot talk, see, touch, or walk. Silent and motionless, they stand in their temples – an abomination to God.

We, of course, would never consider bowing before such things, but that doesn't mean that we don't have idols of our own. We have! The idols of our time are money, materialism, individualism, pleasure, status, health – such things. These are the things that we sacrifice a lot of time and money for, the things we strive for – the things that so easily take God's place.

Let's make sure that we don't build altars to such things in our lives! An altar is a prominence, a high place that we erect by sacrificing time, money, and effort to goals that are not the true purpose of life. There can only be one God in our lives – all the rest are idols!

Lord, You come first in my life.
Help me so that my choices reflect that truth! Amen.

YOU BECOME WHO YOU SERVE

Those who make them become like them;
so do all who trust in them.
PSALM 115:8

You become like your god! The psalmist is making this profound statement in regard to the idols of their time. We know the other side of this biblical truth better, that we as Christians become more like Christ.

It's a general truth, though, that we'll transform into the image of whatever god we worship. Those who bow to mammon can only talk about money, only think of how others can benefit them financially, or are overly anxious about losing what they have.

Those who worship status always brag about their success, act arrogantly toward those under them, and try to work themselves into the right circles. Those who worship their bodies pose relentlessly before the mirror, look down on those who are out of shape, and obsess over their diet.

Yes, our idols change us – they change our thinking and behavior. They make us ugly, selfish, obsessive, and anxious. Idols never liberate us! Of course there is nothing wrong with money as such or with getting ahead or with healthy living. Of course not. But when these things become our driving force, our overriding purpose, we must break their bonds in Jesus' name!

Lord Jesus, help me to serve You alone. Make me more like You! Amen.

BLESSING, BLESSING, BLESSING

The LORD has remembered us; He will bless us; He will bless
the house of Israel; He will bless the house of Aaron;
He will bless those who fear the LORD, both the small and the great.

PSALM 115:12-13

In this psalm the people and the priests are called on to trust God. Then this response comes, probably sung by the temple choir. The Lord *remembered* them! He thought of them, and He blessed them!

Blessing, blessing, and blessing, they sing – read the verse again! Those who serve God are really more blessed than any unbeliever can be. Take note that we said "more blessed," not necessarily richer or healthier. These things can be blessings (or not), but the concept of blessing is actually defined a bit differently.

Blessing is experiencing God's favor over your life. It's the privilege of living with God – in the ups *and* downs! It is to know that God is with you, that you're forever safe, that your purpose is clear. Blessing is to have the peace that surpasses understanding (Phil. 4:7). Those who do not live with God can never have this!

Lord, I receive Your blessing and I thank You for it. Amen.

TILL THE BURDEN HAS LIFTED

Gracious is the LORD, and righteous; our God is merciful.
The LORD preserves the simple; when I was brought low, He saved me.
PSALM 116:5-6

Our unknown psalmist tells us how anxious and desperate he was when he called onto God for help. Then these beautiful verses follow about God's help and care. God saved him! Scripture instructs that we shouldn't worry, but pray (Phil. 4:6-7).

Perhaps we should say it like this: *Whenever* you have worries, you can cast them – all your burdens – onto the Lord (1 Pet. 5:7). *Then* the peace of God will settle over you. Take note, however, that this often entails a process. It takes time for us to experience that peace that surpasses understanding. Therefore, we shouldn't just pray about something and then leave it.

No, we should pray on, push through, *until* we experience the peace that we need, *until* the burden has lifted and we feel we can leave the matter with God. Yes, sometimes peace takes time – yes, often prayer is a real struggle. Carry on praying!

Lord, I pray for Your peace in my heart today. Amen.

RETURN, O MY SOUL

Return, O my soul, to your rest;
for the LORD has dealt bountifully with you.
PSALM 116:7

The psalmist tells us here about a desperate situation and how God intervened and saved him. However, it's as if his spirit is still restless in the aftermath, as if his soul hasn't caught up with the reality yet. It often happens!

Therefore, he reminds himself now to "return," to be calm – God is in control! Elsewhere the Bible also reminds us that it's in "returning and rest" that our salvation lies (Isa. 30:15). Take note: disciplining your soul to peace means to become quiet, to be silent – to stop with all the words! A lot of talking disrupts the soul's rest. Learn to be quiet. Why must we talk?

God has already read your prayers in your heart. Just go into His presence and be still at His feet. Just sit with Him in silence. Do it daily, and you *will* feel your soul returning to rest!

Lord, teach me Your silence. Give me Your peace. Amen.

CONFUSED AND DISAPPOINTED

I believed, even when I spoke: "I am greatly afflicted;"
I said in my alarm, "All mankind are liars."
PSALM 116:10-11

The writer of this psalm went through deep waters. The worst was when he realized that in his greatest need he could depend on no one. No one was trustworthy; no one wanted to help. "All are liars," he writes. He stood alone!

Remember, he is not stating a general truth about humankind here. He is describing a painful, personal experience. There are indeed dependable and loving people around us, but in our confusion and distress we often cannot see or find them. It is really bad for us when we get disappointed again and again and later feel that no one really cares, that everyone is just concerned with their own welfare.

Still, if we put our faith in God – as the psalmist did – He will take us through the affliction and then, when our minds are clearer, we will realize that there were good and kind people all along, that our conclusions were hasty. May God help you, and may you find the support you need!

Lord, I am in need. I need people to help me through this! Amen.

PRECIOUS IS YOUR DEATH

Precious in the sight of the Lord is the death of His saints.
PSALM 116:15

A difficult verse! The idea here is not to glorify death as something valuable to God. On the contrary, it focuses on the fact that *life* is so valuable that God is greatly involved when it is endangered or comes to an end. The verse is translated in the Contemporary English Version as, "You are deeply concerned when one of your loyal people faces death."

It has to do with the question of God's involvement in suffering and death. Does He care? Is He near? Why does He allow innocent people to be killed in accidents, martyrs to be murdered, the sick to die? We first must remember that suffering and death were never revoked by God. They remain a part of life because of the brokenness that sin produced.

Even Christ had to suffer and die! Only in the next world will there be no death. What the Word emphasizes here, though, is that God remains deeply *involved* with us, that He deeply *cares* wherever there is suffering, pain, and loss. In fact, at our death God will be nearer to us than at any other time. He will meet us right there!

Lord, thank You that You are intensely concerned
with my life. Amen.

THE SHORTEST PSALM

Praise the LORD, all nations! Extol Him, all peoples!
For great is His steadfast love toward us, and the
faithfulness of the LORD endures forever. Praise the LORD!

PSALM 117

The above is the entire psalm – the shortest psalm in the Bible! Quickly answer the following questions from this psalm:

With what words does this psalm begin and end? That is the main theme of the whole book of Psalms!

- To whom are these words addressed? Is this injunction observed? What can we do?
- What are the two reasons given to motivate the psalmist's injunction? These are God's most important traits!

Let's summarize: The whole world is obligated to praise God! *All* must acknowledge His love and faithfulness! It is the church's task to proclaim God's goodness to all the world so that all can know Him. Yes, praise testifies. Praise leads to reaching out – to mission!

Lord, I praise You today!
Thank You for Your love and faithfulness. Amen.

THAT'S WHO YOU ARE!

Oh give thanks to the LORD, for He is good;
for His steadfast love endures forever!

PSALM 118:1

This specific pronouncement of praise is found in many psalms. It's actually a well-known song in the Old Testament which was sung at the dedication of the temple, feasts, ceremonies, and even on the battlefield. What does it mean, though?

Well, these words are merely the Old Testament version of the New Testament declaration that God is love. It's a definition and description of God's character. God is good, and God's love is endless. That's who God is! Everything God does emanates from His goodness – even His justice, wrath, and punishment are part of His love! Now consider this: God is defined as love, but love cannot hang in the air. Love needs an object.

You have to love something or someone. Isn't that so? What, then, is the object of God's love? Well, among other things *we* are the objects of God's love – He loves *us*! That brings us to our identities as humans: we are the *beloved* of God. Who are you? You are God's beloved – that's who you are!

*Thank You, loving Father, that I am the object
of Your endless love. I love You also! Amen.*

SING THE BATTLE SONG

The LORD is my strength and my song;
He has become my salvation.
PSALM 118:14

We find this specific formulation at several places in the Old Testament. The first is after Israel crossed the Red Sea and the Egyptians who were following suit all drowned. God became the Israelites' "strength and song," their "salvation."

Make it your personal battle song as well, because God is also your strength. Life entails struggle, but God will help you. David was a warrior. Of course, we don't want to fight, but sometimes we have to fight. Then you'll find God strengthening your hands. He is your strength, and He is your song.

After the victory – the "salvation" – you will have a song of praise in your heart. God will receive glory! Today, go out in the *strength* of the Lord and confront your obstacles in Jesus' name! God will be your salvation. Tonight, then, you will have a song of praise!

Lord, I have challenges to confront.
Be my strength today! Amen.

OCTOBER 16
GOD LOOKS AT YOU

The stone that the builders rejected has become the cornerstone. This is the Lord's doing; it is marvelous in our eyes.
PSALM 118:22–23

The psalmist, walking through the temple grounds, is probably referring to an incident when the temple's cornerstone was initially rejected by the builders but later used after all.

Either that or the temple's huge cornerstone makes him think of a saying that referred to David, who was once rejected as king but afterward became the "cornerstone" of the Israelite nation, so to speak. This saying was later applied to Jesus: rejected by men, but chosen by God as the foundation on which to build His kingdom. The lesson is that God looks at things differently. That which is wise in the eyes of men may be foolish in the eyes of God – or vice versa. Whom we see as weak may be seen by God as a useful instrument to work through. God often takes the least or the humblest to surpass the most important.

So, do you feel as if you don't add much value? Are you at the bottom of the list? Do good things pass you by? Well, blessed are you! God looks at you differently. He *will* use you – and He *will* raise you up in His time!

Lord, thank You that I do not have to compare myself to anyone. You will use me just as I am! Amen.

THIS IS THE DAY, TODAY

This is the day that the LORD has made;
let us rejoice and be glad in it.

PSALM 118:24

The struggling psalmist is experiencing a wonderful day: triumphant and victorious, filled with God's presence. "This is the day that the LORD has made," he rejoices!

Remember, every day is God's day, but we're usually too busy to notice. See *today*, therefore, as a special God-given day. It's filled – from the morning till the evening – with God's presence and with amazing potential. The purpose of today is God's glory. This day is already structured in such a way that God can be honored. We only need to see its possibilities and choose that which will honor Him!

Know that God is in control today, and live this day to His glory as far as possible. Where you fail, God's grace will take over. Whatever happens, remember to "rejoice and be glad in it" – it's *His* day!

Today is Your day, Lord! Open my eyes for its wonder and its joy! Amen.

BLESSED ARE YOU

Blessed is he who comes in the name of the LORD!
We bless you from the house of the LORD.
PSALM 118:26

In this psalm the pilgrim is now entering the temple. There, these wonderful words of blessing come to him pronounced by the priests: "Blessed is he who comes in the name of the Lord!"

In the original context these words were especially directed to the king who, on the day of the feast, led the procession into the temple, but it also included all who followed. In the New Testament the words are applied to Christ, but also to us, following Him into God's sanctuary.

These images make our thoughts wander off to the day that we'll finally and fully enter God's presence – forever. On our eternal arrival into God's abode, a wonderful welcome will await us. A choir will sing a song like this one, and the Church that's already with God will rejoice over yet another believer making it safely home! Jesus will be there with open arms, awaiting us with love in His eyes.

Yes, we know we're speculating. We're dreaming. But still, to enter God's presence is always wonderful, and on that day it will surpass everything we have ever known! Blessed are you, friend, brother, sister, overcomer in Christ!

Lord, thank You for these words of grace.
They bless me! Amen.

START THE CELEBRATION!

The LORD is our God, and He has given us
light! Start the celebration! March with
palm branches all the way to the altar.

PSALM 118:27 (CEV)

This psalm, which has all the characteristics of a Davidic psalm, though it's not presented as such, was used at certain Jewish feasts. It tells us how the king won the victory in God's name and is now leading the festal procession into the temple grounds.

The celebration can begin! This reminds us of the end goal of our faith, which is described as an eternal feast. Actually, that feast starts the moment we enter into a life with God, but because we're so busy we often miss out on the celebration as an everyday reality. Remember the parable of the guests who made excuses not to come to the feast (Luke 14:12-24)? The one wanted to look (again) at his newly acquired land, the other wanted to try out his new oxen. The third was recently married – enough said!

The parable, however, makes it clear that these excuses were not remotely valid and that these guests were missing out on something tremendous. Let's not make the same mistake. Grab every chance to celebrate the fact that you have God in your heart! Join the feast, wave the palm leaves, sing, march to the altar, celebrate!

Lord, I celebrate living with You – I'll change it for nothing! Amen.

YOU ARE BLESSED. PERIOD!

Blessed are those whose way is blameless,
who walk in the law of the LORD!
PSALM 119:1

This longest psalm in the Bible – 176 verses – is about the Word of God. It's an acrostic psalm, meaning its paragraphs correspond to the letters of the Hebrew alphabet. Verses one to eight all start with the Hebrew letter *aleph*, verses nine to sixteen start with the letter *bet*, and so on.

Take note of the simple message of the Bible concerning obedience: obedience leads to God blessing, while disobedience forfeits God's blessing! This is a fundamental truth that we should accept and live by. The blessed life is a life with God, a life in His will. Such a life does not guarantee that you won't have bad times, but the blessing is that we can go through those times *with* God.

That makes quite a difference, because God adds meaning, peace, and victory to all of our seasons. It's *always* blessed to live with God, good times or bad! Do you need to return to the blessed life?

Lord, Your Word is the truth. Help me to walk in that truth. Amen.

THE PROBLEM YOUTHS HAVE

How can a young man keep his way pure?
By guarding it according to Your word.
PSALM 119:9

The psalmist is giving advice to young people who want to remain pure in an impure world. Wouldn't the psalmist be shocked to see the world that *we* are living in?

Because God has been taken out of the picture, the boundary between good and evil has become very vague. Broken homes, free sex, alcohol, drugs, and violence nowadays make up the general context in which young people grow up. A lack of fathers and positive role models leave young people relying largely on their peers. Let's first not blame the youth for these things, though, since *we* have made the world as it is!

Let's rather stand by them and understand how they try to live and get ahead in this world. Young people above all need friends, fathers, and mothers – mentors that will rub off on their lives and prove to them that God's way is the best way. *That* is how young people (and all people) learn values and faith – *not* by condemning or sermonizing. Remember, *we* are the Word that most young people read!

Lord, change my life so that my life can change others. Amen.

MORE THAN RICHES

In the way of Your testimonies I delight as much as in all riches.
I will delight in Your statutes; I will not forget Your word.
PSALM 119:14, 16

This longest psalm in the Bible is devoted to the Word of God – quite a lesson in itself! Without the Word, we would never know God's will for us. Still, the Lord does not just want us to follow His prescripts because it's *His* will for us or in order to receive the blessing it brings.

No! He wants us to follow them because it has become *our* will, because *we* want to, because it delights us, as the psalmist says here. He says following God's decrees brings more pleasure than all the riches in the world! Living with God brings joy and liberty. It's not a burden!

Forget all ideas about a heavy religion or difficult spiritual duties – that is not the biblical emphasis. Ask God to change your heart and start to *enjoy* serving Him! True joy does not come from riches; it comes from a life in God's will. Break away to that joy!

Lord, You are my greatest joy.
Serving You makes my life meaningful, colorful, and rich. Amen!

OPEN MY EYES

Open my eyes, that I may behold wondrous things out of Your law.
PSALM 119:18

We can read Scripture without having it touch our lives in the least. Sometimes the words just roll before our eyes without going into our minds or hearts at all. Our physical eyes may be open, but our spiritual eyes are definitely not!

The Bible often alludes to the fact that we are – spiritually speaking – asleep, in a daze, or blind. We carry on without paying attention to God in our lives, so we never see Him or meet Him. We must *wake up* from our slumber, open our eyes, focus! Then we will perceive God all around us! If we want to "behold wondrous things" from God's Word – the phrase here referring to supernatural things – our eyes must be opened, the psalmist says.

Do the following: Read less, but with more attention. Read audibly, slowly, and intensely. Read with the question, Lord, what do you want to convey to me today? Go back to the phrases that stood out for you, and repeat them slowly. Think about them, mull them over in your mind, explore their meanings and possibilities. Then in faith take a lesson from them into your day. *This* is Scripture meditation.

Lord, open my eyes! I do not just want to read the Bible –
I want to read Your Word for me in the Bible. Amen.

WHAT ABOUT THE LAW?

Teach me Your statutes! Make me understand the way of Your precepts, and I will meditate on Your wondrous works.
PSALM 119:26-27

This psalm is about God's Word, of which the literal meaning here is the Old Testament law. Christians often wonder whether this law still applies to them. Well, for us the ritual law, all about the Jewish religion, has been fulfilled by Christ and does not apply to us anymore.

The moral law, for example the Ten Commandments, expresses God's general will and does apply. Remember that laws are necessary for a meaningful existence. How would man, or a country, survive without them? Will everyone just do as he sees fit? No, we *must* understand what it is that God requires, and we *must* live according to that.

How else can we live but with deference to the only One God, with respect for His name, and with honor toward His precepts? Can we live with murder, adultery, stealing, or false witness? Of course not! Jesus summarizes it when He says God's law is love, love for God and love for others (Matt. 22:36-40). So yes, you need to keep the law!

Lord, I do want to live according to Your statutes, and I do want to love. Help me to do so! Amen.

I AM NOT ASHAMED

*I will also speak of your testimonies before kings
and shall not be put to shame, for I find my delight
in your commandments, which I love.*

PSALM 119:46-47

The psalmist says he is not ashamed of God. He will confidently speak about God, even in the highest circles. It makes us think of Jesus' words that we shouldn't be ashamed of Him before people – and then He will not be ashamed of us before the Father (Luke 9:26).

Why are Christians often timid in speaking about their faith or about God, especially at work or in social settings? Let's be bolder! We should be wise, though. On the one hand, we mustn't hide our light under a bucket – we're not secret agents! On the other hand, our testimony mustn't push more people away from God than it draws nearer.

That defeats our whole purpose! Be fearless and confident, but be wise, in other words. Live your faith, be friendly, be kind, be fair, and be a good worker. When others talk about spiritual matters, you can freely add your own experiences – why not?

Lord, help me to be a bold but wise testimony of Your love. Amen.

TENSION WILL REMAIN

Conceited people sneer at me, but I obey Your Law.
PSALM 119:51 (CEV)

Yesterday we said that Christians should act wisely in the world. We are witnesses of Christ's love. We must also be faithful examples of His love. Our testimony must mainly be seen, not heard. Our words will not draw people to Christ when our lives push them away!

These things are all true, but today we need to add something more. As God's children in the world, we can never fully comply with the world's expectations. Remember, we live *in* the world as people who are not *of* the world. The Bible says those who want to live a godly life *will* be persecuted (2 Tim. 3:12). So a certain tension will remain. Some think of us as narrow-minded, overly conservative, or fanatical.

Let them think what they will! Just continue living with friendliness and kindness, show interest and attention, demonstrate love. Be fair and be gracious – be Jesus to others! Our actual aim, though, is not to please people but to please the Master. To live a godly life and to love others pleases *Him*!

Lord, help me to live with love and respect –
especially in the face of opposition. Amen.

IN-BETWEEN FIRST AND SECOND SLEEP

At midnight I rise to praise You, because of Your righteous rules.
PSALM 119:62

The psalmist says here he gets up at midnight for a time of prayer. That's when he praises God for His law. How wonderful! We, on the other hand, find it very difficult to get up, especially to pray.

There is a very old habit that might work for you, though. In the past people went to bed much, much earlier and had what they called a first sleep from which they awoke very early in the morning hours. Depending on the hours they slept, they were then wide awake. They would go out and perhaps talk for a bit and then could either prepare for the day or get back in bed for a second sleep.

Many staunch Christians of old used that in-between time to pray. This is indeed an ideal time to "watch and pray" (Matt. 26:41) and can become a workable rhythm for you. Let's put it like this: if you're awake, you might be awake for a reason. Use the time to pray!

Heavenly Intercessor, teach me to pray,
and help me to make the sacrifice that prayer asks. Amen.

FAILURES INTO FUEL

It is good for me that I was afflicted,
that I might learn Your statutes.
PSALM 119:71

The psalmist confesses in verse 67 that he "went astray," but the resultant difficulties brought him back on the right track. In that sense, he says now that it was good for him to be afflicted. It is clear from Scripture and everyday life that troubles and obstacles can have a beneficial effect in our lives.

To make mistakes is one way of learning. Some have said that failure is not an option; it is a necessity! We *must* make mistakes, but we also must learn from our mistakes. Yes, the real mistake is to make the same mistake again! Whenever we've made a mistake or experienced trouble of any kind, we can work with it very intentionally.

Try to understand exactly what went wrong and why. Ask yourself: "What must change in my set-up or systems or in my approach to avoid this happening again?" With more serious trouble ask yourself: "Does God want to tell me something?" Turn your failures into fuel for growth!

Lord, I do fail, and I do make mistakes.
Help me to learn from them! Amen.

TURN AROUND AND LOVE

Your hands have made and fashioned me;
give me understanding that I may learn Your commandments.
PSALM 119:73

God made me and knows me. He knows every corner of my body and every turn of my heart. God knows my thoughts, both the good and the bad. He knows my humanity and my nature, my dreams and my fears – He knows me inside out!

The wonder of it is that God loves me in spite of knowing me, especially my wrongdoings and sin, because He sees me as His *child*. Take note, though, of the result of God's loving eyes in this verse. The psalmist now longs to also know *God* better, to understand *Him* more, to serve *Him* fully! Yes, that is the correct response to God's loving engagement: to want to know Him back, to return His love, to serve! In that way a relationship ensues.

Wouldn't it be a terrible sin to reject our own loving Father's reaching out to us? Yes, it would be, and it is! Let's rather just love God back – it still remains the Great Commandment. Then, let's get to know Him better!

Father, thank You for loving me. I love You too,
and I want to know You more! Amen.

WHEN ALL GOES WRONG

For I have become like a wineskin in the smoke,
yet I have not forgotten Your statutes.
PSALM 119:83

The psalmist went through a terrible hardship and now feels "like a wineskin in the smoke." Take note that there are four types of spiritual persons:

- Some do not serve God, whether times are good or bad.
- There are those who live far from God when life goes well since they think do not need Him, but in adversity they turn to God quickly, pray a lot, go to church again, and so on.
- There are those who serve God, especially when life goes well. However, in the bad times they turn away, feeling disappointed by God or believing that their faith does not work.
- Then there are those who remain steadfast, serving God in the good times and the bad. Even when the fields yield no harvest, they still find reason to rejoice in God.

This last type is the faithfulness our psalmist expresses. Let's be like that and remain steadfast!

Lord, I want to remain faithful to You in all circumstances.
Be my strength today! Amen.

MEDITATION AND IMPLEMENTATION

Oh how I love Your law! It is my meditation all the day.
PSALM 119:97

The word *meditation*, in a Christian sense, refers to focused attention, conscious reflection. The psalmist says he intentionally ponders God's Word throughout the day, probably referring to the Jews' daily prayer times.

In our busy days, we may find it difficult to make time for formal Scripture meditation, but the following approach might be of help. Choose one truth or topic that emerges from your daily Scripture reading as the topic of the day – or even the week. Forget all the other things that you read. Now try to keep that specific thing in mind throughout your day, and try to act on it. Let's say you chose *patience* as a fruit of the Spirit. Work then with patience that day or week at work or in your relationships.

Try to understand what patience is and what it isn't, why you become impatient, and how to work toward being more forbearing. Do you see how your Scripture meditation can work its way into your day, become Scripture implementation?

Lord, let Your truth become my truth, my everyday practice! Amen.

November

I lift up my eyes to the hills. From where does my help come?

My help comes from the LORD, who made heaven and earth.

He will not let your foot be moved; He who keeps you will not slumber.

Behold, He who keeps Israel will neither slumber nor sleep.

The LORD is your keeper; the LORD is your shade on your right hand.

The sun shall not strike you by day, nor the moon by night.

The LORD will keep you from all evil; He will keep your life.

The LORD will keep your going out and your coming in from this time forth and forevermore.

PSALM 121

SWEETER THAN HONEY

How sweet are Your words to my taste,
sweeter than honey to my mouth!
PSALM 119:103

In times gone by, sweet things were scarce and considered a luxury. Special events were therefore always celebrated with treats like dates, sweet fruits, or honey. In this verse the psalmist compares the Word of God to honey.

It's a well-known comparison, but take specific note today of the last three words here: "to my mouth." Honey is only sweet when tasted, when in the mouth, isn't that so? In the honey pot or on your bread, its sweetness is merely theoretical. In the same way, the Word of God's goodness is not found between your Bible's leather bound covers but in your mouth: when it is read, repeated, memorized, prayed, sung, recited, preached, confessed – when it is used!

Make the Word part of your everyday life. Repeat its truths, listen to its psalms, learn its verses, pray about its teachings, and live out its instructions. As you ingest the Word, as it becomes part of you, its sweetness will permeate your day – your whole life!

Lord, thank You for these sweet words.
May Your Word fill my words and actions to Your glory. Amen.

LIGHT ON THE PATH

Your word is a lamp to my feet and a light to my path.
PSALM 119:105

Life is a journey and man forever is *Homo Viator* – a man on the way. Life's road twists away into a dark and unknown future, but we have no choice but to take it. We cannot refuse the road that daily presents itself to us. Yes, we must walk it, and we will walk it not knowing what the next turn will bring!

The road can surprise us with unexpected bends or stops, or it can become steep or slippery. At other times the way can become so dark that we cannot even see the next step. It's then that we need a light to guide us. Our psalmist assures us that God's Word is the light we need for life's journey!

His Word will cast light on the road and on our purpose and goal and will guide our actions and decisions. With God's Word, we'll find our way again! Remember that we do not walk life's path alone, although we might think so. Oh no, we have a guide, the Holy Spirit. It is He who whispers God's Word in our ear, shining its light, making sure that we reach the goal!

Holy Spirit, shed Your Light on my path! Amen.

HIDING AND HOPING

You are my hiding place and my shield; I hope in Your word.
PSALM 119:114

Sometimes life can become very stressful. Sometimes everything seems to go wrong! Unexpected obstacles can pop out of nowhere for which we're just not prepared. Other times it can be the same old things that always trip us up.

We come to the place where we just want to get away from it all, even for a little while – where we want to close the door, take a deep breath, and get our thoughts together. At such times we can go and hide with God. Yes, indeed, *He* is our "hiding place." Go to Him, then. As you close your door, open your Bible. Let the Word of God reframe the situation from God's perspective. Read how God feels about you! Let the Word speak into your particular situation and guide your decisions. Realize the riches of God's promises and the power of His presence – right where you are!

Ask yourself: "What would Jesus do? What would Jesus want me to do?" If you do these things, you're doing it right – this is *exactly* how a believer hides away with God! Make His Word your first stop when you need refuge.

Lord, thank You for the encouragement
and strength that Your Word provides. Amen.

YOU OPEN, HE OPENS

The unfolding of Your words gives light;
it imparts understanding to the simple.
PSALM 119:130

In this psalm about God's Word, the psalmist says that the "unfolding" of God's words gives light. In the synagogues, up to this day, the Scriptures are taken out of the ark – the closet where they're kept – with great respect and ceremony and handed to the lector.

Some churches still open the Bible ceremoniously or declare after the Scripture reading: "This is the Word of the Lord!" We know that we should open the Word of the Lord more often since it's God's words for us, His light on our path, His guidance that we so need. What is so beautiful in these verses, though, is that it's not only *we* who open God's Word. *He* also opens His Word for us! By His Holy Spirit He illuminates its meaning to our hearts so that we can understand what He is saying to us personally.

By His Spirit we become able to see the spiritual realities, why things are as they are, and how we should react to them. Yes, when we open God's Word – and when God opens His Word in turn – a holy place and a holy time ensues, a Spirit-filled meeting with the Almighty!

Lord, meet me in Your Word! Amen.

MORNINGS REMAIN SUPERB

I rise before dawn and cry for help; I hope in Your words.
PSALM 119:147

We have said that the Bible does not give specific instructions on how or when a personal quiet time should be taken. We have the examples of many biblical or historical faith heroes, though, and our own personal experience to guide us into a spiritual rhythm, a personal walk with God.

Perhaps you have time over lunch for God's Word or on Wednesday afternoons – perhaps over the week-ends, when it's quiet? Mornings remain superb, though, for meeting with God! Summer mornings are bright and ready for a perfect quiet time, while dark winter mornings will require a cozy blanket and the first coffee of the day. Autumn mornings have that welcomed chill of the seasons turning, while spring mornings are bright, sweet, and full of promise. Mornings are wonderful!

When you're young, you tend to sleep the mornings away, but with maturity you appreciate the freshness of the dawn more and more. It's absolutely fantastic to get up early, go outside, and experience the day breaking. Breathe it in! It's even better to share it with God, as our psalmist did. Try it!

Father, thank You for lovely mornings,
and thank You for sharing those mornings with me. Amen.

CONSTANT AMIDST THE CHANGE

*But You are near, O LORD, and all Your commandments
are true. Long have I known from Your testimonies
that You have founded them forever.*

PSALM 119:151-152

In biblical times the old things were the good things. Old traditions and practices were not tampered with because they were the proven ones. When there was uncertainty, the elders were asked how things were done in the past. Innovations were frowned upon as unnecessary and disruptive.

We, on the other hand, live in a time of constant change. In the last century alone the world has seen two great wars (and many smaller ones), radically changing values, space exploration, and the development and use of computers in all spheres of life. Information, transport, commerce, and media made us world citizens. Old ways of doing and old values have become obsolete and are being replaced by new ones.

Innovation and adaptation have become essential, but all these many changes can be overwhelming, confusing! They create the need for guidance – for discernment, values, direction. The psalmist assures us, however, that God's will remains the same, that His commandments are "forever." Set your compass to God's will – the one true constant amidst the change!

Lord, thank You that You're the same yesterday, today, and forever. Amen.

COME AFTER ME, LORD!

*I am Your servant, but I have wandered away
like a lost sheep. Please come after me,
because I have not forgotten Your teachings.*
PSALM 119:176 (CEV)

Today we conclude this longest psalm in the Bible, which is about God's Word – His will, His law. The psalmist sincerely wants insight into God's Word, and he *wants* to be obedient.

More than that, he *rejoices* in God's law, he *loves* God's will, and he calls up the reader to do the same. Then he ends this beautiful psalm with this verse: "I have wandered away like a lost sheep. Please come after me." The psalmist knows human nature so well! He knows that we are prone to wandering off. We tend to always go after greener grass – and then, when we look up again, the flock is gone! We so easily lose focus, get sidetracked, become busy.

When that happened to our psalmist, he trusted God to come and look for him. Will God seek out His lost sheep? Of course He will! Jesus said the Good Shepherd will leave the ninety-nine to find the one that's not there. Yes, God will come after you! In fact, He is coming for you at this moment. What a relief!

*Thank You, Lord, for seeking me out,
for finding me, for bringing me home! Amen.*

QUARRELS AND CONFRONTATIONS

> Too long have I had my dwelling among those
> who hate peace. I am for peace,
> but when I speak, they are for war!
>
> PSALM 120:6-7

We now come to fifteen short pilgrim songs – also called "songs of ascent." In this first one David, who wrote the psalm according to tradition, says it's terrible to be between quarrelsome people.

There was a time when he lived with such people. Whenever he tried to say something good, it was turned around. Perhaps you also feel this way sometimes – totally misunderstood? When our good intentions are disregarded, we may feel very angry. Remember that we'll often experience conflict in life. We just have to learn to handle it correctly. Frequent, factual, and calm communication is the key. Avoid emotional outbursts or sweeping accusations.

As far as possible, stay objective and mature. Also, try not to attack the person, but the problem. The problem is most often a mere misunderstanding or miscommunication in your relationship. Try to understand first, admit where the other is right, and look for a realistic solution, a compromise. Especially talk with God about the matter – that is what David is doing here!

Lord, I want to bring the following situation to You … Guide me! Amen.

LOOK UP, LOOK *THERE!*

I lift up my eyes to the hills. From where does my help come?
PSALM 121:1

The composer of this pilgrim song is on his way to Jerusalem. Jewish men were obliged to go to the temple three times a year in order to attend the three major festivals. As he walks, he feels worried.

He needs help. The "hills" that he's looking up to are probably not the general hills of Judea. When the psalms refer in these contexts to hills, they usually mean Jerusalem's hills, most especially Zion, on which God's temple stood. It means the pilgrim is looking ahead – to his destination, to the temple, and to Yahweh, the Lord from whom his help comes. Yes, the pilgrim is keeping his eyes on his goal, which is God! We are also pilgrims on our way to eternity, to the celebration that awaits.

Are you perhaps walking with worries or needs, with longings? Do you need help? Your help comes from *Him* to whom your journey leads! His Spirit will daily guide you to that destination. Know that you *will* receive your help, you *will* reach your goal, and you *will* be safe, forever! Let these truths strengthen your strides today.

Thank You, Lord, that my help is from You!
Give me the strength for today's journey. Amen.

GET YOUR FAITH TOGETHER

My help comes from the LORD, who made heaven and earth.
PSALM 121:2

In this psalm a pilgrim is on his way to Jerusalem. He looks at the hills around him and in his mind compares the hills with God, who made the hills, the mountains, and the whole heaven and earth!

Let's take this image as a metaphor for life. Life is a pilgrimage, and our journey often crosses mountains. That's just how it is. We cannot avoid the challenges or obstacles of life. Sometimes the road can become very steep or difficult, though. Sometimes it seems as if the mountains become more abundant the closer you get to the goal! Do you perhaps face a mountain at the moment?

Don't know how you can cross this one? Most often the problem is not with the mountain but with our faith. We are intimidated by mountains, but that's unnecessary! Our God is bigger than any mountain – He is the God of the mountains! Get your faith together now. In Jesus' name address that mountain!

Lord Jesus, in Your name this mountain will be removed –
in Your name I will be victorious. Amen!

TREAD CAREFULLY AND TRUST

He will not let your foot be moved;
He who keeps you will not slumber.
PSALM 121:3

The pilgrim in this psalm is on his way to Jerusalem, and we take his journey as a metaphor for our own life's journey. Just as was *his* road, *our* road to the heavenly Jerusalem isn't neatly paved or evened out. No, it winds up and down through the hills and valleys and often presents us with obstacles or diversions.

If you "lift up [your] eyes to the hills" (Ps. 121:1), you might easily stumble over a stone or a pothole! However, the Word says here that God will keep our feet from wavering – a wonderful promise! Take note, though, that trusting God to keep you from falling means that you're trying not to fall in the first place. No, we don't want to fall, especially into sin, but the problem is this: we're human! We're human and we try, but we fail.

So we *do* stumble and we *do* fall! That's why we need God to pick us up when we have fallen – and He will! As we live with Him and take heed of His guidance, we will learn to avoid many pitfalls. He will teach us not to fall – as much! Steadily, our steps will become more secure.

Author and Finisher of my faith,
keep me from the pitfalls of life – and pick me up where I fall! Amen.

PRACTICE HIS PRESENCE

He who keeps you will not slumber. Behold,
He who keeps Israel will neither slumber nor sleep.
PSALM 121:3-4

Pilgrims traveling to Jerusalem were very aware of the dangers of the road, especially wild animals and robbers that hid out in the hills of Judea. This pilgrim, though, trusts the Keeper of Israel for his safety.

It comforts him that his God never sleeps nor slumbers – that He is always awake and alert, ready to help His people. We do believe that God is always present, because per definition He is omnipresent. It's not just a theological idea. For this Old Testament brother it was also a very practical truth! Practicing the presence of God is a well-known goal of the deeper life and one we can definitely incorporate into our own lives. Become aware of God's presence as part of your spiritual discipline of the here and now.

Learn to experience God when you're sitting, when you're working, when you're eating, or as you go to sleep. Experience His presence in your room right now – next to your chair, at the door, or wherever! Remember to also freely talk with God throughout your day, because God is really, really near!

Omnipresent God, thank You for being with me
right now. Keep me close to You! Amen.

IN THE HEAT AND DUST

The LORD is your keeper;
the LORD is your shade on your right hand.
PSALM 121:5

When a pilgrim walked to Jerusalem, he ended up going through barren and dry desert areas. In summer months, the scorching sun of Palestine could heat things up so much that daytime travelers often had to look for shade in which to rest.

In some areas of the desert, very few trees grew, though. There was literally just ground and stones, and it would have been difficult to find shade. Yet, our pilgrim says that the Lord will be the shade on his "right hand," always the side of help and support in Scripture. What does this mean for life's journey? Well, if the journey gets hard, if you become tired, worn out by the heat and the dust, you can always rest. Right next to you there is shade, there are the "green pastures and still waters" of which David spoke (Ps. 23:2).

Stop for a bit, then. Recover your strength. You can! Our psalmist says that the Lord is our resting place, our strength, that He's always available, always near, always on hand as our help. We just need to make use of His offer.

Thank You, Lord, for being my rest.
I do need Your strength today! Amen.

IN FEARS BY DAY OR NIGHT

The sun shall not strike you by day, nor the moon by night.
PSALM 121:6

This beautiful pilgrim song serves as a metaphor for life's journey. The pilgrim is trusting God for protection during his travels – in this verse against the sun and the moon. In the summer, the desert parts of Judea could become exceedingly hot.

Fatigue, heat exhaustion, or even sunstroke were realities to be taken into account, especially if children travelled along. On the other hand, if they decided to travel during the coolness of night, they were afraid of the moon's rays which were believed to be detrimental. Either that or our verse is referring, in idiomatic form, to the tremendous cold of the desert nights. It's also a fact that the sun and moon were worshiped in those days and were ascribed certain powers. Our pilgrim, however, is *not* afraid of the sun or the moon, because *his* God created them and has full power over them!

The lesson for us is that nothing by day and nothing by night can harm us – nothing at all can happen if the Almighty does not allow it. Our future is firmly in *His* hands! Do not get sidetracked by irrational fears – continue on your journey with confidence.

Lord, whatever happens today or tonight,
You are in control! Amen.

IN THE SPIRITUAL BATTLE

The LORD will keep you from all evil;
He will keep your life. The LORD will keep your going
out and your coming in from this time forth and forevermore.

PSALM 121:7-8

As pilgrims on our way to eternity, we must know that the Lord will protect and keep us in every way. We can *truly* travel with confidence and certainty. In this verse the psalmist tells us that God also protects our life (or literally "soul") from "all evil."

He elaborates by saying that God will protect our "going out" and our "coming in" – ancient formulations referring to going out to war and returning back from the battlefield. This makes us think of the spiritual battles we may face in life. As Christians, we face a real enemy who tries to obstruct our progress and prevent us from reaching our destination.

We experience his onslaught in our minds, on our emotions, and on our strength. Yes, in our soul and spirit we often face a battle far more debilitating to our journey than any physical obstacle. This battle is a reality, but remember – the victory is an even bigger reality! *That* is the promise of this psalm.

Lord, protect me from the dangers of the soul.
Deliver me from the Evil One. Amen.

YOU'LL BE GLAD YOU DID

I was glad when they said to me, "Let us go to the house of the LORD!"
PSALM 122:1

Three times a year Jewish men had to leave everything and go to Jerusalem for at least a week in order to attend a feast. It must have been a disruption, because it involved a long journey, finding accommodation, and definite expenses.

David, however, never complained about a feast! It wasn't just the fact that he already lived in Jerusalem but that his heart was always *glad* to go to the "house of the Lord." Today, to go to the "house of the Lord" still entails effort and a sacrifice of time. Some Christians have become disappointed in the church and readily point to its failures: arrogance, irrelevance, big egos, and many more! Still, whether these be true or not, the church remains Christ's body on earth and remains God's plan for the world.

So do not give up on the church! Rather, find your place in the church – a place where you can hear the Word, simply and directly, where you will grow spiritually, and where you can serve. Don't see it as an effort or a sacrifice but as a necessary spiritual discipline. If you make the space in your life to meet God, you can be sure God will show up! You'll be *glad* you did!

Lord, help me to become more involved in Your church. Amen.

HERE WE ARE, JERUSALEM!

Jerusalem, we are standing inside your gates.
Jerusalem, what a strong and beautiful city you are!
PSALM 122:2-3 (CEV)

Jerusalem! After an arduous journey the weary pilgrims have come to their goal. They relish the sights of the beautiful city, the open market spaces, the impressive homes, the state buildings, the palaces, and, of course, the massive temple complex that takes up a tenth of the whole city area.

Jerusalem was without a doubt the biggest and most beautiful city of their kingdom. Let's allow our thoughts to again wander to the city that awaits our own pilgrimage: the New Jerusalem! The city of God is described as shimmering like a crystal, as having twelve gates made of pearl that are never closed. The streets are of gold, with the main road leading straight to the throne of God.

From out of the throne, the water of life will stream to where the tree of life stands, just as in Paradise. One day we – tired but triumphant – will arrive there and say: "Jerusalem! We are here, in your gates – finally, eternally!" Keep your eye on the goal and keep your faith strong, Christian!

Lord, thank You that my end is with You: in glory, forever! Amen.

THE PEACE OF JERUSALEM

*Pray for the peace of Jerusalem! "May they be secure
who love you! Peace be within your walls
and security within your towers!"*
PSALM 122:6-7

The psalmist is calling on the reader to be just as concerned for Jerusalem as he is himself. He wants us to regularly inquire whether Jerusalem still has peace and also to pray for the "peace of Jerusalem."

How ironic is it, then, that Jerusalem has had so little peace in its history. The city has been captured and destroyed so many times during the ages! Jesus wept for Jerusalem, who rejected Him, and prophesied its destruction, which happened shortly after (Mark 13). Today Jerusalem is still a city in conflict. Jews as well as Palestinians claim it as their own capitol, and it remains a seeming insurmountable problem that Islam's third most important mosque is standing on the site of the ancient temple. Still, we pray for the peace of Jerusalem. We pray that God will fulfill His plan for His city.

We pray for the people of the city, especially for the thousands of Christians staying there. We pray that *they* – the church of God in Jerusalem – will truly shine the light of Him who was crucified there.

*Yes, Lord, I do pray for Jerusalem, the city You love.
Grant them peace! Amen.*

WAIT ON HIS HAND

Behold, as the eyes of servants look to the hand of their master, as the eyes of a maidservant to the hand of her mistress, so our eyes look to the LORD our God, till He has mercy upon us.

PSALM 123:2

What a beautiful image of anticipation and expectation we find here! The psalm reflects a time when servants looked to their masters for instruction and for provision of their daily needs. They had no other task and literally no other place to go.

We find descriptions from ancient times of formal functions in which servants stood silently at the end of tables, arms folded, eyes fixed on their master who could communicate with them through simple gestures. Our psalmist puts us in the position of such a servant of God, and our obedience to God should be as complete as the referenced servant to his master.

Yet, we are often so full of our own will and goals that we remain unhappy and frustrated – and of little use to God. If we could only forget ourselves and look *up* to the Lord, as this psalm says, and wait on His will as our single duty, we would find a much deeper happiness and meaning. We are called to a *total* surrender – God needs to help us with that!

Lord, help me to totally surrender to You! Amen.

SOW THE BAD, REAP THE GOOD

Do good, O LORD, to those who are good,
and to those who are upright in their hearts!
But those who turn aside to their crooked ways
the LORD will lead away with evildoers!
PSALM 125:4-5

The psalmist insists, as always, that those who trust God will be blessed and protected. Wicked people will *not* prevail over the righteous! Then he prays this prayer, in which he asks for God to do good to those who are good. He asks for those who turn away to crooked things to perish along their own crooked paths.

It's once again about the principle of sowing and reaping – each will reap what he sowed. To be blessed – or cursed – was therefore most often the result of personal choices. It's indeed much better to do good than bad, and it's clear that the results in our lives will be concomitant to our choices. Let's therefore always sow *good* seed and nothing else! Yet the Bible teaches us that we do *not* just sow good seed; we also sow bad seed, which will lead, of course, to a bad harvest in our fields.

How fortunate, then, that with God those who sowed the bad can *still* reap the good, that those who deserve the curse of sin can *still* receive the blessing of forgiveness! That is what's so amazing about grace! Jesus made it possible. We just need to ask!

Heavenly Father, thank You for Your grace!
Thank You that I am loved and blessed, in spite of my sin. Amen.

DREAMS COME TRUE

*When the L*ord *restored the fortunes of Zion,*
we were like those who dream.
PSALM 126:1

A miracle happened when the king of Babylon decided after seventy years that the Jews could return to their land. The people danced and rejoiced, for their wildest dream had come true! They would return to the land of milk and honey, which their parents spoke of every day.

Without delay the trek back was organized and implemented – but what a disappointment! Their land was barren and destroyed, inhabited by a new and hostile people. Whatever they built during the day was torn down during the night. They planted, but it didn't rain. They struggled and despaired with their dream collapsed and gone. Now in this psalm they pray that God will change their lot once again. Yes, sometimes we work at a dream we have, a vision, but it doesn't work out.

Everything goes wrong, and we end up with loss after loss. It's a fact, of course, that not every dream can work out, but for now let's look at the outcome for these Jews. They *did* resettle their land, they *did* conquer their challenges, and their dream *did* come true! Speak to God about that dream of yours – it can still happen.

Giver of Dreams, I have a dream in my heart,
and I want to share it with You. Amen.

SOWING AND GROWING

Those who sow in tears shall reap
with shouts of joy! He who goes out weeping,
bearing the seed for sowing, shall come home
with shouts of joy, bringing his sheaves with him.
PSALM 126:5-6

The Jews returned from exile, but they found that their land was barren, destroyed, and inhabited by a hostile people. The expected rains did not come. Now they're sowing again, but they're sowing in tears – they're weeping because their dream has collapsed.

Still, they're sowing because they *had* to sow. What else was there to do? Do you know what happened? They had a harvest, and every year they had a better harvest. Soon they were shouting joyfully during harvest time! Let's draw some general and spiritual truths from these experiences. We *must* sow, because without sowing there can be no reaping. Only sowing can lead to a harvest. Whether you're disheartened or uncertain, you *must* sow! Sow especially what you want to reap be it love, forgiveness, care, provision. Ask God how and when to sow the right seed on the right land. To *sow* is our share of the deal; to *grow* the crop is God's share! Faithfully do what you must – even if it is with many tears – and trust God for the outcome.

Lord, I'm sowing in tears today,
but I'm trusting You for a joyful harvest! Amen.

WORK AND BLESSING

Unless the LORD builds the house, those who build it labor in vain.
Unless the LORD watches over the city, the watchman stays awake in vain.

PSALM 127:1

We're often prepared to work very hard for our goals, to give 110 percent, to work late hours. The pace of modern living is such that we have to work from early to late and to the point that our families are neglected.

Our lives can easily become unbalanced by our focus on work – we'll definitely do harm when we work ourselves to a standstill. Take note that Scripture, as in this verse, is never *against* work. It's always *for* work – for hard work, responsible work. Still, according to Scripture work is not everything. The question always must be, where does God fit into all this working? The lesson of this psalm is emphatically the following: If God is not in our work, we're working in vain.

If His blessing is not upon us, all our efforts are hopeless. "It is in vain that you rise up early and go late to rest, eating the bread of anxious toil" (Ps. 127:2). For those whom God loves, He grants His provision even as they sleep. Let's work then, and let's work hard – but let's also seek God's blessing on what we do, for without that there can be no success. Working is only part of our lives, which wholly belongs to Him!

Lord, bless my work! Help me to balance it
with what is equally important in my life. Amen.

BE A BELOVED!

Without the help of the LORD it is useless to build a home or to guard a city. It is useless to get up early and stay up late in order to earn a living. God takes care of His own, even while they sleep.
PSALM 127:1-2 (CEV)

The psalmist assures us that it's useless to build if God is not building with us, that it's in vain to guard that which God isn't guarding as well. To get up early for work or to work your fingers to the bone is of no benefit at all if the Lord's blessing isn't in the matter.

God can just as well give success to His beloved while they're sleeping. Our first goal, therefore, should not be to work hard but to be God's beloved! That's the *first* requirement for success! How do we become God's beloved? Well, the Bible says that God *already* loves us – that we're *already* the objects of His love. Being a beloved, however, is not a one-sided or passive affair. A beloved is in a two-sided relationship of love: receiving love, but also giving love. God's beloved reacts to God's love by loving God back!

Remember His Great Commandment, that we love Him with our whole heart, soul, and mind? Be a true beloved of God, then, by acting like a true beloved. Nurture and grow the love between you and God, and you will see wonderful things happen!

Lord, thank You for Your love.
Help me to show my love for You as well! Amen.

TWO KEYS TO HAPPINESS

Blessed is everyone who fears the LORD,
who walks in His ways! You shall eat
the fruit of the labor of your hands;
you shall be blessed, and it shall be well with you.

PSALM 128:1-2

Do you want to be happy and prosperous? Do you want God's blessing on your life? Then you're at the right place, because in this verse the Bible gives us two keys to being blessed! Take note:

- "Blessed is everyone who fears the LORD." To serve God leads to happiness and fulfillment. That is just a biblical fact. Do you serve God with all your heart? Then you are blessed and will forever be blessed. Accept it, confess it, and live out your blessing! This is the first key.

- "You shall eat the fruit of the labor of your hands." Remember, first comes the labor and then follows the fruit thereof! That is the second key. There *will* be fruit from the labor of those who serve God. In the Bible work itself was intended as a blessing, so enjoy your work *and* your fruit!

Now you have two keys to happiness: serving God and working meaningfully and productively. A rather basic lesson? Yes, rather. But there's no circumventing its truth. They remain your first two steps!

Lord, I do want to serve You. Help me to work and help me to enjoy! Amen.

NOVEMBER 26
THE CIRCLE OF BLESSING

The LORD bless you from Zion! May you see the prosperity
of Jerusalem all the days of your life!
PSALM 128:5

What a wonderful blessing! In God's beautiful temple on Mount Zion, the priest raises his hands and blesses the people with these words. He *lays* God's blessing on them. God promised Moses that if the priests would pray according to His instructions, He would bless the people (Num. 6:22-27).

Yes, be blessed! Receive your blessing in the name of the Lord! Let's add something to this, though: We cannot just sit and wait for God's blessing to hit us. We must actively receive it. That means that we must appropriate it. We must accept it as a truth and then go and live as if we are blessed indeed. To be blessed is an act of faith and part of our obedience.

There is also another way of appropriating our blessing, and that is by blessing others. To bless others activates the principle of sowing and reaping, remember? To be a blessing is to receive blessing, with which we can be even more of a blessing! Get the circle of blessing going!

Lord, help me to bless wherever I go, whomever I meet. Amen.

THE HUMAN CONDITION

*If You, O LORD, should mark iniquities, O Lord,
who could stand? But with You there is forgiveness,
that You may be feared.*

PSALM 130:3-4

God made us as humans: wonderful, image-of-God humans, but also fallible, prone-to-sin humans! He gave us the choice for either obedience or disobedience, well knowing that we would disobey. Yes, of course God knew we were going to sin, because He knows the history of humankind right to its very last second! Because we would sin, God provided from the start the solution.

He joined mankind Himself in the person of Jesus Christ and addressed the question of man's sin on the cross fully and finally. Remember also that the Old Testament sacrifices drew their validity from the cross. With the door to God wide open, we only need to step into an intimate relationship with Him, as it was in the beginning. This is the gospel invitation! What's more, we must never feel guilty about being human, because God made us human. Let's be human, fully human, then! Embrace your humanity and fully develop it in all its wonder and frailty. The Bible teaches that our humanity is best served when we live as we were designed to live – with God!

*Lord, thank You that I may be who I am.
I want to be my best me – with You! Amen.*

WAIT FOR THE LORD - WAIT!

I wait for the LORD, my soul waits, and in His word I hope;
my soul waits for the Lord more than watchmen
for the morning, more than watchmen for the morning.

PSALM 130:5-6

To "wait for the Lord" is a well-known concept in Scripture but one that we use less today, perhaps because we don't like to wait. To wait on God is just another way of describing faith. It describes our expectation of God's intervention.

It says that we will *stay* before God with the matter, that we will *keep* our eyes on Him until He intervenes! In Scripture, this waiting-on-God wasn't an uncertain matter. Oh no, biblical hope is being *sure* about the outcome but having to wait for it to happen.

It's like a woman who is pregnant and waiting for the birth, or a man on a train waiting for its arrival at the station. It's true that to wait isn't always pleasant, but not everything can happen at once. Sometimes we *do* have to wait. Wait, then, on the Lord: patiently, faithfully – productively!

Lord, give me the patience and the faith to wait! Amen.

LET GO, LET GOD

*O LORD, my heart is not lifted up; my eyes are not raised
too high; I do not occupy myself with things
too great and too marvelous for me.*
PSALM 131:1

David says it's not befitting for him to try and understand the things of God. Some things are too high for any man to know, like the inner workings of the Almighty or the reasons for His actions.

David's wise decision is to be content with *not* knowing, with *not* understanding. He merely halts before the secrets of God. He just accepts the mystery! What a lesson for us, who forever feel the need to define and understand God, to describe Him inside and out, to prescribe and predict His reactions according to the rules we think we have deduced. Remember, it's impossible for man to examine God – it only works the other way around! No, to us God remains the Wholly Other, the undefinable, mysterious, and sovereign Being who does what He chooses to do and is not obliged at all to explain or defend His actions. Yes, we *do* have many questions, but we do *not* have all the answers. Not everything is answered now. God simply demands of us to trust Him – to have faith! Remember, in addition to the above God is also the faithful God, the loving Father!

*Lord, I cannot understand You, but I trust You.
Help me to be content with not understanding! Amen.*

SILENT IN THE STORM

*Surely I have behaved and quieted myself,
as a child that is weaned of his mother:
my soul is even as a weaned child.*
PSALM 131:2 (KJV)

This short psalm is about the fact that we cannot always understand God, that we often just need to trust Him in our incomprehension, our not knowing. God *will* be God, and faith means to *let* God be God in our lives.

Therefore, David says that he has "quieted" his soul before God. He has stopped asking questions. Life's questions remained, of course, because his circumstances remained. His challenges, his onslaughts, were still present. It's not that his problems disappeared! Oh no, *around* him the storm still raged, but *in* him he found a quiet place like the eye of a hurricane. His soul is quiet, his mind is quiet, and his will is quiet. He has the peace of God.

Like a weaned child, he doesn't want something from God – he merely wants God! This, of course, is difficult for us to attain in our walk with God, but this is what faith can do: it can bring about the peace that surpasses understanding (Phil. 4:7). This is a full surrender, and this is what we need!

*Lord, I do so want to have the peace
that surpasses understanding! Amen.*

December

Praise the LORD! Praise God in His sanctuary; praise Him in His mighty heavens!

Praise Him for His mighty deeds; praise Him according to His excellent greatness!

Praise Him with trumpet sound; praise Him with lute and harp!

Praise Him with tambourine and dance; praise Him with strings and pipe!

Praise Him with sounding cymbals; praise Him with loud clashing cymbals!

Let everything that has breath praise the LORD! Praise the LORD!

PSALM 150

HOW GOOD, HOW PLEASANT!

> Behold, how good and pleasant it is when brothers dwell
> in unity! It is like the precious oil on the head,
> running down on the beard, on the beard of Aaron,
> running down on the collar of his robes!
> PSALM 133:1-2

Yes, how wonderful it is when brothers and sisters can live together in peace! This is true for traditional family members and for spiritual brothers and sisters as well.

Scripture uses the imagery of the Holy Spirit to describe God's blessing and unction on such relationships. It's like the anointing oil on the head of Aaron sanctifying him for God's work, like the dew from the mountains of Hermon falling onto Zion. The description of the psalmist makes us think of the Spirit's anointing in this way: First it transforms our thinking, then it flows down to heal our heart's emotions, and then it gets onto our clothes where it becomes part of our behavior.

Finally, it wets the ground around us as a fragrant testimony of God's presence! To be able to live together peaceably is the result of the Spirit's work in our lives and His fruit, which is borne in our behavior: the fruit of love, joy, patience, friendliness, and self-control, among others (Gal. 5:22-23). We need to be filled by the Spirit – then our relationships will be wonderful as well!

Lord, fill me with Your Spirit! Bless us with unity and peace. Amen.

IN THE SANCTUARY, IN THE NIGHT

Come, bless the LORD, all you servants of the LORD,
who stand by night in the house of the LORD!
Lift up your hands to the holy place and bless the LORD!
PSALM 134:1-2

This is the last of the so called pilgrim songs, or songs of ascent. It is probably referring to the end of the feast. The pilgrims journeyed to Jerusalem to spend time with God for a few days of celebration, sacrifice, and worship.

Now they are departing – probably by night – but first they attend the closing ceremonies in the temple. There, in the flickering light of lamps and torches, they pray once more. They raise their hands and thank God for His greatness. Let's leave these beautiful images just there for now. Three thousand years later, you and I are on our own pilgrimage, and we, from time to time, meet with God in the night – the literal night or sometimes the spiritual night.

Spend time with God, then, in your nights. Do not hurry the time! Raise up your hands and praise Him in the night. Especially in the night! Then you will have the strength to resume your journey again.

Lord, teach me to meet with You and to praise
You in the night. Amen.

YOUR HANDS AND GOD'S HANDS

Lift up your hands to the holy place and
bless the LORD! May the LORD bless you
from Zion, He who made heaven and earth!

PSALM 134:2-3

In this psalm the servants of God are called upon to come and worship at night, in God's sanctuary. The literal meaning is that they should go to the temple and pray, probably after the conclusion of the festival.

There, after praying, they received the priests' blessing: "May the LORD bless you from Zion." With this blessing they could proceed on their way. For us, there is also a spiritual application: in our literal or figurative night, we can go into the inner sanctuary of the heart and meet with God. There we can raise our hands and praise Him.

It is difficult to praise God during the dark times of our lives – yes, very much so – but it's so beneficial for the soul! Praise brings us into God's presence; it brings us into obedience – it brings us into faith. Praise leads to a blessing, because upon meeting us in this way God will also raise *His* hands and "bless [us] from Zion." Yes, as we raise our hands in praise, those hands receive His blessing.

Lord, teach me to praise, and bless me, Lord. Bless from Zion! Amen.

DECEMBER 4
AT THE RIVER OF TEARS

By the waters of Babylon, there we sat down
and wept, when we remembered Zion.

PSALM 137:1

This psalm was written during the Babylonian exile. At that time the Jews were living in the capitol of a vast empire, exposed to the best that the world could offer. Rivers crisscrossed the area, the land was fertile, and the vegetation lush and green – the complete opposite of the dry and barren land they came from!

Still, they were weeping. Sitting "by the waters of Babylon," they longed for their land and for Jerusalem. They cried rivers of tears because they felt their God had rejected them. He had turned His back on them, leaving them dejected and forlorn. Yes, it's quite possible to be surrounded by the wealth and beauty of the world but feel far away from God – and far from the place where you *should* be.

Then it all means nothing – less than nothing! Weep, friend. Weep before God! Open your heart to Him, and pour out your longing and regret. Return to God unreservedly! Get back to the place where you belong. Yes, get up and go to your Father. He is already waiting for you!

Father, I am not where I should be. I want to return, Lord! Amen.

DECEMBER 5
HOW CAN WE SING?

How shall we sing the LORD's song in a foreign land?
PSALM 137:4

The Jews were taken into captivity to Babylon. They found themselves subjected by their enemies, humiliated, and despondent – and very far from home! Now their captors, feeling like entertainment, ask of them a typically Jewish song – something upbeat!

Sing us one of the songs of Zion! But there is no way that can happen. The Jews are too sad for happy songs. "How shall we sing the LORD's song in a strange land?" (KJV). There's a time for singing and then there's a time for not singing. Sometimes we just cannot sing! Sometimes we grieve, we withdraw, or we're just without words. It's okay – in fact, it's important – to grieve when you need to grieve.

You may, and you must! Yes, be real with your emotions. Be sad, and be glad. But remember to always share your emotions with God. If you cannot sing now, know this: The Jews' exile was only temporary – back in their land, they sang and they sang! You'll sing again as well!

Lord, You know my heart. I cannot sing at the moment,
but I will sing again! Amen.

THE THREE STEPS

I bow down toward Your holy temple and
give thanks to Your name ... On the day I called,
You answered me; my strength of soul You increased.

PSALM 138:2-3

These verses contain a succinct description of what biblical prayer looks like! Look at the three steps:

- "I bow down toward Your holy temple." Jews still pray in the direction of Jerusalem, and some Christians pray toward the east, from where Jesus is said to return. We, of course, bow in the sanctuary of our hearts – wherever we are – to enter into our time of prayer. Bow often!
- "I give thanks to Your name." We do not start our prayers with a list of requests, wants, or needs. No, we start our prayers by praising and thanking God! Jesus taught us to start with His honor, His kingdom, and His will, not ours.
- "I called, You answered me." Only after we have prayed about God's goodness and grace do we offer up our requests and petitions. We call on God with boldness – and expect His answer!

If you regularly take these three steps to God, you will surely see your "strength of soul" increase.

*Lord, I bow before You, I praise Your name,
and I call on You for my needs. Renew my strength! Amen.*

HE WILL FULFILL HIS PURPOSE

The LORD will fulfill His purpose for me;
Your steadfast love, O LORD, endures forever.
Do not forsake the work of Your hands.

PSALM 138:8

What a beautiful confession: "The Lord will fulfill His purpose for me!" God, who started the good work in you, will also complete it. We, on the other hand, start many things that we never finish!

The Bible is clear, though, that God's future holds *full* completion – yes, *full* and *final* closure of the whole grand drama of His work on earth. Creation leads to consummation! The humans who were driven from Paradise will be welcomed back in the New Jerusalem. Every man and woman ever created will appear before God to account for their lives, where they will be treated justly and appropriately.

Eventually, every good deed will be rewarded and every misdeed punished. Every cause will lead to its effect so that ultimately no loose ends remain. *Then* perfect peace will reign – perfect harmony, righteousness, and love! No, God will *not* forsake the work of His hands. Remember, you and I are still in His hands. He is still busy with us!

Thank You, Lord, that You will bring my life
to its perfect purpose, as You promised. Amen.

DECEMBER 8
YOU LOOK RIGHT THROUGH ME

O Lord, You have searched me and known me!
You know when I sit down and when I rise up;
You discern my thoughts from afar.
PSALM 139:1-2

God knows us better than we know ourselves. His eyes search us and search through us – as if we were made of glass. He knows every cell and organ of our bodies. Even more, He searches our soul and knows our thoughts, our feelings, our motives. Yes, He knows our weaknesses and our sin, our self-centered attitude, our wayward thinking, what we do when no one is watching – how subtly but intentionally we can make others look bad.

God sees our love of money, of honor, and of power. He knows our jealousy and how hard we can sometimes be. God sees ahead in our lives and knows precisely what the future holds: what seasons still lie ahead and how things will change for us. God sees us on our deathbed. He *knows* us! Still – and this is the wonder – God *loves* us! He loves us passionately; He loves every fiber of our being, every motion of our soul. He intends the *best* for us! God makes it abundantly clear that the best life for us is a life with Him, because no one knows us as He does!

Thank You, Lord, for knowing me, and still loving me! Amen.

YOUR HANDS ON ME

You hem me in, behind and before, and lay Your hand upon me.
PSALM 139:5

What a beautiful image: God laying His hands on us! When we pray for the sick in church or consecrate someone for God's service, we lay hands on them – and God does the same!

God's hands on us means that He is busy forming us, like a potter who is working His clay to make something beautiful. What are the Potter's hands busy with in your life? What is He forming? Well, He is forming you into the image of Christ or, better, forming Christ in you (Gal. 4:19). It's your best you! In this psalm, though, God's hands are protecting us, keeping us from harm. What can happen with us with God's hands around us? Well, nothing! Nothing that *He* does not allow! Can the enemy get to you? Can you suffer loss? Can you lose out in life? Never!

Nowhere in the whole world are you safer than in the hands of God. Become more conscious of God's wonderful, strong, and caring hands on your life. Can you feel it? Relax, then. You're in good hands!

Lord, thank You for Your big, strong hands
that protect, comfort, and guide me. Amen.

GOD'S PRESENCE IN LIFE AND DEATH

> If I ascend to heaven, You are there!
> If I make my bed in Sheol, You are there!
>
> PSALM 139:8

David says God is everywhere. If he were to fly to the east or go and live in the west, God would be there. "From east to west" is a well-known biblical phrase used to describe God's deeds over the whole earth.

God is also in the whole vertical dimension: He is up in heaven, down on earth, and even in Sheol, a place beneath the earth where, according to Old Testament thought, the dead resided. Yes, God is there as well! He is the God of the living *and* of the dead. The lesson, though, is this: you cannot go anywhere or do anything where God's hands will not guide you or keep you.

Even amidst your biggest fear, God will be there and, ultimately, and on your last day, God will be right there as well. His hands will safely hold you. Yes, with God on the scene we never need to fear! Have some more faith, will you?

Thank You, Lord, that You are close to me
every day, every place, in life and in death! Amen.

SO NEAR IN THE DARKNESS

If I say, "Surely the darkness shall cover me,
and the light about me be night," even the darkness
is not dark to You; the night is bright as the day.
PSALM 139:11-12

David says that you cannot hide from God. Nowhere on earth, nowhere in heaven – not even in death! God is everywhere! We cannot hide in the darkness because darkness to God is as light as the day.

Remember, darkness and light are mere human perceptions, not God's realities! We have a similar perception that God is far away when we experience spiritual or emotional darkness, but that's equally false. In the dark, *we* cannot see God, but *He* can see us and remains as near to us as ever before! Yes, in our season of confusion and questions, in our tears and fears, He is actually right next to us – all the time!

Scripture says that God draws *near* to those who are despairing or heartbroken. That's how His love works! Our problem, therefore, is not just the darkness but the fact that it hides God from us. We need to focus more on His presence while in the darkness, because He's there! Put out your hand in faith and touch Him.

Lord, thank You that I can always reach out
and touch You. Always. Amen.

WOVEN IN THE DARKNESS

Your eyes saw my unformed substance; in Your book were written,
every one of them, the days that were formed for me,
when as yet there was none of them.

PSALM 139:16

In David's time, the body's working was pretty much a mystery. They could only speculate about all the organs, and they ascribed peculiar functions to, for example, the heart (thinking) and the kidneys (emotions).

How the embryo – here called an "unformed substance" – developed in the darkness of the womb was a tremendous wonder for them. In this psalm David makes one thing clear: it is God's work! In the darkness, God "knits" together a body: bones, muscle, ligaments, veins, blood, and skin. Even more, David says God already knows the person He's making! He knows his name and his days, which are already recorded in God's book. What does this tell us?

Well, we see that God views the developing person as an individual. He is still very immature and dependent, but already valuable, dear – loved by God! He already has all the potential to become someone who can achieve great things for God and for others! This is one of the reasons why we as Christians are always concerned about human life.

Thank You, Lord, that I was made so beautifully
and that You consider me so costly. Amen.

SHINE YOUR LIGHT ON ME

*Search me, O God, and know my heart! Try me
and know my thoughts! And see if there be any grievous way
in me, and lead me in the way everlasting!*

PSALM 139:23-24

In this psalm David says that God is all-present and all-knowing. God "knitted" together every person and knows each one through and through (Ps. 139:13)!

Since this is the case, David is now deliberately stepping forward to stand in God's full gaze. He asks God to shine His light right through him – to "search" him and "try" him. He wants God to "know" his thoughts: to discern the good and the bad. He specifically appeals to God to *test* his heart and see if there is any "grievous way" in him – a term referring to the lure toward idol worship. Although David never outwardly worshiped idols, he is asking God here to show him even the subtlest of motives in his heart that might detract him from God.

What a wonderful love for God is this! We, on the other hand, would rather try to hide, minimize, or excuse our halfhearted devotion to God. Isn't that so? Let's stop with the games and do what David did: stand in the light of God!

*Lord, scrutinize my heart! Show me what is grievous to You,
and help me to grow away from it! Amen.*

PRAYER LIKE INCENSE

Let my prayer be counted as incense before You,
and the lifting up of my hands as the evening sacrifice!
PSALM 141:2

Incense is a powerful symbol of prayer in the Bible. The Old Testament teaches that incense was mixed according to God's instructions and daily sacrificed in the temple. The small, golden incense altar stood directly in front of the veil, opposite God's presence (behind the veil) in the Holy of Holies.

There, only separated by the thick curtain from God's glory, a priest would burn incense every morning and every evening. The haze of the fragrant smoke would permeate the whole temple. In Revelation we read of bowls of sweet-smelling incense brought before God, which symbolizes the prayers of the believers. This symbolism tells us that our prayers are to God as a beautiful fragrance.

It pleases Him! We do still experience prayer as a sacrifice, because it demands our time and effort, but it brings us right into God's presence. It envelops us with His holiness. The fragrance of your meeting with God will hang around you the whole day!

Lord, let my praise be as incense to You. May it please You today. Amen.

DECEMBER 15
A GUARD OVER MY MOUTH

Set a guard, O LORD, over my mouth;
keep watch over the door of my lips!
PSALM 141:3

Believers should talk like believers, not like unbelievers! The following four questions may help you to think before you speak:

- Silence or speech? Sometimes we don't need to react or contribute to what is said. We often speak too much! Let's focus on quality, not quantity – and at times just keep quiet.
- True or untrue? Let's make sure to stick to the truth and nothing else. We may be tempted to embellish a bit, but the spin we put on a story often takes on a life of its own – and then the fingers will point to *you*! No, nothing but the truth!
- Building or breaking? Words can so easily break down or hurt someone. Don't say something behind someone's back that can't be repeated to their face – chances are they will hear it anyway! Rather build up, encourage, compliment, praise!
- Faith or unbelief? Let our words reveal our faith, not our unbelief or our fears!

Words are like flames. Quite unintentionally they can set ablaze the whole forest! Rather, put a guard before your mouth.

Lord, my words must honor You! Give me more self-control. Amen.

DECEMBER 16
READ THE ROAD SIGNS

Teach me to do Your will, for You are my God!
Let Your good Spirit lead me on level ground!
PSALM 143:10

How wonderful when life's journey is easy, like an open road stretching invitingly ahead of us, promising adventure and success. The best times of our lives are shared with loved ones, working hard and dreaming big. Other times, though, especially later in life, the road can become narrower, steeper, strewn with obstacles – the journey more difficult.

Then we become very dependent on the guidance of the Holy Spirit, as David prays for here. The guidance of the Spirit is like the road signs along your way. It tells you where you're heading, what to look out for, and where to turn. To merely know the meaning of the different signs – like when you learned them for your driver's permit – is not enough. To make use of them *on* the journey, at confusing crossroads or where the dangers lie, *that* is helpful!

In the same way, it's not good enough to have a Bible that gathers dust on the shelf, but to use it *as* you journey along, when you need to make decisions or when you need encouragement. Then you'll experience the guidance of the Holy Spirit!

Show me the way, Lord. Lead me, Holy Spirit! Amen.

TEACH ME TO FIGHT

Blessed be the LORD, my rock, who trains
my hands for war, and my fingers for battle.

PSALM 144:1

In this verse we are presented with the important fact that life has its conflict and strife. Yes, unfortunately this is the case. We may have thought that since we're serving God our lives should be all peace and harmony, but that is not the case at all! While we're in the world, we'll definitely deal with its brokenness and sinfulness; therefore, we *will* experience tension, competition, hostility, and struggle!

Yes, as Christians we do need to fight from time to time – for the truth, for what's right, and for those who cannot fight for themselves. We must be able to confront what's wrong and not shy away. Still, we need to learn how to fight correctly, fittingly – as children of God. We must fight our fights with fairness, honesty, empathy, and kindness. God taught David to stand for what was right. He must teach us as well!

Lord, empower me to confront the challenges
in my life. Teach me how to do it in Your way. Amen.

THREE GENERATIONS

*One generation shall commend Your works
to another, and shall declare Your mighty acts.*

PSALM 145:4

David says the one generation will tell the next about God's greatness – and that's how it should be! The passing on of God's testimonies down the ages often happens in the following pattern: The *first* generation of people are those who know God intimately and walk with Him personally.

They have firsthand experiences with God which they can relay to others. The *second* generation also serves God, but they do not experience Him as intensely as the first. They witnessed the previous generation, though, and were impressed by what they saw. They tell *those* stories to the next generation. The *third* generation has heard about the previous generation's walk with God, but they are standing even farther away.

These generations we're talking about are perhaps children and grandchildren, or otherwise the age groups of a congregation. The big question, however, is this: which generation represents you? May it be the first! Don't just see or hear how others walked with God – walk with Him yourself! Tell your own stories!

*Mighty God, I personally want to walk with You
and experience Your greatness! Amen.*

THE GREATEST KINGDOM EVER

Your kingdom is an everlasting kingdom,
and Your dominion endures throughout all generations.
PSALM 145:13

God is king forever, king over all kings! In the New Testament the epithet "King of kings and Lord of lords" is ascribed to Jesus Christ (1 Tim. 6:15). It's a proven fact that Christ, once mockingly called the "king of the Jews" (Luke 23:36-37), is now the greatest king of all time. It's true! Which king has had a reign of two thousand years?

Which king's kingdom is spread out over the whole world? Which king has had as many subjects as our king? Through the ages millions and millions have subjected themselves to Christ! Which king's coming has divided history so radically that new dates and calendars had to be devised?

For which king were so many prepared to change their behavior, their work, their relationships, their plans – or literally give up their lives to die? Well, for King Jesus! Our king is King over all kings – and that is a fact.

Lord, Your kingdom is indeed an everlasting kingdom –
Your dominion is forever! Amen.

FORGET ABOUT PRINCES

Put not your trust in princes, in a son of man,
in whom there is no salvation. When his breath departs,
he returns to the earth; on that very day his plans perish.
PSALM 146:3-4

These verses are about the fact that we so easily depend on "princes." We so readily put people on pedestals as role models or even potential benefactors. Of course it's not wrong to look up to people or to depend on someone, but these verses are about *trusting* people with a trust that no man is worthy of.

The boss, the spiritual leader, the doctor or counselor, the wealthy businessman, or the politician with his connections can perhaps do some things for us, or not, but they will always remain human – and therefore fallible. They cannot save us, however high our expectations of them! Even our significant other can only deliver what he or she can deliver and nothing more.

It's unfair to expect that they fulfill all our needs or save us. No, there is only *one* Savior, and that is Christ Jesus. Only He can be trusted with our happiness, future, prosperity, and salvation. People will disappoint us, but God never disappoints!

Lord, I trust You with my life! Amen.

FOE OR FATHER

The LORD watches over the sojourners;
He upholds the widow and the fatherless,
but the way of the wicked He brings to ruin.

PSALM 146:9

God has two sides, as we see in this verse, although many people only see the one side. For them God is a good-humored character like Santa Claus who understandingly dismisses all misdeeds with a smile. It's true that God is loving, but God is also righteous.

He forgives but also insists that things be *right*. He blesses but also withdraws His blessing, turns away from what is wrong, or disciplines arrogant people. God's not just the Lamb, but also the Lion. He is extremely dangerous as an enemy! Here the psalmist says that God brings the way of the wicked "to ruin" – literally, to turn it upside down, to make it crooked.

The wicked travel on a road that is turned this way and that, taking them left and right but always presenting them with a dead end – how terrifying! Let's make sure that God is with us on the road, not against us! The good news, however, is also given by the psalmist: to travel with God is to have Him *watch* over us, all the way!

*Almighty God, I bow before You. I am so grateful
that You're not my foe, but my Father! Amen.*

DECEMBER 22

STRENGTHEN YOUR SOUL

The Lord builds up Jerusalem;
He gathers the outcasts of Israel.
He heals the brokenhearted and binds up their wounds.
PSALM 147:2-3

What is God doing in these verses? Look at the verbs: He builds up, He gathers, He heals, and He binds up. Isn't it beautiful? Yes, God is in the business of restoration and healing – it's His specialty! Are your walls down? Does the enemy run in and out of your soul with little resistance? Do you feel tired or broken down?

Go, then, to God! Take some rest; catch your breath! Let God heal your heart and strengthen your soul again. You will be restored and rejuvenated, your strength renewed, and your thoughts refocused.

You'll be ready to face the world again! Yes, go the heavenly Healer, go with your confusion or tears or frustrations or questions – just go! You so need it! To go to God is never, ever in vain – you'll see!

Lord, I'm coming to You. Heal my heart! Amen.

ATTRACTIVE, ATHLETIC, POPULAR?

His delight is not in the strength of the horse,
nor His pleasure in the legs of a man,
but the LORD takes pleasure in those who fear Him,
in those who hope in His steadfast love.

PSALM 147:10-11

The question that the psalmist is trying to answer is this one: What is important to God? Is it to be attractive, athletically built, fit, or perhaps popular with many friends? Is it important to God that you're well off, that you live in a sought-after neighborhood with a beautiful home and new car? That you entertain a lot?

Does it count that your children go to the best schools or take expensive music lessons? Is it important that you have a certain standing in the community, that you command respect? Let's emphasize that if you enjoy these things you are blessed indeed – praise God! But the question remains: What is important to God? These things are important to us!

For God, it's important that we are humble, that we can love, that we're grateful for His grace, that we serve *Him* and trust in Him for this life and the next! In such a context wealth becomes irrelevant – as does appearance, popularity, or career. Do you serve the Lord? *That* is the question!

Lord, I do want to serve You. Be the Lord of my life! Amen.

PRAISE GOD FROM THE HEAVENS

Praise the LORD! Praise the LORD from the heavens;
praise Him in the heights! Praise Him, all His angels; praise Him,
all His hosts! Praise Him, sun and moon, praise Him, all you shining stars!

PSALM 148:1-3

These final psalms are all pure praise – they're called "hallelujah psalms" because they all start and end with an exuberant "hallelujah," here translated as "Praise the LORD!" In this psalm the psalmist calls up the whole creation to praise God – from the top to the bottom!

He starts with all the angels who, incidentally, are praising God full time already! Then he calls up the sun, moon, and stars to praise the Lord. We already said that the heathen nations saw these things as gods, but the psalmist makes no provision for false gods. For him they are mere creations that now need to turn and praise their Creator, the only real God.

Do you know what? Idols become idols when we make them idols – when we consider them worthy of unwarranted attention, effort, or honor. When we do not give things undue importance or influence over us, they fade to the background. Let's become conscious of the things in our lives that demand honor, and let's not have false gods lurking around. The only true God deserves our honor and praise!

Lord, nothing compares with You! I praise You alone. Amen.

PRAISE GOD FROM THE EARTH

Praise the LORD from the earth, you great sea creatures
and all deeps ... Mountains and all hills, fruit trees and all cedars!
Beasts and all livestock, creeping things and flying birds!
PSALM 148:7, 9-10

The psalmist calls up the whole of creation to praise God. He starts with the heavenly beings and the heavenly bodies. Then he mentions the earth, the sea, and the air. After that the mountains, plants, and animals are called upon to praise their creator before the psalmist finally turns to man. Everything and everyone must praise God! Let's think: how can a mountain or the wind praise God? Well, nature praises God if nature does what nature was created to do! A mountain glorifies God by its silent majesty, and a brook praises its creator by babbling gently in the forest. When the wind blows it honors God, who caused it to blow, and when plants grow and bear fruit they tell of God's greatness. Birds flit around and chirp to the glory of God! By living out its creation purpose, nature honors the Creator! In exactly the same way we, as the crown of God's creation, must fulfill our creation purpose and so glorify Him. What is your creation purpose? It's to go and be the *best* you that you can be – as wonderful and unique as God made you – *with* God and to His glory! That's your purpose and your calling.

*Lord, thank You that I can and must be myself –
the self that You made me to be. Amen!*

PRAISE FOR NEW REASONS

Praise the LORD! Sing to the LORD a new song,
His praise in the assembly of the godly!
PSALM 149:1

We are often prompted in the Psalms to sing a "new song" to the Lord. Does this mean that God is bored with the old ones? Fortunately not! God first pays attention to the heart of the worshipper, not so much to the words of his song.

It pleases God that we sing to Him – especially that we *want* to sing – whether or not we get the words right. Of least importance is the specific style of music, which depends largely on our cultural context. We can worship God in any variety of music styles as long as we have a heart of worship. So, what is a new song? A new song is the result of a heart that is inspired *anew*, excited *anew* about God's greatness, finding *new* reasons for praising God, using *new* words.

Creative and Spirit-filled artists come up all the time with beautiful new songs, because God is all the time doing new things! Sing a new song – or sing the beautiful old ones for new reasons!

Lord, I do praise and worship You – in the old and in the new ways! Amen.

SING, REJOICE, DANCE, PLAY!

Let Israel be glad in his Maker; let the children
of Zion rejoice in their King! Let them praise His name
with dancing, making melody to Him with tambourine and lyre!
PSALM 149:2-3

What a beautiful song of exuberant praise! The rousing verbs in these first verses call us to join in, to be glad, to rejoice, to praise, to dance, to play to God! These are the emotions and actions that thinking of God should elicit! It's true that temperaments differ and that worship is a very personal matter, but it's also true that we are sometimes emotionally inhibited.

Many of us were raised – especially men – to not express emotions or to be overly aware of what others might think. Shouldn't we rather break free from the expectations of others and be who God wants us to be? Shouldn't we dare to laugh unreservedly, to sing at the top our voices, to dance as if no one is watching?

Can't we rejoice for once and really express gladness over God? He is worth it, and giving praise is so healing! Yes, we should – and we must!

Lord, my heart is full of praise for You.
Teach my mouth and hands and body to praise You as well! Amen.

REVIVE MY HEART!

Let the godly exult in glory; let them sing for joy on their beds.
PSALM 149:5

The psalmist's heart is overjoyed about his God. He praises God, even on his bed, for His goodness and grace. The language the psalmist uses – thinking about God day and night, wanting to talk about Him often – is an expression of what we sometimes call revival.

Revival, which we often pray for in church, has an objective and a subjective side. Objectively, God is still near. He never left, and He is working all the time! Subjectively, though, *we* are not always near where God works. We are sometimes near and sometimes far from Him – our hearts are not always broken before God. The personal revival that we're looking for must be found in our own hearts, not looked for in some church or with some preacher.

It's not the Lord that has to be revived – it's our own cold and calloused hearts that need to be broken for Him again so that we can feel our lost passion again, the Spirit of God moving and working again. We once had it, but we lost it!

*Revive my heart, Lord! Thank You for
drawing near to me when I draw near to You. Amen.*

THE PRAISE AND THE SWORD

Let the high praises of God be in their throats and
two-edged swords in their hands, to execute vengeance
on the nations and punishments on the peoples.

PSALM 149:6-7

The righteous are described here as having the high praises of God in their mouths and two-edged swords in their hands. It makes us think of Israel's holy wars, especially the times when God's praises alone defeated the enemy.

In the New Testament we also find the image of God's Word as the two-edged sword that vanquishes His enemies. Yes, it's the language of spiritual battle! If the enemy threatens us – and his weapon is fear based on lies – we can counter him with the praises of God. Why does it help? Well, to praise God is to exercise faith, to confess that our God has won the victory, that the enemy has been defeated.

Praise is faith building! If the enemy's attack can't lead to fear but only to faith, then he has been overcome. Base your praise on the truth of the Word of God and you'll have a powerful double-edged sword! The Psalms are ideal for this purpose.

Lord, thank You that this fight is Your fight,
and that You always conquer in the fight! Amen.

PRAISE GOD FOR WHO HE IS

Praise the Lord! Praise God in His sanctuary;
praise Him in His mighty heavens! Praise Him for His mighty deeds;
praise Him according to His excellent greatness!

PSALM 150:1-2

The entire book of Psalms, in Hebrew known as *Tehillim* ("praise songs"), flows to a fantastic culmination of praise. The last couple of psalms are all pure praise, of which this final one forms a jubilant climax. Multiple calls to praise are directed at "everything that has breath" (Ps. 150:6).

The song is both introduced and concluded with an exuberant hallelujah! This praise also concludes and summarizes the whole of the book. It's beautiful! In these initial verses we are called to praise God for two reasons: (1) for His "mighty deeds" and (2) for His "excellent greatness." He must be praised for what He did, in other words, but also for who He is! We often want to praise God when things go well for us or when we've experienced one or other blessing.

Still, we can praise God whatever our circumstances, because God is *always* great and powerful, *always* good and gracious – *always* praiseworthy! Circumstances may change, but God does not. What a reason to praise!

*I praise You, Lord, because You're a gracious God
who does good things. Amen!*

PRAISE GOD FOREVER AND EVER!

Let everything that has breath praise the LORD! Praise the LORD!

PSALM 150:6

The book of Psalms ends here with a powerful climax. The calls to praise in this concluding psalm remind us of the Ten Commandments and constitute a new law to praise God forever!

This final psalm describes an enormous orchestra, assembled under the vault of heaven – which has now become one big sanctuary – and praising God with all the instruments known to man. Their song of praise is begun, and the Creator is praised for His mighty deeds and for His greatness. All instruments play, and all people rejoice – the biggest choir imaginable! With these images, and with this commandment, the book of Psalms plays out. God *must* be praised, and God *will* be praised for all eternity!

At the end of the New Testament, in the book of Revelation, we get an insight into *that* eternity in which "every creature in heaven and on earth and under the earth and in the sea, and all that is in them" praises God, saying, "To Him who sits on the throne and to the Lamb be blessing and honor and glory and might forever and ever!" (Rev. 5:13-14).

Amen and amen!

Notes

Notes

Notes

Notes